Structuralist Macroeconomics

Structuralist Macroeconomics

Applicable Models for the Third World

Lance Taylor

Basic Books, Inc., Publishers   *New York*

A version of chapter 10 appeared in the
Journal of International Economics (December 1981).

Library of Congress Cataloging in Publication Data

Taylor, Lance.
  Structuralist macroeconomics.

  Bibliography: p. 220
  Includes index.
  1. Underdeveloped areas—Mathematical models.
2. Macroeconomics. I. Title.
HC59.7.T372 1983   339'.0724   82–72408
ISBN 0–465–08239–4

Contents

Acknowledgments

MOST scholarly books are pastiches of other people's works. This one is no exception, and draws heavily on studies by people from many different parts of the world (though not from different time periods since most of the research on formal structuralist models has taken place during the past three or four years). I am particularly grateful to the following people: Edmar Bacha, Francisco Lopes, Eduardo Modiano, Andre Lara-Resende, and Persio Arida at the Pontifical Catholic University (PUC) in Rio de Janeiro; Alejandro Foxley, Jose Pablo Arellano, and Rene Cortazar at CIEPLAN in Santiago; Alain Ize and Nora Lustig at El Colegio de Mexico in Mexico City; Jørn Rattsø at the University of Trondheim; Hiren Sarkar at the National Council of Applied Economic Research in New Delhi; Jack Duloy, Sweder van Wijnbergen, Alan Gelb, Wafik Grais, Pradeep Mitra, and Desmond McCarthy at the World Bank; Youssef Boutros-Ghali at the International Monetary Fund; Frank Lysy at Johns Hopkins; Jere Behrman and Ed Buffie at the University of Pennsylvania; Graciela Chichilnisky at Columbia; Carlos Diaz-Alejandro at Yale; Bill Gibson at the University of Massachusetts in Amherst; Steve Marglin at Harvard; Eliana Cardoso at Boston University; Amitava Dutt, Paul Krugman, Rudi Dornbusch, Emma Rothschild, and Dick Eckaus at MIT. Cohorts of students at PUC, MIT, El Colegio de Mexico, and in seminars at various other places suffered through successive elaborations of the models here; they paid back their tormentor for his "minor slips" in turn. My wife, children, and pets provided the appropriate quantum of distractions from the algebra. Linda Dorfman did a super job of typing. My thanks to them all.

Structuralist Macroeconomics

1

The Structuralist Perspective

AN ECONOMY has structure if its institutions and the behavior of its members make some patterns of resource allocation and evolution substantially more likely than others. Economic analysis is structuralist when it takes these factors as the foundation stones for its theories.

According to this definition, North Atlantic or neoclassical professionals do not practice structuralist economics. Their standard approach to theory is to postulate a set of interlocking maximization problems by a number of "agents" and ask about the characteristics of the solutions. Institutions are conspicuously lacking in this calculus, as is recognition that men, women, and children are political and social as well as economic animals. Noneconomic, or even nonmaximized, forces affecting economic actions are ruled out of discussion. Moreover, allowable economic actions are curiously circumscribed. For example, markets are almost always postulated to be price-clearing when it is patently obvious that many functioning markets are cleared by quantity adjustments or queues.

In applied economics, this theoretical cabala breaks down, as it must. But the impact of the theory on the practitioner remains strong. If markets are routinely supposed to clear by price, then getting the prices right or, more grandly, assuring a Pareto efficient allocation, becomes an obsession. If neoclassical growth theory teaches that increased saving automatically transubstantiates itself into higher investment and faster growth, then policies that stimulate saving become ends unto themselves.

Until recently, the narrowness of these ways was more apparent in the Third World than the First. The neoclassical synthesis held sway in advanced economies from the 1950s until the mid-1970s, in part because they behaved neoclassically. Such fortune never befell the poor countries of this world, and their economists always talked about structure. So did economists from the richer countries until after the Second World War—John Maynard Keynes is a classic example. Because their epistemology was founded on physics, mathematics, and derivation of economic theories from maximizing "first principles," the framers of the neoclassical synthesis devoted scant thought to issues of structure, though some could do it very well. They passed their bad habit along to their intellectual daughters and sons.

The analysis in this book is an attempt to rectify this omission in the context of developing countries. It amounts to a combination of abstract descriptions of the structures that Third World scholars have always emphasized with analytical models largely developed by Keynes, Michal Kalecki, and their followers of the Cambridge School. Like most blends of two lines of thought, the product will partly displease both sets of progenitors. But—as is clear from the long list of names in the Acknowledgment at the front of the book—it strikes an increasing number of people as a useful way to think about macroeconomics for the majority of countries in the world.

The remainder of this chapter is devoted to three tasks. First, in section 1.1 there is a recital of the structural characteristics of developing countries that are emphasized in the analytical models that follow. No one country has all or even many of the characteristics, but all poor countries have some of them. There is no such thing as a single model of underdevelopment, but certain aspects reappear in different combinations. Not all existing combinations are discussed in this book, but enough models are developed to show how they can be.

In section 1.2 there is a discussion of the main analytical tools applied, the tricks in the models. There is a strong tendency in orthodox economics to make a fetish of technique. In part this book responds to fashion—it purports to show that structuralist thought can be made rigorous. This attempt risks banality. True insight into how the economy functions easily degenerates into boring algebra. Our goal in section 1.2 is to give a preview of how the algebra goes about its tasks.

Finally, in section 1.3 there is a compilation of the topics covered in chapters 2 through 10. Most of what one learns from the analytical models that is of practical or policy use is summarized in chapter 11. The reader mainly interested in inquiring if formalized structuralist macroeconomics is of any earthly use is encouraged to jump directly there.

1.1 Economic Structure

The approach to models taken here begins by asking what variables adjust to assure that overall macro balance is reached—that saving is equal to the value of investment, in the usual shorthand. Three adjustment mechanisms naturally present themselves:

1. Output meets demand, made up of autonomous elements like investment and output-sensitive components like private consumption.
2. Supply is fixed, so demand must adjust to it. One means is through price changes that limit consumption (in the simplest model) to total output minus investment.
3. Some component of demand varies freely to bring overall balance—competitive imports or government spending are two possibilities.

Consider an economy in which commodity production requires inputs of labor, imported intermediate goods, and a stock of durable means of production called "capital." One aspect of structure emphasized here is that the wage is determined institutionally, in effect by class conflict in ways described more fully below. A second key point is the economy's critical need for imported inputs. Since the energy crisis, these have entered North Atlantic theory also, but their importance never eluded economists in the Third World.

In this production setup, which of the three adjustment mechanisms just mentioned can be assumed to apply? The answer is that "it depends." At times and for some purposes the macroeconomy can be assumed to be at "full employment" in the sense that capacity is fully utilized and output fixed; at other times and for other purposes the opposite assumption makes sense. Moreover, some sectors may have fixed outputs, and adjusting prices, whereas others have supply responding to demand. Different structural models follow from different sets of assumptions, as pointed out repeatedly in the following chapters.

Subject to these sorts of hypotheses about commodity market clearing, changes in the functional income distribution are a fundamental part of the economy's approach to macro balance. Classes are distinguished by sources of income and saving and consumption behavior. Some gain and others lose when the macro situation changes; the losers may try to regain their eroded position by forcing further changes in macro variables over time. One example is workers who find their real incomes decline when prices rise to bring macro balance under conditions of fixed output in some sectors. They press for higher wages, and in so doing find that their claims for real income conflict with those of capitalists, the government, foreigners, or other groups in the system. From this process of conflicting claims, inflation, perhaps linked with more severe social disruption, is an inevitable result.

Most structuralist theories of inflation (certainly the ones in this book) proceed along these lines. They can be made subtle when it is recognized that the relative bargaining strength of capitalists and workers changes with the situation of the economy—workers may be in a position to obtain higher real wage gains when employment is high or inflation accelerates. Such assumptions underlie the profit-squeeze theories of cyclical adjustment that appear in the medium-run models presented below.

Foreign trade enters this interplay in several ways. The open economy must adjust so that two balances are satisfied:

1. The trade deficit (foreign saving) must equal investment minus national saving.
2. The trade deficit must also equal the sum of imports (capital, intermediate, and consumer) and net interest payments on debt, minus exports and other net current foreign exchange receipts such as emigrant remittances.

Different models can be constructed around the two variables that adjust to assure these relationships hold. The growth rate, capacity utilization, and the trade deficit are possible accommodating variables among macro quantities, while the exchange rate and the price level (implicitly, the income distribution) play the same role in the price system. Some pairs of adjusting variables are more plausible candidates in the context of development economics than others. The choice defines the structure one chooses to impose for analyzing a particular policy program. Selection requires a judgment from outside the model about the key forces that make the economy operate. Returning to a point made earlier, postulating maximizing behavior on the part of all agents suppresses the need to judge.

Money and financial variables affect the real side of the economy along with trade. Investment responds to the interest rate as well as to the profit rate (or the income distribution) and capacity utilization. But interest payments also enter firms' prime costs if they are required to pay in advance for labor and intermediate inputs. Facing poorly articulated transport and commercialization networks and financial systems with a low degree of intermediation, firms in poor countries may find these working-capital expenses to be a large fraction of their cash flow. One important implication is that by driving up interest rates, contractionary monetary policy is likely to push up prices and reduce activity levels from the side of costs.

Interest rate cost-push is left out of standard models, which inevitably show monetary contraction to be anti-inflationary. Similarly, the fact that exchange-rate devaluation raises costs through intermediate imports does not enter the usual formulations. The implications are that devaluation does not raise prices and stimulates output, when in fact the opposites are true, in the short run, in many developing countries. Models have to include these linkages if they are to be at all relevant to policy formulation in the Third World.

To summarize, structuralist models incorporate important technical and behavioral relationships of the type mentioned above. They focus attention on how the income distribution and output levels vary to satisfy the major macro balance equations in the short run. Longer-run developments depend on the reactions of gainers and losers to these initial adjustments. Finally, judgment is required as to the key forces shaping economic change and the directions they move. An economic world substantially richer than that of orthodox theory is constructed in an attempt to capture the diversity of underdevelopment.

1.2 Analytical Tools

Perhaps surprisingly, in light of the way economic analysis has developed since the 1930s, simple mathematics more than suffices to address the issues considered here. The reason is that separate models are constructed to describe specific economic structures, with no attempt at generalization (in the mathematicians' sense) for its own sake. Eschewing maximization, many agents, general nonlinear or topological descriptions of choice and production sets, and all the other paraphernalia of modern economics means that one can concentrate on essentials—specifically, how do economic groups respond broadly to price and output changes at the macro level?

This question already focuses attention on the two main macro balance equations mentioned above: investment equals foreign plus national saving, and foreign saving equals imports plus net interest, minus exports and net remittances. These two balances hold "identically" in the national accounts data upon which all applied models must be based, but they also describe situations of virtual disequilibrium. Suppose investment momentarily exceeds saving. What can adjust to restore macro balance? Will the adjustment be stable in the sense that once it has occurred, equilibrium will persist? Most analysis in this book is set up in terms of these questions, and for that reason standard local stability analysis of the differential equations describing adjustment toward equilibrium is employed. But the manipulations around the Jacobian matrixes for stability should not shroud the simplicity of the issues involved. Macro equilibrium in which aggregate prices, quantities, and the income distribution all satisfy the "identities" can come about in various ways. We want to explore these paths.

In terms of details, a few formulations are repeatedly employed. They include the following:

1. The price level is often assumed to be determined by a fixed producers' markup over prime cost, including labor, import, and working-capital finance costs. The markup specification broadly fits the data and is far simpler to manipulate than the obvious alternative of neoclassical cost functions.
2. Saving propensities are assumed to differ by class—higher for profit than wage recipients. Once the difference is recognized, one retains little besides detail if the workers' saving propensity is assumed to be positive. Hence, it is set to zero.
3. Even short-run models are often set up in terms of variables normalized by division by the value of capital stock. This trick throws emphasis on growth and profit rates as opposed to levels of investment and payments to factors; one can argue that the former type of variable provides a more intuitive feel for how the system works. Also, setting up initial models in normalized form allows an easy translation to analysis of growth later in the book.
4. In several cases overall macro balance is decomposed sectorally— the stability stories are set up around mechanisms through which excess demand in each sector adjusts toward toward zero in the very short run. As mentioned above, one sector may be assumed to have an adjusting price and the other an adjusting output level. This simple "flexprice-fixprice" model[1] describes a surprising range of economic structures and is employed repeatedly.
5. The two-sector formulation calls attention to differences in consumption patterns, in particular to the fact that some industries face demands that are inelastic with respect to income and price. More or less complicated complete systems of consumer demand equations can be used to formalize this manifestation of Engel's Law. Very simple equations using constant marginal propensities to consume and one or two intercept terms are used here.
6. Financial variables are incorporated on lines set out by Keynes and elaborated by James Tobin. Specifically, a set of assets is postulated, and accommodating variables adjust until rentiers desire to hold the assets in the quantities and at the prices that exist. In the simplest case, for example, firms borrow at a variable interest rate to finance working capital outlays. Rentiers can either lend to firms or put deposits in banks. The interest rate changes until the excess demand for loans (or, given the balance sheets of the banks, the excess supply of deposits)

is equal to zero. Differential equations are deployed to formalize conditions under which this adjustment process stably converges. (Sometimes it does not —a good reason to worry about working-capital cost-push.)

7. Investment demand is determined by firms and plays a key role in both short-run adjustment and longer term growth. The growth rate of capital stock (investment divided by the existing stock, ignoring depreciation) is assumed to depend positively on the profit rate (firms' cash flow divided by the value of capital) or the rate of capacity utilization. This specification reflects Cambridge theory. When the interest rate is brought into the models, capital stock growth depends on the difference between profit and interest rates. This is very Keynesian or Tobinesque. In two-sector models, investment-demand functions may of course differ between industries, with corresponding influence on long-run economic structure.

8. Imports are split several ways. There are, at times, three types of "noncompetitive" imports.[2] Capital-goods purchases abroad are proportional to total investment demand. Intermediate imports depend on levels of output. Consumption imports, when considered, come from demand functions of the type discussed above. Finally, "competitive" imports are sometimes entered as an adjusting variable to close the gap between demand and supply of a commodity produced within the economy. Under this last set of circumstances, the "Law of One Price," which states that internal prices are determined from the world market, may or may not be assumed to hold.

9. Exports may be set exogenously, or assumed to be determined by the difference between the internal and world price of the commodity exported (in a simple linear equation), or vary to equilibrate commodity demand and supply in the same fashion as competitive imports.

10. Long-run issues are investigated by setting up transitions between steady states in which all variables grow at constant rates. For example, in one-sector models with money, the steady-state conditions are two. First, the rate of money expansion should equal the rate of output (or capital stock) growth plus the rate of inflation. Second, the real wage should be constant, or wage inflation should equal price inflation. These conditions are equivalent to stating that the ratios Money Stock/Value of Capital and Price/Wage stay constant. Differential equations are set up in terms of these "state variables," and their stability properties are analyzed. Of course, the equations incorporate hypotheses regarding bargaining or class conflict over wage-adjustment rules, the role of the interest rate in shaping working-capital cost-push and investment demand, and similar matters. In two-sector models, as another example, the relevant state variable is the ratio of capital stocks in the two industries. To hold the ratio constant, both sectors must grow at the same rate in the steady state.

11. Finally, directions of causality among variables differ from model to model— that is what the analysis is all about. A reader carrying this thought at the back of his mind will not be confused by the transitions.

1.3 Readers' Guide

Topics covered in the chapters unwind more or less in the order just set out. Chapter 2 takes up quantity, price, and competitive import adjustment toward macro balance in a one-sector model. Comparative static exercises center around currency devaluation (which can prove "stagflationary," with price increases and output contraction at the same time) and income redistribution. A digression shows that neoclassical formulations give essentially the same results as in the simpler models used here, *except* when macro causality is set up to let saving determine investment. Then the substitutability assumptions at the base of neoclassical models have an important role to play. Finally, a profit-squeeze business-cycle theory is proposed as a first extension of the analysis toward the medium run.

Chapter 3 is devoted to a pair of fixprice/flexprice models, with price-clearing agricultural and infrastructure sectors in order. Industry is the quantity-clearing sector in both models. The effects of big investment pushes, food consumption subsidies, and other matters are discussed in the first agriculture/industry system. The second model focuses on the absorption problems of a mineral exporting economy. Both theoretical specifications underlie chapter 4, where an empirical computable general equilibrium model for India (with two price-clearing and three quantity-clearing sectors) is used to illustrate the vagaries of short-run adjustment in practice.

Financial markets are introduced in chapter 5. The public can hold three assets: money in the form of bank deposits; loans to firms to finance working capital; and a collection of nonproductive assets called "gold." A reduction in money supply increases the interest rate on loans to firms and thus the cost of working capital. A sharp enough increase can drive up the price level from the side of cost-push—monetary contraction can be inflationary in the short run. Similarly, attempts to draw deposits toward the banking system can lead to a contraction in rentiers' desired volume of productive loans to firms instead of holdings of gold. The outcome is once again stagflation. Orthodox financial policy can easily prove counterproductive. This lesson is extended to the long run in chapter 6, where it is shown across different steady states that slower money growth can lead to faster inflation, a lower growth rate of output, and a more unequal income distribution. The skeleton key to these unusual results is again interest rate cost-push resulting from restrictive monetary policy.

Chapter 7 addresses open economy problems of stabilization and growth, using the two balance equations described above. These are first interpreted in terms of the development economists' familiar two-gap model (due fundamentally to Hollis Chenery) and then put through adjustment paces. The chapter also discusses the roles of foreign interest payments and an export push in affecting internal and external balance.

One of the specifications in chapter 7 is short run, with the trade deficit and the level of economic activity responding to investment demand (or the capital stock growth rate), the exchange rate, and other variables. This description of the real side of the economy is combined with financial markets in chapter 8 to inquire about the effects of revising the rate at which the nominal exchange rate is depreciated in a crawling peg. Recent orthodoxy recommends that the rate of crawl be slowed as an anti-inflationary device. This policy is shown to have strongly destabilizing tendencies in the long run. The chapter closes with a review of how the gap equations in chapter 7 plus the monetary system's accounting identity (money supply = bank credit to the private sector + bank credit to the government + foreign reserves) are applied in practical economic work by agencies such as the World Bank and the International Monetary Fund.

Chapter 9 takes up longer-term patterns of growth and income distribution in two two-sector models. The first extends the agriculture/industry model of chapter 3 to discuss food-price inflation and its real effects in steady state. The second model shows how policies aimed at income redistribution may accelerate growth in an economy with "wage" and "luxury" good industries.

Chapter 10 turns to international issues in a long-term context, where the "South" is assumed to export a price-clearing commodity for which the income elasticity of demand in the "North" is less than one. The North exports investment goods and luxuries to the South. It is shown that growth in the South is largely dependent on what happens in the North in these circumstances, and that a productivity increase in its export industry will generate adverse shifts in its terms of trade, available saving, and rate of growth. This last finding is a classic structuralist result.

Finally, as mentioned above, chapter 11 summarizes policy conclusions.

2

Adjustment Mechanisms— The Real Side

MACROECONOMICS begins with the notion that the value of saving generated by all participants in the economy must by one means or another come into equality with the value of investment in the short run. The investment decisions are typically made by public authorities, the managers of firms, and the families that choose to construct new housing. In a capitalist system, saving comes from financial institutions (insurance companies, pension funds, and so forth), retained earnings of firms (over which managers exercise partial control), the public sector's budget surplus, households, and foreign institutions that lend money to accumulate "our" country's financial obligations or cover its deficit on foreign trade. These accounting truisms are repeated here to emphasize one point: the groups making saving and investment decisions only partly overlap; hence, there must be mechanisms that affect their behavior to bring their totals of saving and investment into accord. In any functioning economy, of course, adjustment occurs in many ways at the same time. The art of macroeconomic modeling is to pick out the dominant changes for more careful, at times mathematical, scrutiny. By the same token, fundamental debates in macroeconomics almost always are about which mechanisms are central to the adjustment process.

Although economic history and anthropology show that other modes are possible, saving and investment shifts in modern economies are mediated through money or its close substitutes. The implication is that banks and the financial system play central macroeconomic roles. However, the banks' actions are often (though not always) subordinate—they are overwhelmed by more aggressive actors, like Bertram in *All's Well that Ends Well.* For that reason, this and the next two chapters deal with adjustments in prices and flows of output that stem from the economy's nonmonetary or real side.

The focus here is on countries at middle and low levels of gross domestic product per head. The institutional and class alignments assumed to characterize these economies will emerge during the course of the discussion. With some modification, the models set out here also apply to northern, industrialized nations; indeed, many of the basic ideas are due to progressive economists from that corner of the world. But for the most part the analysis here is directed toward the southern hemisphere.

We begin the discussion in section 2.1 with a simple one-sector model in which three types of short-run macro adjustments are possible—changes in capacity utilization, shifts in the income distribution through "forced saving," and movements in the level of available saving stemming from changes in the foreign trade deficit. Contrasts between these adjustment mechanisms are illustrated by comparative static exercises in section 2.2. The formulation of the model is not neoclassical in the sense that it works with fixed production coefficients and markup pricing. However, the results in practice differ little from more orthodox formulations. This is the topic of section 2.3. How the economy functions under full employment of both labor and capital or capacity is also discussed there. Finally, an initial analysis of growth and distributional issues in the medium run appears in section 2.4.

2.1 An Industrial Economy

Through manufacturing and related activities account for far less than one-half of total value added and an even smaller share of employment in most developing countries, they play a central macroeconomic role. The industrial sector often grows faster than the rest of the system, and is more responsive to government policy tools. Moreover, it is often characterized by excess capacity, and for that reason its macro adjustments take place on the quantity side. By contrast, manufacturing prices are likely to be fixed in the "short run" (one or a few quarters) by relatively stable markups over variable cost. The existence of markups can be rationalized in various ways, but presence of spare capacity and oligopolistic structures among firms (buttressed in most developing countries by ample tariff protection from foreign competition) is probably the best single explanation.[1] For present purposes, we simply postulate a markup rate for such firms (fixed or varying, according to whether capacity is fully utilized) and work out the implications of this pricing rule.

On the cost side, a firm's variable inputs will typically comprise labor, intermediate goods in process, and raw materials. For the economy as a whole, standard input-output calculations show that these input flows can be reduced to labor services and *imported* intermediates. One firm's sale is often another's intermediate purchase, and such transactions can be netted out in macro accounting. To keep the algebra as simple as possible, assume that this consolidation has already taken place.[2]

The costs per unit of labor and intermediates will be taken as fixed in nominal terms in the short run. For imports, this assumption amounts to saying that they can be obtained on the world market at a fixed price in terms of foreign exchange, and that the nominal exchange rate is stable. For labor, a fixed money wage is assumed—workers are hired up to the levels of firms' demand at this wage. Between periods (or "moments" of time) the money wage will adjust according to past inflation rates, labor market conditions, and the relative bargaining strengths of workers and capitalists. The details of what happens when the markup, as opposed to the wage rate, shifts are given in section 2.4.

With fixed nominal input costs and markup pricing in force, the pricing rule for the industrial sector will take the form:

$$P = (1 + \tau)(wb + eP_0^* a_0) \tag{2.1}$$

where P is the sector's output (or producer) price; τ is the markup rate, w is the nominal wage rate; b is a labor-output coefficient (the inverse of average labor productivity); e is the exchange rate or price of the local currency in terms of foreign currency (for example, ten "locals" trade for one dollar, and $e = 10$); P_0^* is the foreign currency price of imported intermediates; and a_0 is the intermediate import-output coefficient. Another decomposition of price, useful later on, is:

$$P = [wb + \tau(wb + eP_0^* a_0)] + eP_0^* a_0 \qquad (2.2)$$

Here, the term in brackets is value-added per unit output, in turn separated into wage and nonwage components wb and $\tau(wb + eP_0^* a_0)$ respectively. Value-added plus intermediate imports per unit output $(eP_0^* a_0)$ sum to the price level P.

Assume that the value of physical capital (plant and equipment) owned by industrial firms is PK. A rigorous justification would be that there is just one type of industrial product that can be used as an intermediate, a final consumption good, and fixed capital: the amount K serving as capital is valued at the current producer price P. Nobody seriously believes such stories but many economists still find it convenient to work with profit rates of the form:

$$r = \frac{PX - wbX - eP_0^* a_0 X}{PK}$$

In this ratio, the numerator is total industrial sales PX (when the output flow is X), less wage and intermediate import costs. Dividing this measure of total profits by the value of capital stock gives the profit rate r. After substitution from (2.1), r can be rewritten as

$$r = \frac{\tau}{1 + \tau} \frac{X}{K} = \frac{\tau}{1 + \tau} u \qquad (2.3)$$

where u is the output-capital ratio. So long as there is excess capacity in the industrial sector, u is free to vary and can serve as a measure of capacity utilization. Equation (2.3) shows that the profit rate is an increasing function of the output-capital ratio. For constant u, r also increases with the markup rate τ, as one might expect.

Now assume for the moment that the industrial sector is the whole economy (or that the rest of the economy behaves just like industry). The purpose of this drastic simplification is to set out the major macro adjustment mechanisms in simplest form. To that end, note that excess demand (demand less supply) for output will equal zero when the condition

$$C + I + E - X = 0 \qquad (2.4)$$

is satisfied. As usual, C in (2.4) stands for household consumption, I for investment (stock changes plus capital formation), and E for net exports (total exports less imports of commodities similar to or "competitive" with domestic products). Note that government purchases of goods and services are not included in the accounting—leaving them out amounts to ignoring fiscal policy in favor of an emphasis on private sector actions in this chapter.

The next step is to reduce (2.4) to a statement of saving-investment equilibrium for the economy. To do so, let the value of total consumption be given by:

$$PC = wbX + (1 - s_r)rPK \qquad (2.5)$$

That is, wage earners consume all their income, while a share, s_r, of profit income is not consumed, or saved. This formulation leaves out whatever saving workers may undertake; however, much of their accumulation ultimately goes to finance housing and purchase of consumer durables and can be left out of a model focused on industrial investment demand. Saving from profits will be undertaken both by firms (retained earnings) and those presumably well-off households that receive significant amounts of property income. Depending on accounting conventions, in many countries surpluses of public enterprises would also contribute to the profit-based saving flow.[3]

Substitution of (2.5) into (2.4) and manipulation based on the cost decomposition (2.2) give the equation:

$$PI - (eP_0^* a_0 X - PE) - s_r rPK = 0$$

This expression can be interpreted as an investment-saving balance. When investment PI less the trade deficit $(eP^* a_0 X - PE)$ less saving from profits $s_r rPK$ is equal to zero, then the economy is in macro equilibrium. An equivalent statement from (2.4) is that excess demand for commodities is zero. In this chapter, excess demands for both labor and financial assets are left out of the picture; hence, (2.4) or the investment-saving balance is equivalent to Walras's law.

In the rest of this chapter, a notation that expresses the investment-saving balance in growth-rate terms will be used to pave the way for analysis of growth models later in the book. Define three new symbols as $\phi = eP_0^* a_0/(wb + eP_0^* a_0)$, or the share of intermediate imports in variable cost; $g = I/K$, or the growth rate of capital stock; and $\epsilon = E/K$, or the ratio of exports to capital stock. Then dividing the above investment-saving balance by PK allows it to be rewritten as:

$$g + \epsilon - (\tau^{-1}\phi + s_r)r = 0 \qquad (2.6)$$

In words, saving per unit of capital in the economy is the sum of saving from profits $s_r r$ and the nonconsumed flow of income resulting from intermediate imports $\phi r / \tau$. Total saving is exhausted by capital stock growth g and net exports of home-produced goods as a fraction of capital stock, ϵ.

To close out a description of the macroeconomy, we have to write down demand functions for investment and net exports. Export demand ϵ can most usefully be held constant for the moment. Investment demand can be expressed as:

$$g = z_0 + z_1 r + z_2 u$$
$$= z_0 + \left[z_1 + \frac{1 + \tau}{\tau} z_2 \right] r \qquad (2.7)$$

The theory underlying the equation in the first line is that there is some base level z_0 of public and private investment that is unaffected by current economic conditions—in the traditional phrase, z_0 reflects the "animal spirits" of private corporate managers and public enterprise functionaries. Investment will rise with both the profit rate r and the index of capacity utilization u as indicators of future profitability. The variable u resembles an accelerator term in investment demand functions; econometric evidence suggests that the accelerator coefficient z_2 is likely to exceed the profit rate coefficient z_1 in (2.7). The second line in this formula uses (2.3) to reduce investment behavior to a function of the profit rate and the markup τ.

Equation (2.6) is drawn as the "Saving supply" curve in figure 2.1, under the assumption of an exogenously fixed level of net exports. Even if investment demand g is zero, domestic saving is required to finance the corresponding trade surplus. The intercept of the saving supply curve on the r-axis represents the profit rate that will generate the needed saving flow.

The "investment demand" schedules in the diagram correspond to (2.7), with two different levels of the animal spirits parameter z_0. In the middle quadrant, capacity utilization and the profit rate are related positively according to (2.3) until a capacity limit $\bar{u}$ is reached. Thereafter, capacity use stays constant while profit rate increases are accompanied in the bottom quadrant by a falling real wage ω or w/P:

$$\omega = \frac{W}{P} = \frac{w}{(1 + \tau)(wb + eP_0^* a_0)} = \frac{1 - \phi}{(1 + \tau)b} \qquad (2.8)$$

The markup rate is constant so long as capacity utilization is below its maximum value $\bar{u}$. The real wage takes on corresponding value $\bar{\omega}$. When

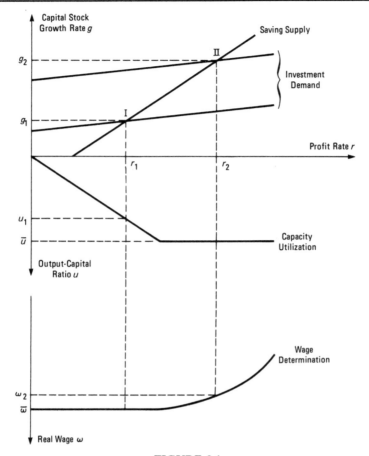

FIGURE 2.1

Macro Equilibrium with Capacity Adjustment (Point I) and Forced Saving (Point II)

the economy reaches full capacity, further increases in the profit rate can only come from a higher markup rate and a falling real wage. In formal terms, transition to full capacity imposes an additional restriction on the macro system. It can only be met by an additional dependent variable, and the obvious candidate is the markup rate. As described in detail below, a rise in τ drives up the price level P, which in turn limits demand to the available capacity level $\bar{u}K$.

Now consider the investment-saving equilibrium points in figure 2.1. At point I, the growth rate is g_1, the profit rate is r_1, and there is excess capacity since u_1 lies below $\bar{u}$. Any small increase in investment (or export) demand could be met by increased capacity use at a constant real wage $\bar{\omega}$.

Macro adjustments in the vicinity of equilibrium I follow the classical Keynesian rules.[4] From (2.6) and (2.7) the mechanism can be described in formal terms as an adjustment in the profit rate of the form:

$$\frac{dr}{dt} = f[g + \epsilon - (\tau^{-1}\phi + s_r)r]$$

$$= f\left\{z_0 + \epsilon + \left[\left(z_1 + \frac{1 + \tau}{\tau}z_2\right) - \left(\frac{\phi}{\tau} + s_r\right)\right]r\right\} \quad (2.9)$$

where $f(0) = 0$ and the first derivative of f is positive. The profit rate (and capacity utilization) will be constant when commodity excess demand is zero and saving equals investment, but will rise when excess demand is positive. The adjustment is stable if the derivative of f with respect to r is negative, so that a rising r will drive excess demand back toward zero. It is easy to verify that this will be the case when the slope of the investment function is less than that of the saving function, as shown in figure 2.1.

At point II, the saving-investment equilibrium occurs at full capacity $\bar{u}$. As argued above, the markup rate and real wage are endogenous in this situation. Any increase in animal spirits or exogenous investment z_0 will create excess demand for output that can only be reduced by rising price level P and markup rate τ. From (2.8), there will be a falling real wage ω. Since the propensity to consume from wage income exceeds that from profits, total consumption will be reduced and excess demand driven back to zero. This is a forced saving adjustment, of the type emphasized by Kalecki and Kaldor.[5] Note that its efficacy requires a constant money wage w in (2.8), or at least wage increases that lag prices. Forced saving is impossible when (1) saving propensities of workers and profit recipients (or of all groups) are the same, *or* (2) wages (or all nominal payment flows) are instantaneously and fully indexed to price increases. In an economy with a plausible set of medium-term contract obligations, behavioral parameters and apparatus for class repression, these conditions will not be satisfied and forced saving is a viable adjustment mechanism.[6]

To give a formal version of the adjustment, note from (2.3) that at full capacity the profit and markup rates are linked by the equation $(1 + \tau)/\tau = \bar{u}/r$. Substitution into (2.9) then gives the profit rate response to excess demand as:

$$\frac{dr}{dt} = f[z_0 + \epsilon + (z_2 - \phi)\bar{u} + (z_1 + \phi - s_r)r]$$

For a plausibly high saving rate, $df/dr < 0$, and the forced saving adjustment will be stable.

So far, the variable ϵ, representing net exports as a share of capital stock, has been held constant. Moreover, little would be changed if net exports adjusted according to a rule such as $\epsilon = \epsilon(eP_E^*/P)$, where P_E^* is the foreign currency price of "our" exports. This equation simply states that exports are an increasing function of the ratio between the price at which they can be sold and the domestic producer price. Depending on the circumstances, export price responsiveness may or may not be macroeconomically important, but it does not modify the adjustment mechanism underlying figure 2.1 in any essential way.

Adjustment can be affected, however, if net exports are treated as completely endogenous. Assume that the economy is at full capacity and, moreover, that workers can muster sufficient power to stabilize the real wage at level ω_2 in figure 2.1. At full capacity, the profit rate will then be fixed at r_2 and saving supply (per unit of capital) at g_2. How could a further increase in investment demand be accommodated? Figure 2.2 illustrates one means —an upward shift in the saving function mediated by falling net exports.

FIGURE 2.2

Macro Adjustment by Reduced Net Exports at Full Capacity Utilization and a Fixed Real Wage

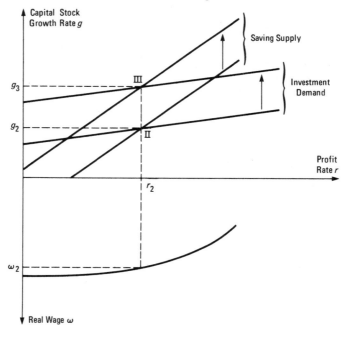

As ϵ declines for a given profit rate r, (2.6) shows that more saving is made available to finance investment demand. The saving supply curve shifts up while the country's foreign trade surplus declines (or its deficit increases). "Foreign saving" provides the means for the economy to move its equilibrium from II to III while the real wage stays fixed.

Evidently, other saving flows could be made endogenous to satisfy a similar function. Changes in the public sector surplus by continuously adjusting tax or subsidy rates are examples. As we will see in subsequent chapters, such adjustments almost always have monetary repercussions that may not be easy to control. But along with variations in capacity use and forced saving, endogenous shifts in the levels of foreign or public sector saving are an important adjustment device.

2.2 Comparative Statics

The best way to illustrate the economic significance of these mechanisms is through exercises in comparative statics. Two main variants are presented here—a reduction in the markup rate τ and currency devaluation or an increase in the exchange rate e.

Cutting the markup rate amounts to an income redistribution from profit recipients to wage earners. In a relatively closed economy, lower markups could be achieved by profit taxes coupled with income transfers or with price controls or more forceful state intervention in the affairs of industrial firms. In an open economy, reduction of tariff barriers and other forms of trade liberalization could do the trick. If these moves are made when there is excess capacity, there will be three major effects. First, there will be an increase in aggregate demand as income flows are redirected toward relatively low-saving workers. At a given level of capacity utilization u, the real wage will rise and the profit rate will fall when τ is reduced, as shown respectively by (2.8) and (2.3). The curve relating u and r will rotate clockwise, as shown in the middle quadrant of figure 2.3. The outcome will be higher output from increased demand at the initial profit rate r_1.

The second effect is on investment demand. When the coefficient z_2 exceeds zero in (2.7), investors will respond to increasing capacity use by raising their rate of capital accumulation. The investment demand function will rotate counterclockwise in the upper quadrant of figure 2.3, and the result, when the saving function doesn't shift, would be higher rates of growth, profits, and capacity utilization.

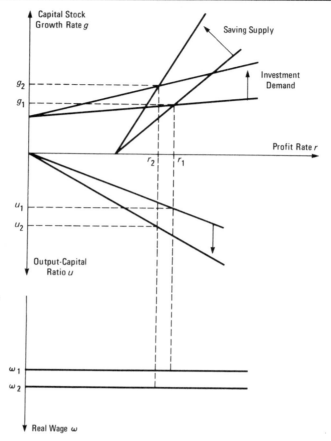

FIGURE 2.3

Effects of a Reduction in the Markup Rate τ

The third effect—a shift in the savings function—works in the opposite direction. From (2.6) saving supply at a constant r increases when τ declines; in effect, imports amount to a larger share of redirected income flows. The resulting leftward rotation of the saving function is contractionary, reducing aggregate demand. The joint movement of investment and saving functions has an ambiguous impact on both r and g, as can be seen from the following algebraic expressions for their changes:

$$\frac{\partial r}{\partial \tau} = \frac{r}{\Delta \tau^2}(\phi - z_2)$$

and

$$\frac{\partial g}{\partial \tau} = \frac{r}{\Delta \tau^2}[\phi z_1 + z_2(\phi - s_r)]$$

where $\Delta = (\tau^{-1}\phi + s_r) - [z_1 + \tau^{-1}(1 + \tau)z_2]$ is positive from the overall stability conditions.

These equations show that the growth rate will increase with a decline in τ so long as the saving rate s_r exceeds the import cost share ϕ. The conclusion is that profit and growth rate increases are more likely consequences of a reduction in the markup rate when the economy is not highly dependent on intermediate imports. Otherwise, the profit rate could easily fall, as illustrated in figure 2.3. Note also that capacity utilization increases, though this change could go in either direction as well. In the diagram, a reduction in markups gives rise to faster growth, more capacity utilization, and a higher real wage (bottom quadrant). At the same time, the profit rate falls. Resistance on the part of capitalists toward such a policy would be likely.

This model is often interpreted the other way round, with a high markup presented as the root cause of economic stagnation—low capacity utilization and slow growth. This line of thought has been frequently repeated in India, as in the following quotation from Deepak Nayyar:[7]

Clearly, a large proportion of the demand for industrial products originates from a narrow segment of the population. However, manufactured goods sold to the relatively few rich can use up only so much, and no more of the capacity in the intermediate and capital goods sector. Only a broad-based demand for mass consumption goods can lead to a full utilization of capacity . . . but that in turn requires incomes for the poor. Thus an unequal income distribution operating through demand functions might well restrict the prospects of sustained industrial growth.

The simple model used here does not capture Nayyar's intersectoral nuances, but does reflect his emphasis on lagging aggregate demand. Indeed, with a low enough intermediate import share, even capitalists might benefit from the sort of income distribution he implicitly favors. Such a condition may hold in India. Also, as shown in chapter 9, effects of the type discussed here carry over to a multisectoral macro model.

To pursue this theme further, one might ask about the consequences of income redistribution under full capacity use. Since τ is an endogenous variable when there is full capacity, income shifts via forced reduction in markups are not feasible. To explore other devices we can use the price decomposition:

$$P = wb + \frac{rP}{u} + eP_0^* a_0 \qquad (2.10)$$

which follows from (2.2) using the substitution $rPK = \tau(wb + eP_0^* a_0)X$ for total profits. Equation (2.10) can in turn be solved as:

$$r = u\left[1 - \frac{wb + eP_0^* a_0}{P}\right]$$

where, under full capacity, u will take the value $\bar{u}$.

The trade-offs in this equation are between real wage w/P (or ω) and profit rate r. Suppose that it is possible to raise w/P, for example, by money wage increases under strict price controls. Then r will fall, as in response to an increase in ω above the value ω_2 in figure 2.2. As r declines from r_2, the first effect would be macro disequilibrium. The excess of investment over saving (excess commodity demand) might be met by some endogenous saving source—for example, the balance of payments deficit or fiscal surplus. After the resulting upward shift in the saving supply schedule, the final effects would be slower growth, a higher real wage, and some dampening of aggregate demand from the fiscal or trade balance change. If demand were not damped, prices would tend to rise and the result would be reestablishment of macro equilibrium at point II after the wage increases had fully been passed along into the price level. Unless accompanied by policies to contract demand, attempts at income redistribution under full capacity can easily set off an outburst of inflation, resulting in no redistribution at all. The trick when attempting to shift income toward low-saving classes is to recognize when capacity bottlenecks are reached and the appropriable surplus from excess capacity has run out. Although other circumstances were adverse, the experience of historically slow-growing Chile in the early 1970s suggests that the feasible once-for-all increase in GDP might be about 8 to 10 percent.[8]

Income redistributions also play a substantial role in devaluation, the other comparative static shift explored here. An increase in the exchange rate e has several macro effects. It will initially lead to a rise in ϕ, the share of imported intermediates in variable cost. From (2.8) the real wage will fall when there is excess capacity and the markup rate is fixed. From (2.6) there will be more saving generated for a given profit rate r. As shown in figure 2.4 the saving supply schedule will rotate to the left. Finally, net exports may respond to a higher exchange rate, raising the initial surplus on trade of competitive goods, and shifting the intercept of the saving schedule to the right.

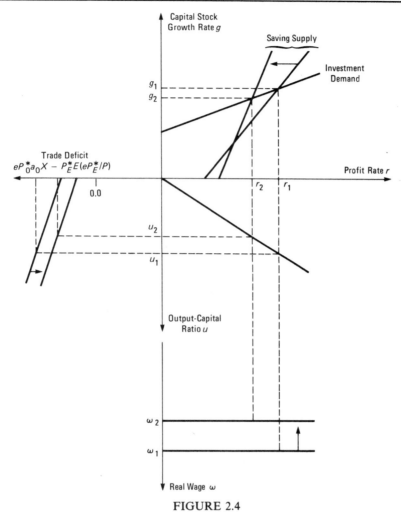

FIGURE 2.4

Effects of a Devaluation (an Increase in the Exchange Rate e)

The macroeconomic result of these changes is ambiguous. Figure 2.4 shows a case in which export response is relatively weak and the share of imported intermediates in variable cost is high. The leftward rotation of the saving schedule outweighs its rightward shift, leading to slower growth and reduced capacity use. Or, to put it another way, the initial increase in the local currency trade deficit from higher import costs exceeds its reduction from more exports, leading to increased foreign saving and lower aggregate demand. Put either way, the resulting output contraction is also accompanied by a price increase from (2.1) and a lower real wage. As illustrated on the "Trade deficit" axis, the devaluation does lead to balance of payments improvement, at least in terms of foreign prices. However, the deficit in domestic prices (the foreign price deficit multiplied by the higher exchange rate e) may get larger. As discussed in chapter 8, the higher deficit can lead to contraction in the money supply, which will strengthen the effects being discussed here.

Empirical evidence suggests that the output contraction and adverse income redistribution from devaluation illustrated in figure 2.4 may be fairly common; however, much depends on the export response. To get a formal expression, let η be the elasticity of exports with respect to their relative profitability, viz:

$$\eta = \frac{\partial E}{\partial(eP_E^*/P)} \frac{(eP_E^*/P)}{E}$$

Using this elasticity, one can show that, leaving aside changes in investment ($z_1 = z_2 = 0$), the response of output to devaluation is given by:

$$\frac{\partial X}{\partial e} \frac{e}{X} = \frac{(1 + \tau)(1 - \phi)}{s_r \tau + \phi} \left\{ \frac{\eta}{(eP_E^*/P)} \frac{E}{X} - \frac{\phi}{1 + \tau} \right\}$$

From this expression it is easy to see that output expansion requires the export elasticity to satisfy the condition:

$$\eta > \frac{eP_E^*}{P} \frac{(eP_0^* a_0 X/PX)}{E/X} \tag{2.11}$$

In an application, the price ratio eP_E^*/P should be fairly close to one (depending on the extent of export taxes or subsidies). In chapter 7 it is argued that exports will often exceed intermediate imports. Most developing countries import substantial quantities of capital goods as well as intermediates; indeed, the stylized fact is that financial capital inflow or the trade deficit is *less* than the value of imports of physical capital goods. Under such circumstances, exports exceed intermediate imports to generate sufficient foreign exchange to pay for the balance of capital goods imports.

The implication from condition (2.11) is that the lower bound on the elasticity for devaluation not to be contractionary is likely to be less than one. After a few quarters for sales to build up, η might be expected to take a value around unity. Hence, devaluation may be initially contractionary, and then lead to economic expansion after the export response takes hold.

However, riding out the contractionary phase may not be easy. The expected tenure of finance ministers who devalue is often very short.[9]

The effects of devaluation at full capacity can vary, depending on the specific assumptions about the responses of different classes of income recipients that one chooses to make. When u is fixed at $\bar{u}$ and the markup rate is endogenous, the saving supply and investment demand functions (2.6) and (2.7) can respectively be written as:

$$s_r r = g + \{\epsilon(eP_E^*/P) - (eP_0^*a_0/P)\bar{u}\} \qquad (2.12)$$

and

$$g = (z_0 + z_2\bar{u}) + z_1 r \qquad (2.13)$$

Suppose that the domestic price level P is held constant when e is raised so that the nominal devaluation is also "real." Then the relative cost of imported intermediates $(eP_0^*a_0/P)$ will go up while the return to exports (eP_E^*/P) will rise. The change in the bracketed term on the right side of (2.12) can, in principle, take either sign, but a "successful" devaluation would improve the trade balance and lead it to increase. It is easy to see from (2.12) and (2.13) that the outcome would be a higher capital stock growth rate g and profit rate r (so long as the basic stability condition $s_r > z_1$ is satisfied).

What about real wages? The cost decomposition (2.10) can be restated as:

$$\omega = \frac{1}{b}\left[1 - \left(\frac{r}{\bar{u}}\right) - \left(\frac{eP_0^*a_0}{P}\right)\right]$$

Evidently, if both r and the relative cost of intermediate imports $eP_0^*a_0/P$ rise, the real wage must fall. And the fall in the real wage is the mechanism by which consumption demand can decline so that exports and investment can rise when output is held constant by full capacity utilization. Under both fixed and variable capacity, devaluation basically works by cutting real wages. Once again, its political liabilities stand out strikingly.

2.3 A Neoclassical Digression

The model sketched so far has scant possibility for substitution of labor and capital, capital and imports, and other such trade-offs that neoclassical economists adore. The omission stems in part from a desire to simplify—fixed coefficients and markup pricing permit easy algebra and diagrams that emphasize directions of causation underlying macro adjustment paths. At the same time, the basic neoclassical hypotheses of perfect competition, facile substitution of production inputs, and all the rest lack credibility in industrial economies, let alone the Third World. Finally, a neoclassical formulation adds little to what has already been said, except under strong additional hypotheses. Demonstration of this last point is the purpose of this section.

To begin, note that the standard story about substitution in production can be closely mimicked with the apparatus already developed. The key neoclassical hypothesis is that the rate of profit should rise with the output-capital ratio. This relationship is already built into equation (2.3) for a fixed markup rate τ. Making τ a nonlinearly increasing function of output (there is conflicting econometric evidence on this idea[10]) would not change the fundamentals of macro adjustment as previously analyzed. However, there *would* be a blending of the two first adjustment mechanisms described above. That is, there would be forced saving from the increasing markup even before high levels of capacity utilization were reached, whereas if the function $\tau = \tau(X)$ were made steep near "full capacity," the kink in the capacity utilization function of figure 2.1 and the abrupt switch between Keynesian and forced saving adjustment regimes would not show up. For applied models, smoothing out adjustment processes in this way is often convenient—it helps prevent the numbers coming out of the computer from taking disconcerting jumps. One strength of neoclassical formulations comes from the fact that they have a lot of smoothness built in.

To illustrate smooth adjustment in more detail, it is simplest to work with a model in which there are no intermediate imports, so that only labor and capital enter as production inputs. Suppose further that there is an economywide constant elasticity of substitution (CES) production function of the form[11]:

$$X = \{ \mathbf{B}_L L^{(\sigma-1)/\sigma} + \mathbf{B}_K K^{(\sigma-1)/\sigma} \}^{\sigma/(\sigma-1)}$$

where L is the level of employment, σ the elasticity of substitution, and $\mathbf{B}_L$ and $\mathbf{B}_K$ distribution parameters in the CES function.

If producers minimize costs subject to this production technology, then the labor-output and capital-output ratios they choose will be given by:

$$\frac{L}{X} = \mathbf{B}_L{}^{\sigma} \left(\frac{w}{P} \right)^{-\sigma} \tag{2.14}$$

and

$$\frac{K}{X} = \mathbf{B}_K{}^{\sigma} \left(\frac{rP}{P} \right)^{-\sigma} = \left(\frac{\mathbf{B}_K}{r} \right)^{\sigma} \tag{2.15}$$

That is, the intensity of use of each factor is a decreasing function of its real cost to the producer.

To fit these relationships into a macro model, assume in the neoclassical spirit that there are no differences in saving parameters between recipients of wage and profit incomes. Then the value of consumption is given by:

$$PC = (1 - s)PX$$

where s is the economywide saving ratio. Insertion of this condition into the commodity excess demand function (2.4) and use of (2.15) then give an investment-saving balance of the form:

$$g + \epsilon - s \left(\frac{r}{\mathbf{B}_K} \right)^{\sigma} = 0 \tag{2.16}$$

This equation should be compared to (2.6). The two relationships clearly have the same general form, though when σ is not unity (the production function is not Cobb-Douglas), (2.16) is nonlinear in the profit rate r.

There is one more apparent difference between the neoclassical formulation and the one used before, in that the CES function permits capital-labor substitution. Observe that the CES production function can be rewritten as:

$$\frac{L}{K} = \frac{1}{\mathbf{B}_L} \left[\left(\frac{X}{K} \right)^{(\sigma - 1)/\sigma} - \mathbf{B}_K \right]^{\sigma/(\sigma - 1)} \tag{2.17}$$

This relates the labor-capital ratio uniquely to the output-capital ratio, or u. The relationship is not a straight line, as we have been assuming so far. Rather, it shows decreasing returns to labor in generating output as in the southwest quadrant of figure 2.5.

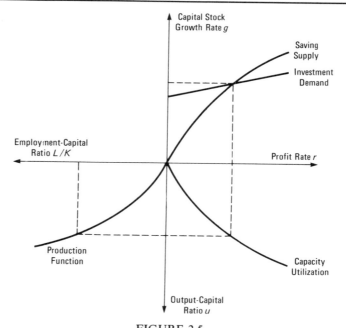

FIGURE 2.5

Macro Equilibrium When There Is a CES Production Function ($\sigma < 1$) and Producer Cost Minimization

Adding decreasing returns to the analysis suggests that wage-cutting ought to be an effective way to raise employment in the neoclassical model. However, such optimism is not well founded when the price level is free to vary. The reasoning is as follows:

1. The profit rate r is set in the macro equilibrium condition (2.16) when exports and the growth rate are predetermined variables.
2. The output-capital ratio follows from (2.15) and the labor-capital ratio from (2.17).
3. Solving (2.14) and (2.15) for the real wage w/P gives:

$$\frac{w}{P} = \left[\frac{L}{K}\right]^{-1/\sigma} \frac{B_L B_K}{r}$$

so that w/P is determined macroeconomically. Any attempt to reduce w will just pull P down along with it, and the real wage and resource allocation will be left unchanged. Unless the price level is set from outside (by fiat as the numeraire, or else by foreign trade), a nominal wage reduction will not reduce employment despite ample possibility for labor-capital substitution.[12]

The equilibrium model is illustrated in figure 2.5. Equation (2.16) becomes the nonlinear saving function in the northwest quadrant. Immediately below, the output-capital ratio is an increasing function of the profit rate, while in the southwest quadrant employment rises along with output. The saving supply and capacity utilization curves are drawn under the empirically based assumption that the elasticity of substitution σ lies below unity. The implication is that successively higher levels of the profit rate are associated with decreasing increments in the output-capital ratio. This hypothesis approximates the shape of the kinked capacity utilization schedule in figure 2.1

An increase in investment demand would lead to higher levels of the profit rate and output-capital ratio in figure 2.5. The labor-capital ratio would also rise, and from (2.17) the real wage w/P would have to fall. The adjustment to increased investment is a mixture of forced saving and Keynesian responses.

One final observation is that the economy might be supposed to function with full employment of both capital and labor. In that case, the labor/capital ratio would take on a predetermined value. From figure 2.5 one can see that the output-capital ratio, the profit rate, and [from equation (2.17)] the real wage would all be determined. What about saving and investment? With exports either fixed or depending strictly on price relationships, equation (2.16) is a condition for macroeconomic equilibrium that must be respected. Hence, investment and the capital stock growth rate would have to adjust to the level of g following from the full employment assumption and the economy's technological and savings parameters.

Along with output changes, forced saving, and endogenous shifts in the saving function, an investment function that always moves to meet saving supply is a fourth macro adjustment mechanism that one might consider. The problem is that it is not obvious *what* is changing to permit the investment function to shift (as opposed to the trade deficit or government budget surplus when there is an endogenous saving function). In fact, it is probably simpler to dispense with the investment function altogether, and assert that the capital stock growth rate results only from the forces of productivity and thrift. This sort of macro adjustment might properly be labeled neoclassical since it is based on the notion that the wage, profit rate, and labor- and capital-output ratios can always vary in such a way as to permit full employment of both inputs. That investment has to be endogenous is a natural corollary of such a system.

To illustrate the implications of this interpretation of neoclassicism, the comparative statics experiment of increasing the saving rate is useful. In a version of figure 2.5 with the investment function suppressed, the outcome would be a counterclockwise rotation of the saving supply and a higher capital stock growth rate g. Neither the profit rate nor the ratios describing labor and capital use would change. The contrast with previous formulations is striking since in those a higher saving rate is associated with slower growth, a lower profit rate, and either a lower level of output or a higher real wage.

Which set of responses is more realistic is a question of the institutions and historical circumstances in which an economy happens to be. Presumably, neoclassical economists tend to think that there really is full employment, while Keynesians and structuralists do not. The main thing to recognize is that a neoclassical formulation of production relationships is not fundamentally different from a story involving excess capacity and markups unless full employment is also assumed. But that amounts to a statement about the grand structure of the macro system and not its specific details.[13]

2.4 Profit Squeeze and Growth Dynamics in the Medium Run

As a final exercise, we can use the nonneoclassical model of sections 2.1 and 2.2 to explore growth and distribution over time as a prelude to the models of chapters 6, 8, and 9. Suppose that the markup rate τ is fixed at any moment, determining the level of capacity utilization u as in figure 2.1. If we treat u as the adjusting variable, then its value follows from the condition that excess demand equal zero.

$$\left(z_0 + z_1 \frac{\tau}{1 + \tau} u\right) - \left(\frac{\phi + s_r\tau}{1 + \tau}\right)u = 0 \qquad (2.18)$$

where the first term in parentheses represents investment demand (assumed to depend only on the profit rate $r = \tau u/(1 + \tau)$ (because of the coefficient z_1) and the second term is saving supply. The stability condition is that saving responds more strongly to an increase in capacity utilization than investment, or $(\phi/\tau) + s_r > z_1$.

Dynamics in the medium run will center around changes in the markup rate. Specifically, we adopt a chronology that appears in American business cycles, as follows:

Phase of Cycle	Profit Rate	Capacity Utilization	Profit Share
Upswing	Rises	Rises	Rises
Peak	Falls	Stable	Falls
Downswing	Falls	Falls	Falls

Radical economists (especially) interpret these cyclical variations in terms of a theory of profit squeeze. At the top of the cycle, employment and labor's bargaining strength rise. Workers can force a reduction in the share of profits in output, or a decline in the ratio $\tau/(1 + \tau)$. The resulting fall in markups also reduces the profit *rate,* leading to a contraction in investment demand. Aggregate demand as a whole declines in a multiplier process, and the cycle turns down. Over time, these effects may cumulate to lead to a secular decline in profits and the rate of growth, unless the central government intervenes to prop up demand.[14] Profit-squeeze or class-conflict theories of distribution and growth of this type state that the effect of capacity utilization on the markup is opposite to that in the neoclassical model in the last section. The evidence for advanced economies (at least) seems to run against the neoclassical hypothesis.[15]

To work out a formal model, we need to know the comparative statics of responses of the profit rate r, the capacity utilization rate u, and the capital stock growth rate g to changes in τ. From (2.18) an increase in τ will raise investment demand by the amount $z_1 u/(1 + \tau)^2$. It will cut savings generated directly and indirectly from intermediate imports by $-\phi u/(1 + \tau)^2$, and raise savings from profits by $s_r u/(1 + \tau)^2$. Assume investment minus saving rises, or $z_1 > s_r - \phi$. Then capacity utilization will go up with the markup rate. The solutions for the other variables are:

$$r = \frac{z_0}{\Delta}$$

and

$$g = (\tau^{-1}\phi + s_r)\frac{z_0}{\Delta}$$

where

$$\Delta = \tau^{-1}\phi + s_r - h > 0$$

By direct calculation, $\partial r/\partial \tau > 0$ and $\partial g/\partial \tau > 0$.

The profit-squeeze story depends on the notion that τ falls when employment and labor militancy are high. The labor-capital ratio L/K is equal to bu. Let the labor supply consistent with high employment be $\bar{L}$—in the Marxist idiom the reserve army of the unemployed would shrink toward a low level as L rose toward $\bar{L}$. Let $\lambda = L/\bar{L}$ and $k = K/\bar{L}$. Then by easy substitution:

$$\lambda = \left(\frac{L}{K}\right)\left(\frac{K}{\bar{L}}\right) = buk$$

Assume that the markup rate varies over time according to the rule

$$d\tau/dt = \alpha(1 - \lambda) = \alpha(1 - buk) \qquad (2.19)$$

so that τ falls when λ grows and full employment is approached.[16]

If the fully employed labor force grow at the rate g^*, then the growth rate of k is given by:

$$dk/dt = (g - g^*)k \qquad (2.20)$$

since (lettering a "hat" over a variable denote its growth rate)

$$\hat{k} = (dk/dt)/k = \hat{K} - \hat{\bar{L}}$$

and

$$\hat{K} = (dK/dt)/K = g$$

In growth models such as the system (2.19) and (2.20), it is simplest analytically to consider dynamics around a steady-state solution like the one defined by $\lambda = 1$ and $g = g^*$. That is, there is full employment of labor and the capital stock is growing at the same rate as the labor force at the steady state.

Around such an ideal growth trajectory, the variables adjust according to the Jacobian of (2.19) and (2.20):

$$\begin{bmatrix} -\alpha bk(\partial u/\partial\tau) & -\alpha bu \\ k(\partial g/\partial\tau) & 0 \end{bmatrix} \qquad (2.21)$$

where the entry in the southeast vanishes since $g = g^*$ at equilibrium.

Following tradition for applied economists, in this book we will consider only conditions assuring local stability of differential equations for adjustment around an equilibrium solution where time derivatives of "state" variables such as τ and k are equal to zero. For a two-dimensional system like (2.19) and (2.20), the stability conditions are that the trace of the Jacobian matrix must be negative and the determinant positive.[17]

The determinant of the matrix in (2.21) is positive, while the trace will be negative when $\partial u / \partial \tau > 0$. The conclusion is that when the level of capacity utilization responds positively to the markup rate, then distributional changes induced by a profit squeeze will lead the economy toward steady growth. As indicated by the spiral path sketched in figure 2.6, cyclical convergence toward the equilibrium could be expected.

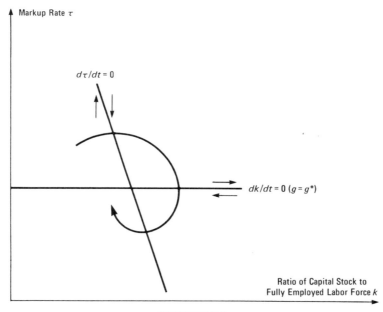

FIGURE 2.6

Dynamics of Adjustment to Steady-State Growth in a Profit-Squeeze Model

The key linkages underlying the stable adjustment are the positive association of capacity utilization with the markup rate due to

1. a strong investment response to a rise in τ, and
2. a saving decrease at the bottom of the cycle due to a lower relative domestic valuation of intermediate imports as τ starts to rise.

Forced dissaving from imports at low values of τ together with the investment response cause an initial expansion that is finally throttled by the profit squeeze. Stability of the process evidently requires that there exist a source of saving separate from that by capitalists. Fluctuations in the real value of this saving source as well as a Keynesian adjustment underlie the cyclical dynamics of figure 2.6. This adjustment process is complex, but it does broadly fit the data. It would fit even better if it took into account the role of inflation in prolonging forced saving processes over time. Such topics are addressed in the version of the present model for an inflationary economy, which appears in chapter 6.

A final question regards secular changes in τ as the economy shifts from the vicinity of one steady state to another. From the condition $g = g^*$, the equilibrium value of τ is:

$$\tau = \frac{\phi(g^* - z_0)}{z_1 g^* - s_r(g^* - z_0)}$$

A positive value of τ requires labor force growth to exceed autonomous investment demand ($g^* > z_0$) and a relatively high investment response parameter z_1.

Comparisons across steady states follow from observing that in the short run $\partial g/\partial \tau > 0$, $\partial g/\partial z_1 > 0$, and so forth.

Holding g equal to g^* and then taking the total differentials shows that the markup rate will fall secularly as labor force growth declines, investment responsiveness to the profit rate rises, or the saving rate falls. Any or all of these shifts could contribute to a long-run profit squeeze.

3

Adjustment Mechanisms— Two-Sector Models

ONCE any model of the economy is extended from one to several sectors, changes in relative prices of the different outputs can play a key role in the short-run adjustment process. The specific details, however, vary from system to system. In this chapter, the price mechanism is illustrated in two models corresponding to economic structures that appear widely in the Third World. The first describes an economy in which food production accounts for a large share of economic activity and consumer demand. There is a nonagricultural sector similar to the industrial economy described in the last chapter, with a fixed markup and capacity adjustment. The food, or agricultural, sector, by contrast, has fixed (or price-inelastic) supply in the short run, while its price varies to clear the market. A model is presented in section 3.1, with comparative statics in section 3.2.[1]

The other kind of economy described in this chapter is one in which there are large mineral exports. The mineral sector provides resources in foreign exchange, and the problem is how to transform dollars into effective nonmineral production within the country. There is assumed to be a sector producing nontraded goods with fixed capacity in the short run (think of the construction sector, transport and energy, and other infrastructure services). The price of such "universal intermediates" varies to clear the market. One effect of a price increase will be to raise production costs in the rest of the economy, assumed to have excess capacity and markup pricing (over wage, national intermediate, and imported intermediate costs). Products from the "manufacturing" sector are assumed to be used for export and consumer demand.

The details of the model are set out in section 3.3, where it is shown that expansion of mineral production can lead to a reduction in output and exports of the manufacturing sector (as well as increases in prices and a fall in the real wage). Hence, reduced internal and external diversification of the economy may go hand in hand. These results are extended to describe balance of payments problems in section 3.4, where the merits of devaluation and manipulation of the mining sector to improve the balance of trade are assessed.

3.1 An Economy with an Important Food Sector

Two sectors are assumed to be macroeconomically important. We will call them the agriculture (or the A-sector) and nonagriculture (or the N-sector) sectors for short. The N-sector resembles industry and urban services in most market economies by operating with chronic excess capacity and a fixed markup. If intermediate imports as an item of cost are ignored for simplicity, then the N-sector price P_n is given by:

$$P_n = (1 + \tau)wb_n \tag{3.1}$$

where τ is the markup rate, w is the money wage, and b_n is the labor-output ratio.

The agricultural sector, by contrast, is resource-limited: supply does not respond to price or other incentives in the short run.[2] For purposes of formal modeling, land can be assimilated with capital so that sustained food output increases can only come from investment activities such as land-clearing, mechanization, and works for irrigation. Available employment opportunities are limited by capital in the A-sector in terms of full-time equivalent jobs. For macroeconomic purposes here, we do not go into details about how full-time jobs may be split among numerous family members and employed workers. Also, no distinction is drawn between food sector capitalists and employees. All income flows go to "peasants," who are assumed to share common saving and consumption functions.[3]

In formal terms, agricultural output is determined by available capital stock:

$$X_a = aK_a \qquad (3.2)$$

where a is the output-capital ratio. Variations in a can reflect good or bad weather and other supply shocks in food production.

Total income in agriculture is $P_a X_a$, where P_a is the market-clearing food price. Nonagricultural workers are assumed not to save, while the saving propensities for agriculturalists and nonagricultural profit recipients are s_a and s_n, respectively. Then the value of total consumption demand D is given by:

$$
\begin{aligned}
D &= (1 - s_a)P_a X_A + w_n b_n X_n + (1 - s_n)\tau w_n b_n X_n \\
&= \gamma_a P_a X_a + \gamma_n P_n X_n
\end{aligned} \qquad (3.3)
$$

where $\gamma_a = 1 - s_a$ and $\gamma_n = [1 + (1 - s_n)\tau]/(1 + \tau)$ are the propensities to consume from agricultural and nonagricultural income flows, respectively. Note that $\partial \gamma_n / \partial \tau = -s_n/(1 + \tau)^2 < 0$. Not surprisingly, an increase in the markup rate reduces the propensity to consume from the N-sector income.

Consumption spending is split between the two sectors. Probably the best-established stylized fact in economics is Engel's law, which states that food consumption is inelastic with respect to income—a 10-percent rise in real income will lead to substantially less than a 10-percent increase in real food consumption. The simplest way to capture Engel's law in a formal specification is to write sectoral consumption functions as:

$$P_a C_a = \alpha D + \Theta P_a \qquad (3.4)$$

and

$$P_n C_n = (1 - \alpha)D - \Theta P_a \qquad (3.5)$$

where C_a and C_n stand for consumption of food and nonfood, respectively. It is easy to verify that food demand will be income-inelastic (and nonfood demand income-elastic) when $\Theta > 0$. These equations have the great advantage of being linear in income and prices. They are a simplification of the econometrician's well-known linear expenditure system (described more fully in chapter 4).

Excess demand functions for the two commodities can be written as:

$$ED_a = C_a + E - X_a \tag{3.6}$$

and

$$ED_n = C_n + I_a + I_n - X_n = C_n + I - X_n \tag{3.7}$$

where E stands for net exports of food, and I is investment demand (the sum of sectoral investment demands I_n and I_a, on the assumption that capital goods are produced only in the N-sector).

The conditions for macro equilibrium in the economy are $ED_a = ED_n = 0$. One can multiply (3.6) by P_a and (3.7) by P_n, sum the equations, and simplify to get the investment-saving balance:

$$P_n I + P_a E - s_a P_a X_a - s_n (\tau w_n b_n X_n) = 0 \tag{3.8}$$

As in the last chapter, investment and net exports are financed in equilibrium by domestic saving, the sources this time being agricultural and profit incomes.

Rather than express all variables as growth or profit rates, it is simplest in the present model to work out adjustment processes in terms of "level" variables of the form presented so far. The price P_a rises when there is excess demand in the food market, while X_n balances the N-sector. The formal specification depends on the excess demand functions, which can be written in detail as:

$$ED_n = -[1 - (1 - \alpha)\gamma_n]X_n + \frac{[(1 - \alpha)\gamma_a X_a - \Theta]P_a}{P_n} + I \tag{3.9}$$

and

$$ED_a = \frac{\alpha \gamma_n P_n X_n}{P_a} - (1 - \alpha \gamma_a)X_a + \Theta + E \tag{3.10}$$

The specific adjustment rules are:

$$\frac{dX_n}{dt} = f[ED_n(X_n, P_a)]$$

and

$$\frac{dP_a}{dt} = g[ED_a(X_n, P_a)]$$

where the functions f and g satisfy $f(0) = g(0) = 0$ and have positive first derivatives. These derivatives only describe speed of adjustment (which is presumably fast since we are dealing with a short-run model). Stability itself depends on the properties of the Jacobian matrix of the excess demand functions, which can be written as:

$$\begin{bmatrix} -[1 - (1 - \alpha)\gamma_n] & \dfrac{(1 - \alpha)\gamma_a X_a - \Theta}{P_n} \\ \dfrac{\alpha\gamma_n P_n}{P_a} & -\dfrac{\alpha\gamma_n P_n X_n}{P_a} \end{bmatrix}$$

Stability analysis follows the usual procedures.[4] To check the trace condition, note that the bracketed term in the northwest is one minus the propensity to consume nonagricultural products from nonagricultural income, which will be a fraction. Similarly, the term in the southeast (aside from the minus sign) is proportional to the propensity to consume food from nonagricultural income, also a fraction. Both terms are clearly negative, and so is the trace (their sum). The determinant of the Jacobian is:

$$\Delta = \frac{\alpha\gamma_n P_n}{P_a}\left[\frac{X_n}{P_a}[1 - (1 - \alpha)\gamma_n] - \frac{(1 - \alpha)\gamma_a X_a - \Theta}{P_n}\right] \quad (3.11)$$

For Δ to be positive, the condition:

$$X_n > \frac{(1 - \alpha)\gamma_a X_a - \Theta}{P_n[1 - (1 - \alpha)\gamma_n]}P_a$$

must be satisfied. But note that when excess demand for the nonagricultural product is zero, then from (3.9) X_n is given by:

$$X_n = \frac{[(1 - \alpha)\gamma_a X_a - \Theta]P_a}{P_n[1 - (1 - \alpha)\gamma_n]} + \frac{I}{1 - (1 - \alpha)\gamma_n} \quad (3.12)$$

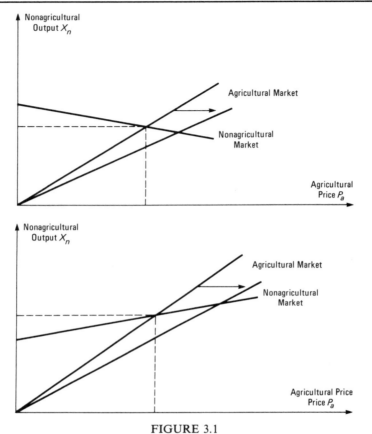

FIGURE 3.1

*Equilibrium in the Two-Sector Model When Demand for Food Is Relatively
Income-Inelastic (Upper Diagram) or Elastic (Lower Diagram)*

NOTE: The shifts in the Agricultural market lines represent increased net exports or lower production
in the agricultural sector.

So long as investment demand I is positive, (3.12) shows that the above
condition for a positive determinant will be satisfied. The conclusion is that
the adjustment process based on X_n and P_a is locally stable.

Equation (3.12) is one relationship between the two endogenous variables
in the model. Either the investment-saving balance (3.8) or the food excess
demand function (3.10) could be used to finish solving the system. For
present purposes, it is clearer to use (3.10). With ED_a set to zero, X_n can
be expressed as:

$$X_n = \frac{[(1 - \alpha\gamma_a)X_a - \Theta - E]P_a}{\alpha\gamma_n P_n} \tag{3.13}$$

To see how the system works, begin with the excess demand function for the N-sector, equation (3.9). Demands are from investment I and nonagricultural and agricultural incomes. An increase in the agricultural price reduces real incomes in the N-sector while it increases those of agriculturalists. Thus, a rise in P_a causes demand for X_n from N-sector incomes to fall (from both income and substitution effects) and demand from A-sector incomes to rise. The former effect is likely to dominate when Engel effects are strong, leading to a relatively large real income loss in the N-sector as P_a goes up. In the algebra, a large value of Θ is what matters since this parameter represents the portion of food demand that is insensitive to changes in incomes and prices. In formal terms, $\Theta > (1 - \alpha)\gamma_a X_a$ is the condition for X_n to respond negatively to P_a, as can be seen directly from (3.12). The two possible cases are illustrated by the "Nonagricultural market" schedules in figure 3.1, with the upper diagram showing what happens when Engel effects are strong.

The analysis of food market equilibrium is simpler. As (3.13) shows, X_n will be an increasing function of P_a so long as food output X_a exceeds the sum of marginal food demands from farmers $(\alpha\gamma_a X_a)$, the constant demand level Θ, and net exports E. Equation (3.13) is graphed as "Agricultural market" schedule in figure 3.1.

3.2 Comparative Statics for the Economy with an Important Food Sector

As usual, changes in policy or exogenous variables can be viewed as shifting one or both of the curves in figure 3.1. The diagrams then show how the agricultural price and nonagricultural output adjust to reestablish the disturbed equilibrium. Several examples are presented in this section. They reveal that the interaction of the two sectors creates enough potential surprises to keep the macro policy team alert.

First, figure 3.1 itself demonstrates what happens when there is an increase in net food exports. At a given level of X_n, excess food demand in (3.10) rises in response to the increased sales abroad. The only way it can be driven back to zero is via reduced domestic demand induced by higher prices, so P_a must rise. The outcome is a clockwise rotation of the agricultural market schedule. Hence the domestic food price goes up in response to increased export demand. If Engel effects are strong, the price increase will choke off demand for N-sector products and X_n will decline (upper diagram). Otherwise, both P_a and X_n will rise in response to the higher net exports.

This result can be used to illustrate institutional responses in several countries. When Engel effects are strong, nonfarmers would benefit in two ways from lower net food exports (or higher imports)—the food price would be lower and there would be a higher level of N-sector economic activity. Under such circumstances, a political coalition in favor of gaining easy access to imports could form. Examples might be the groups favoring repeal of the Corn Laws in England in the last century, or nationalistic supporters of low-cost Japanese acquisition of rice from Taiwan and elsewhere before World War II. By contrast, export promotion might well be favored politically when Engel effects are not important at the macroeconomic level, and the lower diagram of figure 3.1 applies. Exports would stimulate both farm prices and industrial activity in this case, perhaps characteristic of food exporters such as the United States in recent years.

These examples are implicitly based on the notion that the volume of agricultural trade is controlled by the government, perhaps through a state trading corporation. In fact, regulation of both internal and external commerce in food products is the rule in most countries because of the extremely low demand and supply elasticities that characterize the market in the short run. Low elasticities naturally give rise to large fluctuations in food prices and quantities offered for sale, which governments do their best to avoid by regulatory maneuvers.[5]

If, improbably, free trade in food products were allowed, then the domestic price P_a would in principle be determined from the world market. Food traders could make a profit by importing for domestic resale until such time as the internal price came down to the world level. In practice, such convergence to the "Law of One Price" may be glacial, but the assumption is often maintained in theoretical discussions.[6]

If P_a as determined by the world market increases from an initial equilibrium position in figure 3.1, then adjustment would occur by a clockwise rotation of the agricultural market schedule as net food exports go up. It is easy to see from the excess demand function (3.10) that the immediate export response would be given by:

$$\left.\frac{\partial E}{\partial P_a}\right]_{ED_a} = \left(\frac{1}{P_a}\right)[X_a(1 - \alpha\gamma_a) - \Theta - E]$$

Note that this response will be weak insofar as net surplus production beyond fixed food demands (the term in brackets) is small. Indeed, one could imagine cases in which this surplus would be negative, for example when the propensity to consume food from food producer's incomes $(\alpha\gamma_a)$ is high. The particular model developed here does not have a solution with positive values of X_n and P_a under these circumstances, and other models are unstable. Nonetheless, a perverse or very weak export response to world price increases has often been pointed out in the literature as a serious policy problem confronting such food exporters as Argentina or Thailand.[7]

Turning to other experiments, note that increased investment demand will shift up the intercept of the nonagricultural market schedule in figure 3.1, driving up both X_n and P_a. A push toward more rapid growth should then be accompanied by a shift in the terms of trade toward agriculture.

This possibility is of considerable historical interest, for example, in the rapid growth spurt experienced by the Soviet Union in the first five-year plan between 1928 and 1932. During that period, the share of investment in national income rose from 14.8 percent to 44.1 percent, and national income itself rose by 60 percent. By the end of the period, the investment share in national income was more than twice as big as that of agriculture.

The traditional interpretation is that much of the increment in savings necessary to support the extra investment came from the agricultural sector. However, the above comparison of the income shares of investment and agricultural value-added shows that the role of agriculture as a savings source cannot have been great. Rather, the terms of trade shifted strongly in favor of food producers (from 100 in 1928 to 164 in 1930 and 130 in 1932), and real urban wages dropped by about 50 percent. The resulting forced savings on the part of workers supported much of the investment effort. At the same time, Stalin's dekulakization campaign generated an ample supply of displaced agricultural labor for employment in urban industries—in many ways capacity limitations on industrial output could be broken by (inefficient) use of raw labor.

This interpretation of Soviet experience is broadly consistent with the model at hand, where an investment push is bound to raise the agricultural terms of trade.[8] Other historical conjunctures would be interesting to explore.

A more contemporary policy issue regards consumer food subsidies, which have been installed in a number of poor countries. They satisfy political necessity to pacify urban workers' pressures to maintain their living standards, but also are often criticized by international agencies as being "distortions" leading to improper resource allocation. It is reasonable to ask about the macro implications of modifying subsidy policies.

Suppose the consumer price of food is $(1 - z)P_a$, where z is the subsidy rate. From appropriately extended versions of (3.12) and (3.13), one can show that an increase in z will shift both schedules in the diagrams of figure 3.1 upward. The food price P_a will assuredly rise, and in fact one can show that the consumer price $(1 - z)P_a$ will also go up. The economics is simple. The extra subsidy gives an increment in purchasing power to consumers, but food supply is fixed. Hence, the consumer price must rise more than proportionately to the subsidy to limit demand. Incremental food imports would permit the consumer price to fall and real food intake to rise, but of course could lead to balance of payments problems. One practical reason for objections to food subsidies by regulatory agencies such as the International Monetary Fund becomes clear.

Another observation is that decreases in food subsidies may possibly reduce manufacturing output. In the upper diagram of figure 3.1, a downward shift in both schedules can lead X_n to fall. With strong Engel effects present, the loss in purchasing power induced by the fall in the farmgate price P_a can actually cut nonfood demand. By contrast, an increase in subsidies will raise the level of economic activity. Evidently, food subsidies can have important macro repercussions. Their installation or modification should be subject to serious prior consideration.

Next consider a fall in food production. In figure 3.1, the agricultural market schedule will rotate clockwise (just as from increased net exports), while the nonagricultural schedule will move the same way. In the diagrams of figure 3.1 the results are ambiguous; however, total differentiation of (3.12) and (3.13) shows that X_n must fall and P_a rise in response to this supply shock.

To illustrate the economics, figure 3.2 presents a four-quadrant diagram of the model. From (3.9) total demand for N-sector output can be split into the sum of investment and demand from the A-sector, or $I + (P_a/P_n)$ $[(1 - \alpha)\gamma_a X_a - \Theta]$, and also demand resulting from N-sector income itself. The first component is shown (with strong Engel effects) in the northwest quadrant of figure 3.2; the other component is the straight-line function of X_n beginning at point B. For the agricultural price $\bar{P}_a$, nonagricultural output $\bar{X}_n$ is determined by the intersection of total demand for N-sector output with supply along the 45°-line.

The lower quadrants show how the model can be solved using the investment-saving balance (3.8). An amount $P_n I - s_n \tau \omega_n b_n X_n$ of saving is required in equilibrium from agriculture, after nonagricultural saving supply is subtracted from investment demand. This declining function of X_n appears in the southeast quandrant. Finally, saving supply from agricul-

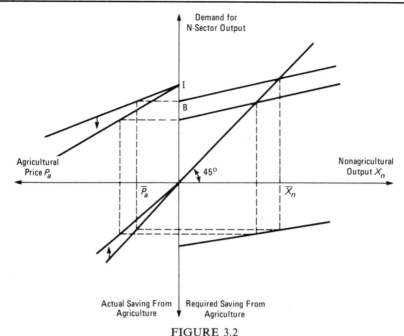

FIGURE 3.2

A Four-Quadrant Diagram for the Economy with an Important Food Sector

NOTE: A reduction in agricultural supply reduces both demand for nonagricultural output and potential saving from the sector, leading P_a to rise and X_n to fall.

ture is $(s_a x_a - E)P_a$, shown in the southwest quadrant. For overall equilibrium, both excess demand for the nonagricultural commodity and economywide excess demand (investment minus saving) must be driven to zero at $\bar{P}_a$ and $\bar{X}_n$. In the diagram, adjustment occurs via upward or downward shifts of the X_n demand function in the northeast quadrant.

Now consider a food supply shortfall, or a fall in X_a. For a given P_a, both farmers' demand for X_n and their supply of saving will decline. In the diagram, the schedules in both the northwest and southwest quadrants rotate toward the P_a axis, and the outcome is a higher P_a and lower X_n.

The sort of supply shock shown in figure 3.2 can easily set off a burst of inflation if money wages respond to the rising agricultural price and drive up N-sector costs in turn. A sequence of such shocks could keep inflation going if, for example, population growth runs ahead of the growth rate of agricultural supply. This sort of inflationary process is discussed formally in chapter 9.

Two final exogenous shifts of interest are increases in the urban nominal wage w and the markup rate τ. Observe from (3.12) and (3.13) that the

whole model is linearly homogeneous in P_a and P_n—the output side would
be unaffected by any proportional increases in the two prices. An increase
in w is automatically passed along into P_n via the markup without affecting
other variables or parameters. Because of homogeneity, the only response
of the system would be an equiproportionate increase in P_a. A money wage
increase is purely inflationary and has no effects on resource allocation at
all. Of course, this result would not carry over if intermediate imports were
introduced as elements of N-sector cost, as in the model of the last chapter.
A money wage increase would then make imports relatively cheaper, reduce
potential foreign saving, and lead to both higher X_n and P_a.

An increase in the markup rate both drives up P_n and reduces the
nonagricultural consumption propensity γ_n. As with a wage increase, the
first effect is purely inflationary in the present model. However, the decrease
in γ_n will reduce demand for food. The implication is that P_a will rise less
than proportionately to τ, and might even fall. N-sector output unambiguously declines in response to lower aggregate demand. As shown in the
growth version of this model in section 9.2, these results regarding price
(and inflation) effects of changing the markup carry over into the long
run.[9]

3.3 Intermediate Inputs in a Mineral-Exporting Economy

The sort of model used for agriculture and industry in the previous
sections can be extended to deal with many other economic structures in
which prices vary to clear some markets and output movements clear
others. In this section, we sketch a model in which intermediate inputs play
a crucial role. The economy in question exports a fixed quantity of a
commodity, such as a mineral, which requires nationally produced nonim-
portable intermediates like transport services, energy, and other infrastructure. These "universal" inputs are assumed to be in fixed supply, and feed
either mineral production or another "manufacturing" sector with markup
pricing. Mining itself typically generates only modest wage flows that lead
to demand for manufactured goods since export profits come in the form
of foreign exchange. If mineral output expands it will pull intermediates
from use in manufacturing on the one hand, and generate demand for
manufacturing output on the other. In addition, there can be cost-push
price increases in manufacturing if the intermediate goods price rises to
clear that market. The final outcomes for manufacturing prices, exports (if

they are price-responsive) and outputs is unclear. And the situation becomes even more complicated if foreign exchange is in relatively short supply (the case for most mineral exporters except those with major petroleum pools). With a binding restriction on the amount of foreign exchange the country can spend, short-run variations in the exchange rate may be required to stimulate manufacturing exports and keep imports in line. Feedbacks from the exchange rate to the rest of the system then have to be taken into account.[10]

To set this up formally, let mineral output (equals volume of exports) be X_m, which is fixed in the short run. The volume of output of universal intermediates, X_u, is also fixed, but output of manufactures (or, really, the rest of the economy) can vary. The level of production in this N-sector is X_n, and the price P_n is given by:

$$P_n = (1 + \tau)[wb_n + P_u a_{un} + eP_0^* a_{0n}] \qquad (3.14)$$

In this equation, the markup (at rate τ) is taken on wage cost per unit output wb_n, cost of the universal intermediate $P_u a_{un}$, and imported intermediate costs $eP_0^* a_{0n}$. The input-output coefficients b_n, a_{un}, and a_{0n} are assumed constant in the short run.

On the demand side, assume that Engel elasticities are unity. To save notation, all profits will be assumed to be saved and all wages spent on consumption. Then the consumer demand functions for N-sector outputs will be

$$P_n C_n = (1 - \alpha)w[b_n x_n + b_u X_u + b_m X_m]$$

and

$$P_u C_u = \alpha w[b_n X_n + b_u X_u + b_m X_m]$$

where it is assumed that the same wage w is paid in all three sectors.[11] The coefficient α will presumably be positive but small, as much less than one-half of consumer spending goes toward energy, transport, and other products from the U-sector. In these equations, the contribution of the mineral sector to consumption demand is likely to be low since only wage income is consumed. (The share of mining wages in the total across the economy might be as low as 5 percent.[12]) In practice, some share of the export receipts from mining will go to the national government, and will be spent. This important potential source of demand is left out in the present formulation, which concentrates on short-run responses.

Excess demand balances for the nonmineral sectors are:

$$C_n + E + G - X_n = 0$$

and

$$C_u + a_{un}X_n + a_{um}X_m + \Theta I - X_u = 0$$

In the second equation, demands for the universal intermediate come from consumption, intermediate sales $(a_{un}X_n + a_{um}X_m)$, and investment. The key assumption regarding the latter is that a fraction, Θ, of the demand level I is produced nationally by the U-sector. In practice, ΘI represents the construction component of capital formation, and the implicit hypothesis is that output of construction services is limited by skilled labor and equipment shortages. Such an assumption makes sense in some countries but not in others; it is mostly adopted to generate an interesting story here.

On the side of manufacturing, assume that volume of sales abroad E is given by:

$$E = [\epsilon_0 + \epsilon_1(eP_n^*/P_n)]X_n = \epsilon X_n \qquad (3.15)$$

An essentially noncompetitive market in exports is assumed. The price of national products sold abroad is P_n/e, or domestic price divided by the exchange rate. The price in the international market of products against which "our" manufactured exports compete is P_n^*. As P_n^* rises relatively to P_n/e, a larger share of domestic output goes abroad. The elasticity of this share with respect to eP_n^*/P_n can easily be shown to exceed one when $\epsilon_0 < 0$, and be less than one when $\epsilon_0 > 0$. With any magnitude of the elasticity, this export response will of course take time to build up, but such lags are ignored for simplicity.

Putting all these equations together gives excess demand functions for the manufacturing and intermediate sectors as:

$$\frac{(1 - \alpha)w}{(1 + \tau)[wb_n + P_u a_{un} + eP_0^* a_{0n}]}[b_n X_n + b_u X_u + b_m X_m]$$
$$+ G + \left[\epsilon_0 + \epsilon_1 \frac{eP_n^*}{(1 + \tau)[wb_n + P_u a_{un} + eP_0^* a_{0n}]} X_n\right]$$
$$- X_n = 0 \quad (3.16)$$

and

$$\frac{\alpha w}{P_u}[b_n X_n + b_u X_u + b_m X_m] + a_{un} X_n$$

$$+ a_{um} X_m + \Theta I - X_u = 0 \qquad (3.17)$$

The adjusting variables are X_n for (3.16) and P_u for (3.17).[13] The equations are written out in all their glory to illustrate the fact that inclusion of intermediate inputs in a model substantially complicates its accounting. Compared to (3.9) and (3.10) for the agriculture/industry model, these excess demand functions both have more entries and (more importantly) are nonlinear. Because the intermediate price P_u enters into the determination of the N-sector price P_n, terms in products or quotients of P_u and manufacturing output X_n are unavoidable in (3.16) and (3.17).

Even without writing the Jacobian, it is straightforward to see that (3.16) gives a negatively sloped relationship between P_u and X_n. Excess demand for manufacturers falls when X_n rises (more supply) and also when P_u goes up (less consumer and export demand from intermediate cost-push into a higher P_u). Hence, the two adjusting variables must trade off inversely in the (P_u, X_n) plane. By contrast, an increase in X_n generates more consumer demand for the U-sector in (3.17), which must be limited by an increase in P_u. A positively sloped curve results.

The two schedules are shown in figure 3.3. The shifts are due to an

FIGURE 3.3

Response of the Mineral-Exporting Economy to an Increase in Mineral Output

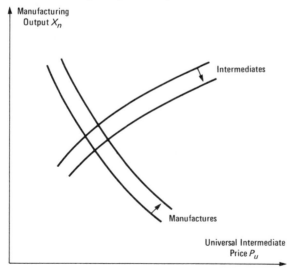

NOTE: The intermediate price rises and manufacturing output can shift either way.

increase in mineral output. More mining activity generates greater intermediate demand, so the "Intermediates" schedule must shift to the right as
P_u rises to ration the fixed supply. At the same time, the mineral wage bill
goes up, stimulating demand for manufacturers, and that schedule shifts up.
The outcome is a rise in P_u and an ambiguous response in X_n.

To track down the ambiguity, we can begin with an algebraic expression
that determines the sign of the N-sector output response:

$$\frac{\alpha wL(1 - \alpha)wb_m}{P_u}$$

$$- \frac{\alpha wb_m + a_{um}P_u}{P_n}[(1 - \alpha)wL + \epsilon_1 eP_n^* X_n](1 + \tau)a_{un} \quad (3.18)$$

in which $L = b_n X_n + b_u X_u + b_m X_m$, or total employment.

The first positive term represents the consumer demand generated by
more mining employment. The negative entries show how an increase in
P_n from intermediate cost-push reduces consumption and export demand
for manufacturing output. Depending on which effects are stronger, the
output response can go either way.

Figure 3.4 illustrates the comparative statics for two special cases. In the
upper diagram, a_{un} is set to zero, so that manufacturing does not require
intermediates. With unitary income elasticities (no Engel effects), X_n is
independent of P_u in (3.16) and rises along with miners' consumption
demand from X_m. By contrast, α is set to zero in the lower diagram, so that
there is no consumer demand for U-sector products. N-sector output is
determined in (3.17), and falls as its available intermediates inputs are
reduced by an increase in X_m. The relative importance of these two effects
depends finally on the relative magnitudes of α and a_{un}.

The ambiguous response of X_n to an increase in mineral production
illustrates a classic problem of single-export economies. When output in the
export sector goes up, it may choke off or at best weakly stimulate nonexport production. Indeed, if manufacturing exports are reduced by intermediate cost-push, declines in both "external diversification" (of the export
basket) and "internal diversification" (of the production structure) go
together.[14] More mining drives down both exports and output levels in the
rest of the economy. The loss in production flexibility and the noneconomic
retardation caused by lagging domestic production of everything but a
mineral can both be very great.

Other comparative static responses depend on the linkages just discussed.
A higher level of investment demand puts pressure on the intermediate

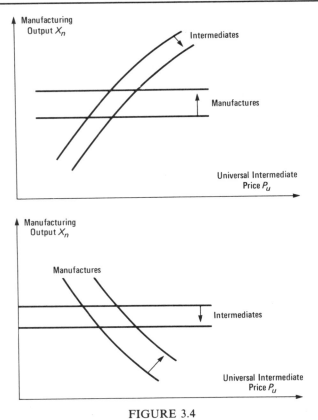

FIGURE 3.4

*Effects of an Increase in Mineral Output When the Manufacturing Sector Does
Not Require Intermediate Inputs (Upper Diagram) and When There Is No
Consumer Demand for Products of the Intermediate Sector (Lower Diagram)*

goods market, so that P_u rises and X_n falls. An increase in intermediate
output X_u has the opposite effect, with corresponding responses in the
endogenous variables. Higher government spending G pulls up both X_n and
P_u. Finally, a rise in the wage rate w drives up P_u by creating consumer
demand. The effect on X_n is ambiguous but positive if additional consumption demand by workers for N-sector products outweights the reduction in
exports resulting from a higher price level (P_n/e) of national products
abroad.

Finally, note that the real wage defined in terms of the workers' consumption basket is:

$$\omega = \frac{w}{(P_n)^{1-\alpha}(P_u)^\alpha} = \frac{w}{(P_u)^\alpha \{(1 + \tau)[wb_n + eP_0^* a_{0n} + P_u a_{un}]\}^{1-\alpha}}$$

so that the real wage falls when P_u goes up. On the saving-investment side of the model, the corresponding increase in real profits underlies a forced saving macro adjustment process. Setting out the details is left to the reader. The derivations are tedious, but follow directly along the lines of the models already described.

3.4 Balance of Trade Complications

Though there are striking exceptions (mostly in the Persian Gulf), mineral-exporting countries by and large suffer from balance of payments pressure. The historical sequence is that after an initial phase of building up foreign exchange holdings when mineral wealth arrives, pressures to increase imports rise and the corresponding coefficients shift up. The government learns that it can finance more spending on N-sector goods by holding foreign exchange in the form of central bank reserves and creating national money against that base.[15] The outcomes in terms of the model sketched in last section are relatively high levels of G, $(1 - \Theta)$, and a_{0n}. The balance of payments deficit in terms of dollars becomes:

$$
\begin{aligned}
B = {} & P_0^* a_{0n} X_n + P_{0i}^* (1 - \Theta) I - P_m^* X_m \\
& - [\epsilon_0 + \epsilon_1 (e P_n^* / P_n)] X_n (P_n / e) - F
\end{aligned}
\qquad (3.19)
$$

where F is an endogenous level of capital inflows net of interest and amortization costs. The deficit B may be near zero or positive (indicating loss of central bank reserves) even though F is high because a mineral-exporting country often has good credit in Eurocurrency and similar financial markets abroad. The other new terms in the equation are P_{0i}^* or the cost of imported investment goods in the world market, and P_m^* or the world price of mineral exports.

Suppose that the trade deficit suddenly gets worse, from drying up of foreign loans, an increase in investment demand, or some such similar shock. Reserve outflow can accelerate for a time, but finally some sort of adjustment must be made. Devaluation is one standard policy choice.

The effects of an increase in the exchange rate e on the trade deficit basically run through intermediate imports and manufactured exports since the mineral export price P_m^* is fixed in terms of dollars. The longhand expression can be derived by totally differentiating (3.19) and plugging in expressions for dX_n / de and dP_u / de from the model of last section. The result is lengthy but enlightening. It is:

$$\frac{dB}{de} = \frac{1}{\Delta}\frac{X_n}{P_n}[\epsilon_1 P_n^* - (1 - \gamma - \epsilon_0)(1 + \tau)P_0^* a_{0n}]$$

$$\left\{\frac{awL}{(P_u)^2}\left(P_0^* a_{0n} - \epsilon\frac{P_n}{e}\right) - \frac{awb_n + P_u a_{un}}{P_u}\epsilon_0\frac{X_n}{e}(1 + \tau)a_{un}\right\}$$

$$+ \epsilon_0 X_n\frac{P_n - (1 + \tau)eP_{0n}^* a_{0n}}{e^2} \tag{3.20}$$

where $\Delta > 0$ is the Jacobian determinant of the (stable) system of two excess demand functions, and $\gamma = G/X_n$.

To disentangle the knots, begin with the last expression in (3.20). This term comes from the expression multiplied by (P_n/e) in (3.19), and shows that when $\epsilon_0 > 0$ devaluation makes the trade deficit *worse*. The explanation is that an increase in e lowers the world price of national exports (P_n/e) immediately. However, export volume presumably rises in response to the price improvement. If a time lag is involved, the trade surplus may first grow smaller and then gradually increase. Graphed against time, the surplus looks like a fish hook, or the letter J. Hence we have a "j-curve" dynamic export response.[16] For present purposes it is simplest to ignore this process, though it may take well over a year to work itself out. The main point is that the overall payments response must include the world price increase induced by a rise in e.

The bracketed term at the beginning of (3.20) shows how N-sector demand responds to devaluation. When the export response term ϵ_1 is small, X_n will decline when e goes up—this is the contractionary response to devaluation illustrated in figure 2.4. By way of variety, we assume an expansion in output when e rises, or in other words when the export response is strong.

However, to get an improvement in the balance of payments ($dB/de < 0$), not all hurdles have been crossed. One helpful effect (at least when the exchange rate elasticity of exports is less than unity, or $\epsilon_0 > 0$) comes from the second term in the curly brackets, showing how P_n rises from intermediate cost push, partly offsetting the decline in competitiveness resulting from the initial increase in e. But finally, we also require $\epsilon(P_n/e) - P_0^* a_{0n} > 0$, or the export share in N-sector output (measured in dollar prices) exceeds that share of intermediate inputs. If this condition is satisfied by a wide enough margin, then the j-curve will turn up and devaluation will improve the balance of payments. The strength of the response clearly depends on many parameters in the system.

The conclusion is that devaluation, if expansionary, will help the mineral exporter's trade deficit, with both internal and external diversification. One policy cost would be a reduction in the real wage, from an increase in P_u and e in (3.18). This shift, plus possibly weak responses of manufactured exports to exchange rate changes in the medium run, makes a devaluation strategy possibly infeasible and certainly difficult to implement over time.[17]

The alternative is always to manipulate the level of mineral exports in response to a payments crunch. How feasible such a policy is depends very much on the characteristics of the commodity involved. Changing oil production volume or even capacity may be fairly simple; for copper or tin the required modifications in output flows could be fairly hard.

There is also a question of which way to go. The obvious response is to increase production from the mines and suffer the loss of economic flexibility entailed in lower internal and external diversification (as discussed above). But in some cases it is possible that *reduced* mineral production would lower P_n and raise X_n enough to *increase* net exports. Contemplation of the model suggests such an outcome is more likely when export responses to price are strong and the share of nonmineral exports in the total is already high. Such a situation might apply for a country that has already pursued the devaluation strategy for quite some time. But until then, devaluation and (more plausibly) export incentives may be an unavoidable policy choice. The details in the incentive case are interesting, but are left to the reader to work out.

4

Short-Run Adjustment
in Practice

THE previous chapters described four mechanisms through which aggregate saving supply is brought into equality with the value of investment demand. These are variation in the level of output; forced saving caused by changes in prices relative to a nominally fixed magnitude such as the wage or exchange rate; variation in the value of sales or purchases of a commodity (for example, endogenous determination of exports or competitive imports through the condition that excess demand for a commodity must equal zero); and determination of the level of investment by available saving. Now we will illustrate the roles that the first three mechanisms play in a practical model. We leave neoclassical determination of investment by saving for others to pursue.

The model described here is for the Indian economy in the national accounts year 1980–81 (beginning April 1st). It generally follows the theoretical structure of the agriculture/industry model set out in sections 3.1 and 3.2, but with five production sectors (two with flexible prices and three with varying outputs) instead of just two. Similar systems have been constructed for several countries besides India, so the discussion really refers to a class of models in active use for macroeconomic analysis in the early 1980s rather than an isolated example.[1]

The data base for the India model (and all the others) is arranged in the form of a social accounting matrix, or SAM. The Indian SAM is described in section 4.1—it amounts to a blown-up version of the accounting relationships developed above. Section 4.2 sets out the equations for the model, which are closely linked to the structure of the SAM. A brief discussion of how values are assigned to the parameters appears in section 4.3. Section 4.4 describes the numerically calculated Jacobian of the Indian model's excess demand equations. This leads to the analysis in section 4.5 of a number of comparative static exercises with the model, as parameters or exogenous variables are perturbed to shift it away from its base solution (which is described by the SAM). The emphasis is on the role that different adjustment mechanisms play in this applied model. Conclusions are summarized in section 4.6.

4.1 A Social Accounting Matrix for India, 1980–81

A social accounting matrix is a tabular representation of the accounting identities stating that incomes must equal outlays for all sectors of the economy. Typically, deliveries of commodities or incomes are put in the rows of the matrix, and receipts in the columns. Corresponding row and column totals must be equal to make the double-entry income/outlay book-keeping balance out. During the 1970s, such matrices were constructed for a large number of countries—they seem to be generally accepted as a compact device for presenting input-output and national income accounts.[2]

The structure of the Indian matrix is illustrated schematically in figure 4.1. The principal blocks are labeled in the diagram. It makes sense to describe them briefly before going on to the numerical SAM.

In the northwest corner is the interindustry matrix, which gives the values of intermediate commodity flows among the five sectors distinguished in the economy. Because the matrix identities are valid only in value (and not "real" or quantity) terms, these flows are in 1980–1981 Indian prices (in units of crores, or 10 million rupees). The five sectors are food-producing crop agriculture (cereals, pulses, and vegetables), other agriculture, manufacturing and construction, infrastructure and energy-producing sectors (transport, mining and quarrying, electricity, gas, and water), and services. In the model described below, the two agriculture sectors are assumed to be price-clearing, whereas the others reach demand-supply balance through changes in output.

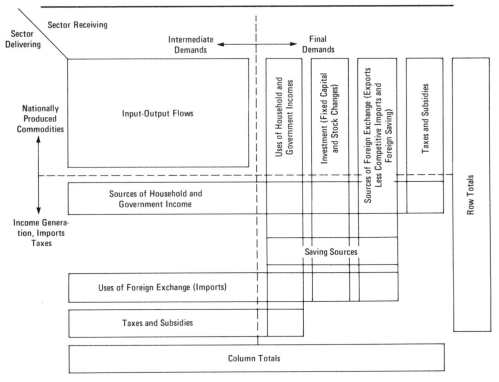

FIGURE 4.1

Block Diagram of the Indian Social Accounting Matrix

Immediately below the input-output flow table are blocks giving sources of household and government revenues, sources of foreign commodities (or uses of foreign exchange for imports), and taxes and subsidies. All the accounting in these rows is in current Indian price terms *except* the import row, where purchases are valued in c.i.f. border prices (multiplied by the rupee/dollar exchange rate). Differences between prices of imports at the border and the prices at which they are sold internally are captured in entries in the tax and subsidy rows of the SAM.

The first five column sums give the cost structures of the producing sectors, exhausted by intermediate purchases, payments to the government and households, import costs, and indirect taxes less subsidies. By the standard SAM accounting rule, these column sums must equal the corresponding row sums, which represent total sales by the sectors.

To the right of the input-output matrix are blocks for uses of resources. The household sector purchases outputs of the sectors, saves, receives subsidies, and pays direct taxes. The government also buys commodities on its current account (its capital expenditures are in the investment column), and saves and pays subsidies. In the investment columns appear outlays for gross fixed capital formation and stock changes—their total is of course balanced by the sum of the entries in the saving block. Exports (positive) and competitive imports (negative) are valued in border price terms. The difference between border and internal prices of exports is made up in the export subsidy column. Exports less competitive imports comprise sources of foreign exchange; the other major sources are remittances from emigrant workers that go into household income, and foreign saving, which comes into the economy on foreign capital account to balance the current account deficit.[3]

Table 4.1 is the numerical SAM for our Indian model.[4] Some of its details are worth pointing out. Note first that income flows to households are split three ways. Agricultural households in row 6c get income from the first two sectors, while income generated in nonagriculture goes to wage-earning and nonwage-earning households. The nonagricultural households get government wage, transfer, and interest payments (column 7) and emigrants' remittances (column 9a). Note also that government revenues in row 7 include income from public sector production activities outside of agriculture.

Household uses of income appear in column 6. Only totals are shown in the matrix, though in the model described below distinct consumption patterns are postulated for agricultural and nonagricultural households. Note the entry with negative value −545 in row 11. This represents subsidies to food consumption; along with producers' subsidies signed with a minus in columns 1–3, it is offset by the government's total subsidy outlay of 1327 in column 7.

Besides its production activities, the government's revenue sources in row 7 include indirect and direct taxes (columns 11 and 12). The sources of these taxes appear in rows 12 and 13. All direct taxes are assumed to be paid by households (2941 in column 6), whereas the indirect tax burden falls on production and sales in the nonagricultural sectors. Government uses of funds appear in column 7.

Transactions with the rest of the world are recorded in row 9 for imports and columns 9a and 9b for exports and competitive imports. The negative entries for the latter in the commodity balance rows 1 through 5 are offset by a positive total of 3782 in row 9, so that the column 9b sum is zero. Most competitive imports come into the manufacturing sector. Besides exports and remittances, the other source of foreign exchange include 1800 as the current account deficit or foreign saving in row 8. Household saving is 22637 and government current saving is 2980; their total of 27417 is equal to investment demand, or the sum of the column totals 8a and 8b.

TABLE 4.1

A Social Accounting Matrix for India, 1980–81

	Food Agriculture	Other Agriculture	Industry (Manufacturing)	Infra-Structure & Energy	Services	Use of Private Income	Use of Government Revenue	Cross Fixed Investment	Stock Changes	Export	Competitive Import	Export Subsidy	Indirect Taxes	Direct Taxes	Total (Gross Output)
	1	2	3	4	5	6	7	8a	8b	9a	9b	10	11	12	13
1. Food agriculture	1895	463	907	—	509	29383	173	—	(–)528	—	—	—	—	—	32802
2. Other agriculture	1117	3396	8164	—	382	11190	60	—	—	2272	(–)35	—	—	—	26546
3. Industry (Manufacturing)	2700	2167	27054	1201	8944	23479	2499	23186	3428	4473	(–)3747	328	—	—	95712
4. Infrastructure and energy	107	86	3203	1994	1423	2574	354	—	120	355	—	—	—	—	10216
5. Services	1450	1183	18665	850	9988	28811	4438	—	—	—	—	—	—	—	65385
6a. Nonagricultural wage income	—	—	10736	3053	19455	—	7633	—	—	—	—	—	—	—	43277
6b. Nonagricultural nonwage income	—	—	9146	2035	19848	—	1388	—	—	—	—	—	—	—	32417
6c. Agricultural income	25530	19246	—	—	—	—	—	—	—	—	—	—	—	—	44776
6. (6a + 6b + 6c) Private income	25530	19246	19882	5088	39303	—	9021	—	—	2400	—	—	—	—	120470
7. Government income (Revenue)	—	—	1738	141	566	—	—	—	—	—	—	—	15794	2941	21180
8. Gross savings	—	—	5719	—	—	22637	2980	—	—	1800	—	—	—	—	27417
9. Imports	312	276	5719	—	—	—	—	1211	—	—	3782	—	—	—	11300
10. Export subsidy	—	—	—	—	—	—	328	—	—	—	—	—	—	—	328
11. Production/consumption subsidy	(–)309	(–)271	(–)202	—	—	(–)545	1327	—	—	—	—	—	—	—	0
12. Indirect taxes	—	—	10582	942	4270	—	—	—	—	—	—	—	—	—	15794
13. Direct taxes	—	—	—	—	—	2941	—	—	—	—	—	—	—	—	2961
14. Total (Gross Output)	32802	26546	95712	10216	65385	120470	21100	24397	3020	11300	0	328	15794	2941	—

NOTE: All values are in crores (ten million rupees) at current prices.

With its double-entry bookkeeping, the SAM provides a data base around which it is easy to construct a general equilibrium model. The SAM in fact represents the base solution of the model since, as we will see in section 4.3, the parameters of its equations are calculated to make their numerical solution agree with the SAM. Of course, one has to first produce a SAM to be able to follow this procedure.

Fairly complete recipes for constructing social accounting matrixes are available in the literature, so there is no need to go into great detail here.[5] The usual approach is to begin with an input-output table, the national accounts, and information from a household survey on patterns of consumer spending. In general outline, the following steps will produce the matrix:

1. Sectoral levels of value-added from the input-output and national accounts data must be made consistent, typically by adjustment of both.
2. Next comes disaggregation of the value-added totals into income flows to household and government sectors to be distinguished in the analysis. For example, sectoral value-added in the Indian SAM had to be split among the entries in rows 6a, 6b, 6c, and 7 of table 4.1, following national accounts and other information about the functional distribution of income.
3. The national accounts will give a control total for household saving. Savings levels from the different income recipient classes (H of them) have to be estimated to satisfy this total, typically on the basis of cross-sectionally estimated saving parameters.
4. After taxes and saving are subtracted from household incomes, one is left with H totals for values of household consumption by income recipient class. If there are N sectors in the economy, the input-output table gives N totals for consumption of the different sectoral outputs. One thus has the row and column sums (perhaps after correction for consumer taxes and subsidies) for the $N \times H$ matrix of values of household consumption by type of product and income recipient group. Subject to these control totals, the matrix has to be filled in. One typically begins with existing estimates of household expenditure patterns, then modifies them until the control totals are satisfied. The computations can either be done informally or with a matrix-balancing computer algorithm such as the procedure called RAS.[6]
5. Input-output and foreign trade information can be utilized to fill in the rest of the sectoral final demand columns and the import row. Government fiscal data usually suffice for the tax, subsidy, and government expenditure accounts. The final check on filling in the matrix is that saving supply should equal investment demand. After enough informal reconciliations between inconsistent data sources are made, overall balance can usually be worked out.

4.2 A Macro Model for India

With the SAM constructed, the next step is to set out equations for the model around it. The Indian model is based on the notion that the two agricultural sectors are price-clearing, while output levels vary to satisfy demand in the rest of the economy. Much literature in India points to an "infrastructure bottleneck," which suggests that sector four might best be treated as price-clearing subject to fixed supply (like the U-sector in the model of sections 3.3 and 3.4). However, numerical results show little demand variation for sector four, so it was deemed simpler to treat it as quantity-clearing to avoid complications in the model solution algorithm described below.

The model's equations appear in table 4.2 and the variables and parameters are described in table 4.3. The equations are set out in blocks, to be described in succession.

Block I contains input-output balances, which set demand (to the left) equal to supply for the five sectors. The entries correspond to the first five rows of the SAM, with the convention that base-period prices for sectoral outputs are all set to one. Note in equation (4.1) an entry $(GP_1 - FA_1 - FN_1)$ that reflects government food market interventions described below. Also, in (4.3) national production of intermediate inputs to sectors one and two is pegged at the level X_f. This quantity represents an exogenously specified level of fertilizer output. The balance of fertilizer demand $(a_{31}X_1 + a_{32}X_2 - X_f)$ is assumed to be met by imports.

Block II contains an equation making accumulation of private food stocks an increasing function of the market food price. The equation is included in an attempt to capture the macroeconomic effect of food stock speculation, which is often pointed out as a possible source of inflation in India. Equation (4.6) gives a positive feedback from a rise in the food price to increased stock accumulation and hence to a still higher price. The practical importance of this potentially destabilizing demand response is discussed below.

Block III has equations defining agricultural and wage incomes Y_a and Y_w. Value-added in the two agricultural sectors is calculated in (4.7) to give Y_a. Note that farmers pay a regulated price P_f for their fertilizer inputs. The government also gives them a guaranteed "procurement price" P_1^* for a fixed quantity GP_1 of food sales (the procurement). Production above the procurement level $(X_1 - GP_1)$ is sold at the market price P_1. The government's accounts for this complex set of food market interventions are set out below.

TABLE 4.2
Equations for the India Model

I. Demand-Supply Balances by Sector

$$\sum_{j=1}^{5} a_{1j}X_j + (GP_1 - FA_1 - FN_1) + C_1 + \Delta S_1 + G_1 + E_1 - M_1 = X_1 \tag{4.1}$$

$$\sum_{j=1}^{5} a_{2j}X_j + C_2 + \Delta S_2 + G_2 + E_2 - M_2 = X_2 \tag{4.2}$$

$$X_f + \sum_{j=3}^{5} a_{3j}X_j + C_3 + E_3 + I_3 + \Delta S_3 + G_3 + E_3 - M_3 = X_3 \tag{4.3}$$

$$\sum_{j=1}^{5} a_{4j}X_j + C_4 + \Delta S_4 + G_4 + E_4 - M_4 = X_4 \tag{4.4}$$

$$\sum_{j=1}^{5} a_{5j}X_j + GS_5 + C_5 + \Delta S_5 + G_5 + E_5 - M_5 = X_5 \tag{4.5}$$

II. Cereal Stock Speculation

$$\Delta S_1 = \Delta S_1^{\circ}(P_1/P_1^{\circ})^{\sigma}s \tag{4.6}$$

III. Generation of Nonprofit Income Flows

$$Y_a = P_1^*(GP_1) + P_1(X_1 - GP_1) - \left(\sum_{i=1}^{2} a_{i1}P_i + a_{31}P_f + \sum_{i=4}^{5} a_{i1}P_i\right)X_1$$

$$+ \left(P_2 - \sum_{i=1}^{2} a_{i2}P_i - a_{32}P_f - \sum_{i=4}^{5} a_{i2}P_i\right)X_2 \tag{4.7}$$

$$CPI = \sum_{i=1}^{5} \alpha_i P_i \tag{4.8}$$

$$w_i = w_i^{\circ} + k_{wi}(CPI - CPI^{\circ}), \ i = 3, 4, 5 \text{ and } g \tag{4.9}-(4.12)$$

$$Y_w = \sum_{i=3}^{5} w_i b_i X_i + w_g L_g + eR + TR \tag{4.13}$$

IV. Price Equations for Nonagricultural Sectors

$$\tau_i = k_{\tau i}(X_i/K_i)^{\sigma}i, \ i = 3 \text{ and } 5 \tag{4.14}-(4.15)$$

$$P_3 = \frac{(1 + t_3)(1 + \tau_3)}{1 - (1 + t_3)(1 + \tau_3)a_{33}(1 - sub_3)}[a_{13}P_1 + a_{23}P_2 + a_{43}P_4 + a_{53}P_5$$

$$+ w_3 b_3 + a_{03}eP_{03}^*(1 - t_{03})] \tag{4.16}$$

$$P_4 = \frac{(1 + \tau_4)(1 + t_4)}{1 - (1 + \tau_4)(1 + t_4)a_{44}}[\sum_{i=1}^{3} a_{i4}P_i + a_{54}P_5 + w_4 b_4 + a_{04}eP_{04}^*(1 - t_{04})] \tag{4.17}$$

$$P_5 = \frac{(1 + \tau_5)(1 + t_5)}{1 - (1 + \tau_5)(1 + t_5)a_{55}}[\sum_{i=1}^{4} a_{i5}P_5 + w_5 b_5 + a_{05}eP_{05}^*(1 - t_{05})] \tag{4.18}$$

V. Equations for Variable Costs in Nonagricultural Sectors

$$B_3 = \sum_{i=1}^{5} a_{i3}P_i + w_3 b_3 + a_{03}eP_{03}^*(1 - t_{03}) - sub_3 P_3 a_{33} \tag{4.19}$$

$$B_j = \sum_{i=1}^{5} a_{ij}P_i + w_j b_j + a_{0j}eP_{0j}^*(1 - t_{0j}), j = 4 \text{ and } 5 \tag{4.20}-(4.21)$$

VI. Generation of Income from Nonagricultural Markups

$$Y_z = \sum_{i=3}^{5} (\tau_i B_i X_i - GR_i) - (1 - \phi)DEP + GINT \tag{4.22}$$

VII. Consumption From Agricultural and Nonagricultural Incomes

$$D_a = (1 - s_a)Y_a \tag{4.23}$$

$$D_n = (1 - s_w)Y_w + (1 - s_z)(1 - t_z)Y_z - eP^*_{0c}C_0 \tag{4.24}$$

VIII. Sectoral Consumption Functions

$$\hat{D}_a = \sum_{i=1}^{5} \Theta^a_i P_i \tag{4.25}$$

$$\hat{D}_n = \sum_{i=1}^{5} \Theta^n_i P_i \tag{4.26}$$

$$C^a_1 = \Theta^a_1 - FA_1 + (m^a_1/P_1)(D_a + P_1 FA_1 - \hat{D}_a) \tag{4.27}$$

$$C^a_i = \Theta^a_i + (m^a_i/P_i)(D_a + P_1 FA_1 - \hat{D}_a), i = 2, \ldots, 5 \tag{4.28–4.31}$$

$$C^n_1 = \Theta^n_1 - FN_1 + (m^n_1/P_1)[D_n + (P_1 - \bar{P}_1)FN_1 - \hat{D}_n] \tag{4.32}$$

$$C^n_i = \Theta^n_i + (m^n_i/P_i)[D_n + (P_1 - \bar{P}_1)FN_1 - \hat{D}_n], i = 2, \ldots, 5 \tag{4.33–4.36}$$

$$C_1 = C^a_1 + FA_1 + C^n_1 + FN_1 \tag{4.37}$$

$$C_i = C^a_i + C^n_i, i = 2, \ldots, 5 \tag{4.38–4.41}$$

IX. Model Closure

$$X_i - \bar{X}_i = 0, i = 1 \text{ and } 2 \tag{4.42–4.43}$$

X. Governmental Balances

$$T^{\text{ind}} = \sum_{i=3}^{5} t_i(1 + \tau_i)B_i X_i \tag{4.44}$$

$$GREV = t_z Y_z + T^{\text{ind}} + \sum_{i=3}^{5} GR_i \tag{4.45}$$

$$GEXP = P_1 FA_1 + (P_1 - \bar{P}_1)FN_1 + (P_1 - P^*_1)GP_1 + P_5 GS_5 + \sum_{i=1}^{5} P_i G_i$$
$$+ (P_3 - eP^*_{0f})X_f + (eP^*_{0f} - P_f)(a_{31}X_1 + a_{32}X_2) + w_g L_g + TR$$
$$+ \phi DEP + GINT + sub_3 a_{33} X_3 + \sum_{i=1}^{5} (P_i - eP^*_{ei})E_i$$
$$+ \sum_{i=1}^{5} a_{0i} eP^*_{0i} t_{0i} X_i \tag{4.46}$$

XI. Trade Deficit

$$DEF = \sum_{i=1}^{5} P_i M_i + eP^*_{0c}C_0 + \sum_{i=1}^{5} eP^*_{0i} a_{0i} X_i + eP^*_{0f}I_0$$
$$+ eP^*_{0f}(a_{31}X_1 + a_{32}X_2 - X_f) - \sum_{i=1}^{5} eP^*_{ei}E_i - eR \tag{4.47}$$

XII. Saving-Investment Balance

$$s_a Y_a + s_w Y_w + s_z(1 - t_z)Y_z + (GREV - GEXP) + DEF$$
$$= P_3 I_3 + eP^*_{0f}I_0 + \sum_{i=1}^{5} P_i \Delta S_i + P_1(GP_1 - FA_1 - FN_1) \tag{4.48}$$

TABLE 4.3
Symbols for the India Model

I. Sectors

---

1. Food agriculture
2. Other agriculture
3. Manufacturing industries
4. Intermediate production (energy and transportation)
5. Services

II. Endogenous Variables

X_i — sectoral output levels, $i = 1, \ldots, 5$
P_i — sectoral price levels, $i = i, \ldots, 5$
C_i — sectoral levels of consumption demand, $i = i, \ldots, 5$
C_i^a — sectoral consumption levels from agricultural income, $i = 1, \ldots, 5$
C_i^n — sectoral consumption levels from nonagricultural income, $i = 1, \ldots, 5$
w_i — sectoral wage rates, $i = 3,4,5$
w_g — government wage rate
B_i — variable costs per unit of output, $i = 3,4,5$
τ_3 — markup rate in sector 3
τ_5 — markup rate in sector 5
Y_a — income in agriculture
Y_w — wage income
Y_z — markup income
D_a — consumption spending from agricultural income
D_n — consumption spending from nonagricultural income
$\hat{D}_a$ — floor-level consumption from agricultural income
$\hat{D}_n$ — floor-level consumption from nonagricultural income
ΔS_1 — change in private stocks of sector 1 products
CPI — consumer price index for urban consumption
T^{ind} — indirect taxes
$GREV$ — government revenue
$GEXP$ — government spending
DEF — trade deficit

III. Exogenous Variables

GP_1 — procurement of cereals at prespecified price P_1^*
GS_5 — government demand for services on development budget
G_i — government demand for commodities, $i = 1, \ldots, 5$
ΔS_1^o — base-year change in stocks in sector 1
ΔS_i — change in sectoral stocks, $i = 2, \ldots, 5$
E_i — sectoral exports, $i = 1, \ldots, 5$
M_i — competitive imports, $i = 1, \ldots, 5$
X_f — domestic production of fertilizer
I_3 — investment demand for sector 3 products
I_0 — investment demand for imports
P_{0I}^* — border price of I_0
P_1^* — procurement price
P_f — subsidized price of fertilizer from sector 3

e	—	exchange rate
R	—	remittances
L_g	—	government employment
TR	—	transfer payments
P_{0i}^*	—	border prices of intermediate imports, $i = 1, \ldots, 5$
t_{0i}	—	subsidy rates on intermediate imports, $i = 1, \ldots, 5$
sub_3	—	subsidy rate for manufacturing industries
τ_4	—	markup rate in sector 4
t_i	—	indirect tax rates, $i = 3,4,5$
DEP	—	total depreciation
ϕ	—	share of depreciation for government capital
GR_i	—	government profits from enterprises, $i = 3,4,5$
t_z	—	tax rate on profit income
FA_1	—	food distribution under rural food-for-work program
FN_1	—	food distribution in ration shops, "issue"
$\bar{P}_1$	—	issue price
C_0	—	consumption of imported goods
P_{0c}^*	—	border price of consumption imports
P_{0f}^*	—	border price of fertilizer imports
P_{ei}^*	—	border price of sectoral exports, $i = 1, \ldots, 5$
K_i	—	capital stock in sector i, $i = 3$ and 5
$GINT$	—	government interest payments
$\bar{X}_i$	—	fixed output levels, $i = 1,2$

IV. Parameters

a_{ij}	—	sectoral input-output coefficients, $i, j = 1, \ldots, 5$
a_{0i}	—	input coefficients for intermediate imports, $i = 1, \ldots, 5$
m_i^a	—	marginal propensity to consume from agricultural income, $i = 1, \ldots, 5$
m_i^n	—	marginal propensity to consume from nonagricultural income, $i = 1, \ldots, 5$
Θ_i^a	—	floor-level consumption from agricultural income, $i = 1, \ldots, 5$
Θ_i^n	—	floor-level consumption from nonagricultural income, $i = 1, \ldots, 5$
b_i	—	sectoral labor-output ratios, $i = 3,4,5$
s_a	—	savings ratio for agricultural income
s_w	—	savings ratio for wage income
s_z	—	savings ratio for profit income
α_i	—	weights in the consumer price index, $i = 1,5$
$k_{\tau i}$	—	constants in the supply-response functions, $i = 3$ and 5
σ_i	—	elasticity in the supply-response function, $i = 3$ and 5
k_{wi}	—	wage-indexation coefficient
σ_s	—	elasticity of stock speculation

V. Initial Values

w_i°	—	beginning-of-period wage level, $i = 3,4,5$ and g
CPI°	—	beginning-of-period consumer price index
P_1°	—	beginning-of-period price level of sector 1

Wages in the nonagricultural commodity-producing sectors and for government employees are assumed to be partially indexed to the cost of living *within* the model's solution period of one year. Equations (4.8)–(4.12) give the details of how wages respond to changes in the consumer price index *CPI*. Wage income Y_w in (4.13) comes from production activities, government employment, emigrant remittances (eR), and transfer payments from the government (TR).

Block IV gives price equations for the nonagricultural sectors, with prices determined by a markup over variable costs. In manufacturing and services (sectors three and five) the markup rates τ_3 and τ_5 are assumed in equations (4.14) and (4.15) to rise with levels of output, again to capture a potentially inflationary phenomenon emphasized by Indian economists. Prices themselves are given in the simultaneous system (4.16)–(4.18), which includes terms for sales taxes at rate t_i for sector i, as well as subsidies granted manufacturing production (sub_3) and intermediate imports (at rates t_{0i}).

With the prices computed, it is an easy matter to give final expressions for variable costs per unit of output in block V. The level of income from profits then follows in block VI, as the sum of markups over variable cost less prespecified government revenues GR_i from public enterprise production. Depreciation on capital stock is subtracted from markup incomes and government interest payments are added to give the final value of Y_z.

In block VII appear equations for levels of consumer spending from agricultural and nonagricultural incomes (D_a and D_n, respectively). Agricultural saving at rate s_a is subtracted from income Y_a to give D_a in (4.23). Along with saving parameters, income taxes at rate t_z on profit income Y_z also enter the determination of D_n in (4.24). A term for a prespecified (small or zero) level of noncompetitive consumption imports is also subtracted.

Block VIII specifies sectoral consumption levels according to the widely used complete set of demand equations known as the linear expenditure system, or LES.[7] There are two sets of parameters for the LES—base levels of commodity consumption (Θ_i^a and Θ_i^n, $i = 1, \ldots, 5$), which are assumed to be independent of income and prices, and marginal propensities to consume (m_i^a and m_i^n, $i = 1, \ldots, 5$) from incomes above the levels $\hat{D}_a$ and $\hat{D}_n$ required to pay for the base-level purchases. Both price and income responsiveness of consumption are summarized by these parameters.

In the Indian context, further complications come from the facts that agricultural families receive food-for-work cereal donations at zero price in quantity FA_1, while nonagricultural families can get an "issue" of grain (total quantity FN_1) at a subsidized price $\bar{P}_1$ in the largely urban ration shops. Working through the utility maximization that underlies the LES when these food subsidies are included in budget constraints gives the demand equations that appear as (4.27)–(4.36). Adding the subsidy quantities gives sectoral consumption levels in (4.37)–(4.41). Finally, note back in equation (4.1) that the net change in the government's food stocks is given by its procurement GP_1 less food-for-work distribution FA_1 and the ration issue FN_1.

So far, we have described 41 equations in 43 variables (that is, all the endogenous variables in section II of table 4.3 except T^{ind}, *GREV, GEXP,* and *DEF,* which are described below). The two equations of block IX that specify that demand less the fixed supply for each agricultural commodity must equal zero serve to close the system. Thinking in terms of excess demand functions shows how it can be solved. An algorithm contains the following steps:

1. Guess sectoral output levels $X_1, \ldots, X_5$ and a trial pair of prices P_1 and P_2 for the agricultural sectors.
2. Calculate nonagricultural markup rates and prices from the equations in block IV (incorporating the feedback from price levels to wage rates in equations (4.8)–(4.12) when it is assumed to apply).
3. Using the trial values of prices and outputs, calculate wages and wage and agricultural incomes in block III, variable costs per unit output in block V, and profit income in block VI.
4. Calculate sectoral levels of consumer demand from blocks VII and VIII, and the foodstock change from block II.
5. Add up totals of sectoral demand, using the expressions to the left of the equality signs in equations (4.1)–(4.5). If any sectoral demand level differs from its corresponding trial value by more than a prespecified tolerance, set the trial value equal to the demand level and go back to step 2. Continue until demand levels are very close to trial output values for all sectors.[8]
6. Check if output levels X_1 and X_2 are very close to the prespecified agricultural supply levels $\overline{X}_1$ and $\overline{X}_2$. If not, modify the prices P_1 and P_2 and return to step 1. Continue until excess demands for the agricultural products are effectively equal to zero.[9]

When this solution procedure is complete, all sectors are in demand-supply equilibrium and as a consequence saving must equal investment. This *derived* relationship appears as equation (4.48) of table 4.2. To get to this expression for macro balance, government and foreign trade accounts are defined in (4.44)–(4.47). These equations summarize the fiscal and balance of payments effects of all the tax and subsidy programs described above.

For the government, (4.45) gives its current revenue *GREV,* made up of direct tax receipts, indirect taxes [calculated in (4.44)], and revenues from enterprise. The first two terms in equation (4.46) for current expenditure *GEXP* are costs of food-for-work and ration shop food subsidies; the cost differential associated with grain procurement, $(P_1 - P_1^*) GP_1$, follows. The next terms represent purchases of sector outputs from the development budget $(P_5 GS_5)$ and current outlay accounts; then come two terms capturing the effects of the fertilizer subsidy. The following five terms, respectively, represent wage payments to functionaries, transfers, depreciation on government capital stock, government interest payments, and the subsidy to manufacturing industry.

The next term is the sum of export subsidies in the five sectors and merits some commentary. The law of one price is not imposed in the model; as a consequence domestic and border prices of commodity exports may differ. The price differential creates an income gain or loss to be absorbed by someone in the system. In practice, both firms and the government will share the benefit or burden, but in the Indian institutional context where the government actively subsidizes exports, it is appropriate in a simplified model to give it the full role. The penultimate term in (4.46) shows that the government pays a variable export subsidy to firms, so that they can sell at the same price both internally and externally. This outlay, of course, represents government dissaving, and plays a role in the model's overall adjustment to equilibrium. (A corresponding entry, which should appear for variable tariffs on competitive imports, is omitted since its magnitude is likely to be small.) The final term shows that the government also subsidizes intermediate imports, at fixed sectoral rates t_{0i}.

Equation (4.47) defines the trade deficit in rupee prices. Because taxes or subsidies on competitive imports are not included in the specification, they enter the definition of the deficit *DEF* at internal prices (first term to right of the equality sign). The other terms are at border prices multiplied by the exchange rate e, and represent items of foreign commerce already described.

The saving-investment balance (4.48) is of standard form. Saving to the left of the equals sign comes from households, the government current account, and the trade deficit. Investment on the right includes capital formation and stock changes. The other item is the government's net stock acquisition $GP_1 - FA_1 - FN_1$, valued at the market price P_1.

As in all the models of this book, the saving-investment balance is not an independent restriction; for that reason it is equation number 48 in a system of 47 endogenous variables. However, it provides a convenient numerical check on the computer solution of a model like the one here. In solving the India model, tolerance limits were set to make saving equal to investment to five or six significant figures. This degree of precision assures that the algorithm to solve the model will generate a balanced SAM; it is well beyond the accuracy of the data at hand.

4.3 Parameterization

The main reason for setting up a model based on a social accounting matrix is that it can be used to address questions of income distribution and intersectoral interaction that are aggregated away in one- or two-sector specifications. A corresponding drawback is that time series information can be used to estimate only a few relationships in the model, since the national accounts do not appear in the requisite detail. Indeed, as described above, even the construction of a SAM is usually based on a process of imposing accounting identities on disparate and inconsistent data sources. A social accounting matrix will scarcely ever be a correct description of the macro economy, but at least it is a consistent one.[10]

If one takes consistency and accounting identities as central to the exercise, then it is clear that model equations must be parameterized in such a way as to satisfy the SAM. The main parameters are listed in part IV of table 4.3. Observations on their calculations follow:

1. The input-output coefficients a_{ij} and a_{0j} follow directly by division of intersectoral flows by gross outputs of the sectors. The main complication in figuring out these "physical" coefficients is to make sure that taxes and subsidies are taken out of the valuation of commodity flows in their numerators and denominators, but getting the details straight essentially requires only tenacity and respect for the accounting identities.
2. Parameters of the LES are not independent. Like all demand systems based on additive utility functions, it has only $N + 1$ independent parameters for an N-sector demand structure. Recipes are available for estimating the complete parameter set based on (for example) income elasticities and minimal information regarding price response.[11]
3. Saving rates must be computed to satisfy the overall saving-investment balance of the SAM. In practice, both saving rates and levels for the different income recipient classes are calculated together, incorporating whatever econometric information happens to be available about saving behavior.
4. Labor-output ratios b_i come from the wage bill and the wage rate by sector. In a dynamic model, one would have to worry about rates at which the b_i decline from productivity change. Note also that in realistic country data, wage and profit rates will always differ across sectors; an a priori assumption that they should be equalized by competition does not fit the facts.

5. The other parameters in the table were estimated more or less ad hoc for the India model, again subject to sensitivity analysis and the results of formal statistical estimation.
6. The initial values of the variables of the model either can be read directly from the SAM or else follow from simple manipulations (like dividing sectoral gross output levels by total variable costs to get markup rates). Again, accounting consistency permits straightforward computation of the long list of symbols in table 4.3.

Key parameters from these manipulations appear in table 4.4. Saving propensities from the various income flows differ but are all in the range from 0.12 to 0.23. Income elasticities for consumer demand are plausible, and there is substantial price-responsiveness in the consumption functions. Note the value of 0.3081 for m_1^a, the marginal propensity to buy cereal products from total consumer spending generated from agricultural in-

TABLE 4.4

Main Parameters of the Model

Uses of Agricultural Income				
$s_a = 0.12$				
Sector	m_i^a	Θ_i^a	Income Elas.	Own Price Elas.
1	0.3081	1.36314	0.6162	−0.5213
2	0.13239	0.18677	1.1654	−0.6380
3	0.35388	0.14801	1.6497	−0.8869
4	0.01743	0.07376	0.6354	−0.3296
5	0.1882	0.19846	1.3027	−0.7170

Uses of Nonagricultural Income				
$s_w = 0.1482$		$s_z = 0.2223$		$t_z = 0.10936$
Sector	m_i^n	Θ_i^n	Income Elas.	Own Price Elas.
1	0.09665	0.69737	0.7548	−0.4409
2	0.14771	0.25756	1.2207	−0.6731
3	0.33929	0.5521	1.2528	−0.7572
4	0.02103	0.09038	0.7816	−0.4074
5	0.39532	1.20443	0.9488	−0.6850

Sectoral Markup and Indirect Tax Rates		
Sector	Markup Rate	Indirect Tax Rate
3	0.1466	0.1243
4	0.3066	0.10157
5	0.50158	0.06987

comes. The parameter shows that about 30 percent of agriculturalists' extra spending goes for consumption of products of sector one. This economically reasonable assumption strongly influences behavior of the model, as discussed in the following section.

4.4 The Jacobian

The basic equations are (4.1)–(4.5), which can easily be rewritten as excess demand functions for the five sectors. When excess demands are not zero, equilibrium is reestablished via price increases in the first two sectors and output increases in the other three. For the variables P_1, P_2, X_3, X_4, and X_5, three adjustment matrices are shown in table 4.5: the Jacobian for the five-equation excess demand system, a matrix of elasticities of excess

TABLE 4.5

Response Matrices for the India Model

Jacobian Matrix for Excess Demand Functions					
	P_1	P_2	X_3	X_4	X_5
$\dot{P}_1$	−0.561	0.500	0.026	0.039	0.053
$\dot{P}_2$	0.091	−0.481	0.111	0.059	0.075
$\dot{X}_3$	0.217	0.190	−0.658	0.254	0.296
$\dot{X}_4$	0.010	0.020	0.037	−0.796	0.032
$\dot{X}_5$	0.012	0.128	0.264	0.242	−0.662
Column total	−0.231	0.357	−0.220	−0.202	−0.206
Elasticities of Excess Demand Function with Respect to Investment					
	−0.242	0.216	0.107	0.017	0.149
	0.039	−0.207	0.458	0.026	0.212
	0.094	0.082	−2.716	0.112	0.835
	0.004	0.009	0.153	−0.351	0.090
	0.005	0.055	1.090	0.107	−1.867
Inverse of the Jacobian Matrix (x − 1)					
	3.133	4.317	1.534	1.419	1.497
	1.267	4.309	1.347	1.193	1.252
	2.010	4.052	3.282	2.114	2.193
	0.212	0.457	0.273	1.467	0.261
	1.179	2.693	1.697	1.636	2.750

demand with respect for goods from sector three (industry and construction), and the inverse of the Jacobian.[12]

An increase in any one of the five adjusting variables will reduce excess
demand in its corresponding sector—that is, the meaning of the negative
entries along the main diagonal of the Jacobian. Note, however, that there
are strong feedbacks from some sectors to others. The most important
example is the coefficient in row one, column two. Its value of 0.5 comes
directly from the parameter value of 0.3081 for the marginal propensity to
consume m_1^q pointed out in connection with table 4.4 above. The linkages
go as follows:

1. An increase in P_2 raises agricultural income proportionately to sector two output
   of 2.6546 (the entry in row 14, column 2 of table 4.1 with quantities measured
   in ten thousand crores, or one hundred billion rupees in 1980–81).
2. The direct effect on sector one consumer demand is given by $2.6546 (1 - s_a)m_1^q$
   $= 2.6446(0.88)(0.3081) = 0.717$.
3. Subtracting intermediate input costs ($a_{12} = 0.0174$ in the input-output matrix),
   substitution effects in consumption and other minor feedbacks gives the coefficient of 0.5 appearing in table 4.5. Despite these emendations, there remains a
   strong income effect from increases in the noncereal price P_2 on demand for
   products of sector one. Through this linkage, an increase in the price of a major,
   relatively stable production flow has macroeconomic repercussions throughout
   the system.

Along similar lines, there are strong demands from all other sectors for
sector three, and from sectors three and four for sector five. Perhaps surprisingly, not much additional demand for infrastructure services from sector
four is generated by price or quantity increments in the other sectors. The
Jacobian replicates the finding mentioned earlier that output in the infrastructure sector is relatively independent of activity in the rest of the economy.

In algebraic terms one can write the response of the endogenous variables
to a change in investment demand for sector three products as follows:

$$
\begin{bmatrix}
j_{11} & j_{12} & \cdots & j_{15} \\
j_{21} & & & \cdot \\
\cdot & & & \cdot \\
\cdot & & & \cdot \\
j_{51} & \cdots & \cdots & j_{55}
\end{bmatrix}
\begin{bmatrix}
dP_1 \\
dP_2 \\
dX_3 \\
dX_4 \\
dX_5
\end{bmatrix}
+
\begin{bmatrix}
0 \\
0 \\
dI_3 \\
0 \\
0
\end{bmatrix}
=
\begin{bmatrix}
0 \\
0 \\
0 \\
0 \\
0
\end{bmatrix}
$$

where the j_{ik} are the elements of the Jacobian. From this formulation it is evident that the column sums of the Jacobian (multiplied by minus one) provide a differential form of the saving-investment balance in the model, that is

$$- (j_{11} + j_{21} + \cdots + j_{51})dP_1 - (j_{12} + j_{22} + \cdots + j_{52})dP_2$$
$$- \cdots - (j_{15} + j_{25} + \cdots + j_{55})dX_5 = dI_3$$

The numerical matrix in table 4.5 shows that a unit increase in P_1 generates 0.231 units of saving, and so on.[13] All saving responses are positive except for P_2. The increase in demand for food and other products that a rise in this price generates actually reduces saving overall. Such an effect could potentially make the excess demand functions unstable, but it is not strong enough to do so in the present model.[14]

The elasticity matrix shows how prices and quantities respond in relative terms to an increase in investment demand. Since the rise in investment first affects sector three, its own elasticity of 2.716 is the largest in absolute terms in the matrix, as might be expected. The elasticities for the prices are in general less than for the quantities, basically because consumers' price elasticities of demand for food are fairly small, as shown in table 4.4. The consequence is that wide swings in prices as equilibrium shifts may be expected. This observation is verified by the inverse of the Jacobian (with all entries multiplied by minus one) in table 4.5. It shows that all the endogenous variables will respond positively to an increase in any sector's demand. The elements in the first two rows giving price responses are large, especially in comparison to the initial normalization of both prices at unity. The direct and indirect elasticities of the endogenous variables to an increase in sector three investment demand (calculated from the third column of the inverse Jacobian matrix) are: P_1, 3.557; P_2, 3.123; X_3, 0.819; X_4, 0.62; X_5, 0.602. The fivefold difference in magnitude between price and quantity elasticities comes from the economics of the system. The price-clearing agricultural sector plays a major role in the Indian economy, and is characterized by inelastic supply and low elasticities of demand. Hypersensitive prices are the structural outcome.

4.5 Numerical Results

In this section, trial variations in parameters and data for the India model are described, with emphasis on its adjustment mechanisms. We first take up how the system responds to changes in investment demand, coupled with foodstock speculation, partial wage indexation, rising markup rates, and variations in the level of agricultural supply. Next comes an analysis of the possible effects of devaluation, followed by a discussion of how the government might adjust its food procurement policy to compensate for output fluctuations in sector one. Results from the model, including a demand-supply balance for money, are given in section 5.5.

Table 4.6 shows how the system responds to an increase in investment demand for products of sector three from 2.3186 to 2.41 hundred billion rupees (about 4 percent). The rise in aggregate demand is reflected in increases of both agricultural prices and nonagricultural levels of output, as shown in the second column of panel A of the table. The arc elasticities of response are close to those calculated from the Jacobian in table 4.5, and the output multiplers are X_3, 3.335; X_4, 0.281; X_5, 1.743. These values are consistent with the usual Keynesian "leakages" from the income-demand linkage through saving and intermediate imports, coupled with the feedback of increases in agricultural prices to demand for nonagricultural products.

Panel B of table 4.6 shows how saving flows adjust to meet higher investment demand. The value of investment rises from 2.7417 to 2.928 hundred billion rupees. This increase reflects both the greater quantity of capital goods demanded and the rise in the sector three price (due to cost-push of intermediate inputs purchased from agriculture) from 1.0 to 1.0318. As shares of investment we have the following changes in sources of saving:

Saving Sources	Initial	Final
Agricultural incomes	0.196	0.213
Wage incomes	0.234	0.224
Profits	0.194	0.192
Trade deficit	0.066	0.072
Government saving	0.049	0.055
Depreciation	0.261	0.244

There is a forced saving in the sense that real wages in nonagricultural sectors decline as prices go up, causing the proportion of saving from wages to the total to fall. The real value of nominal depreciation allowances goes down for the same reason. The share of saving coming from nonagricultural

TABLE 4.6

Effects of a Four-Percent Increase in Investment Demand for Sector Three Products

A. *Prices and Quantities*

			Investment Increase Coupled With		
	Base Run	Only Investment Increase	Foodstock Price Responsiveness	Wage Indexation	Rising Markup Rates
P_1	1	1.1484	1.1917	1.2182	1.1988
P_2	1	1.1325	1.1527	1.1916	1.1748
P_3	1	1.0318	1.0372	1.0597	1.0666
P_4	1	1.0098	1.0015	1.0336	1.0229
P_5	1	1.0138	1.0164	1.0388	1.0435
X_3	9.5712	9.8760	9.9012	9.9299	9.8833
X_4	1.0216	1.0473	1.0501	1.0530	1.0505
X_5	6.5387	6.6980	6.7128	6.7350	6.7052

B. *Savings and Investment*

			Investment Increase Coupled With		
	Base Run	Only Investment Increase	Foodstock Price Responsiveness	Wage Indexation	Rising Markup Rates
Agr. sav.	0.5373	0.6237	0.6437	0.6626	0.6511
Wage sav.	0.6414	0.6546	0.6558	0.6702	0.6552
Prof. sav.	0.5324	0.5635	0.5675	0.5850	0.6094
Trade def.	0.1800	0.2108	0.2142	0.2246	0.2243
Gov. sav.	0.1357	0.1606	0.1607	0.1516	0.1720
Deprec.	0.7148	0.7148	0.7148	0.7148	0.7148
Total	2.7417	2.9280	2.9567	3.0087	3.0268

C. *Income Shares*

			Investment Increase Coupled With		
	Base Run	Only Investment Increase	Foodstock Price Responsiveness	Wage Indexation	Rising Markup Rates
Agr. income	0.3895	0.4171	0.4239	0.4248	0.4198
Wage income	0.3765	0.3545	0.3497	0.3479	0.3420
Profit income	0.2340	0.2384	0.2264	0.2273	0.2382
Total	1.0000	1.0000	1.0000	1.0000	1.0000

profits stays about constant, while the output increases in the nonagricultural sectors draw in more intermediate imports and drive up the trade deficit's share.

Both price and quantity changes enter into the adjustment. In distributional terms, the outcome in panel C of table 4.6 is an increase in agriculturalists' share of income, and a fall of that of wage earners. In relative terms, profit incomes hold roughly stable.

These patterns change when additional price and quantity reactions are introduced into the system, as shown in the other columns of the table. The columns headed "Foodstock price responsiveness" show what happens when the speculation parameter σ_s in equation (4.6) is changed from zero to one. There are sharper price increases, and some output response in the nonagricultural sectors. More forced saving occurs at the expense of workers, and the income distribution shifts further toward agriculture.

In practice, partial indexation of urban wages in India to price increases within the year appears to be the rule. The columns headed "Wage indexation" show what happens when 20 percent of the increase in the consumer price index as calculated in (4.8) is passed along to nominal wages in (4.9)–(4.12). Not surprisingly, the effect is inflationary. Moreover, workers *lose* from the indexation, as their income share falls from 0.3545 when investment increases without indexation, to 0.3479. The reason is that food supplies are assumed fixed, so that an initial increase in demand resulting from higher money wages has to be cut back by still sharper food price increases. The outcome is an additional shift of the income distribution toward agriculture and a lower real wage. Profit recipients gain from bigger markups on higher nominal variable costs.

The columns headed "Rising markup rates" summarize the effects of raising the parameters σ_3 and σ_5 from zero to 2.0 and 1.5, respectively, in equations (4.14) and (4.15). With these changes in specification, markup rates rise along with the output-capital ratios in sectors three and five, essentially reflecting demand-pressure on prices.[15] Once again, price increases go beyond those induced by a simple increase in investment demand. In panel C of table 4.6, it can be seen that the distributional effect favors agriculturalists and harms wage earners; the profit share as usual holds steady.

Each of the three shifts in the specification—foodstock speculation, wage indexing, and markups rising in response to demand—is mildly inflationary taken by itself, adding 5 percentage points or so to the average 14 percent rise in agricultural prices caused by higher investment demand. However, when the three effects are put together, the feedbacks between them are extreme.

The agricultural prices rise by 64 and 49 percent, as shown in the "Inflationary effects" column in panel A of table 4.7. There are also substantial increases in sectoral outputs, and the income distribution swings 7 percentage points toward agriculture.

TABLE 4.7

*Effects of an Investment Increase Linked with All
Inflationary Mechanisms and Either Increased Imports of
Sector Two Commodities or Supply Response in Sectors
One and Two*

A. *Prices and Quantities*

	Base Run	Inflationary Effects	Increased Imports	Agric. Supply Response
P_1	1	1.6396	1.1853	1.0998
P_2	1	1.4856	1.1342	1.0850
P_3	1	1.2133	1.0689	1.0511
P_4	1	1.1184	1.0377	1.0270
X_3	9.5712	10.1302	9.8628	9.8551
X_4	1.0216	1.0798	1.0473	1.0466
X_5	6.5387	6.8687	6.6906	6.6955

B. *Savings and Investment*

	Base Run	Inflationary Effects	Increased Imports	Agric. Supply Response
Agr. sav.	0.5373	0.8826	0.6353	0.6006
Wage sav.	0.6414	0.7083	0.6660	0.6617
Prof. sav.	0.5324	0.7456	0.6123	0.6026
Trade def.	0.1800	0.2954	0.2464	0.2234
Gov. sav.	0.1357	0.1596	0.1688	0.1710
Deprec.	0.7148	0.7148	0.7148	0.7148
Total:	2.7417	3.5063	3.0435	2.9742

C. *Income Shares*

	Base Run	Inflationary Effects	Increased Imports	Agric. Supply Response
Agr. income	0.3395	0.4626	0.4110	0.4000
Wage income	0.3765	0.3006	0.3489	0.3563
Profit income	0.2340	0.2368	0.2401	0.2432
Total:	1.0000	1.0000	1.0000	1.0000

These shifts are too large to be credible, but do reflect the model's (and to a degree the Indian economy's) sensitivity to the agricultural sectors. However, they are easily moderated by supply changes. In table 4.7 two options are presented. First, "Increased imports" columns show the effects of raising competitive imports into sector two from 0.0035 to 0.0235 hundred billion rupees (about 0.75 percent of initial supply). Second, the "Agricultural supply response" columns show what happens when output during the year in each of the agricultural sectors rises in the response to higher prices. The supply elasticities were set at values 0.1 and 0.2 in sectors one and two, respectively, on the notion that there is likely to be somewhat less market sensitivity for the staple commodities produced by cereal growers. For short-run elasticities these values are perhaps on the high side, but were chosen to reflect as much stabilization from supply response as might reasonably be expected.

In both cases, the price increases are greatly moderated, as one could already anticipate from the large entries in the northwest corner of the inverse Jacobian matrix of table 4.5.[16] Both import manipulation and farmers' price-responsiveness (as well as other policies such as changes in publicly held foodgrain stocks) have very important macroeconomic effects in the model. This observation also applies to the real economy of India.

Turning to another topic, we examine the effects of a 15-percent devaluation of the rupee in table 4.8. Three simulations are given, with elasticities of export volumes from all sectors with respect to the exchange rate assumed to be zero, 0.5, and 2.0, respectively.

When there is no export response, the model follows the contractionary devaluation scenario of chapter 2. Devaluation drives up the costs of intermediate imports, which are directly transmitted to higher prices of nonagricultural products. Real wages fall, pulling down aggregate demand. The outcome is reduced production in the quantity-adjusting sectors, and lower agricultural prices. There is an overall inflationary push, despite the reductions in P_1 and P_2.

Increased nominal values of exports and remittances and the reduced volume of intermediate imports dominate higher import costs, so that the trade deficit in rupee terms declines (panel C).[17] At the same time, the nominal value of investment demand rises along with nonagricultural prices. The required saving comes mainly from the government (panel B) as its nominal export subsidies fall. The net increase in saving from government and the trade deficit is $(0.2247 - 0.1357) + (0.1539 - 0.1800) = 0.0629$. As discussed in section 5.5, where money is brought into the present model, the outcome is a reduction in money creation by 0.0629 as well. At a time when devaluation is driving up nonagricultural prices, money supply drops with a contractionary effect on output and growth. Finally, note that devaluation shifts the income distribution slightly away from agriculture (panel D) as the sector's prices fall.

When exports respond to the exchange rate, the contractionary effects vanish. Already an exchange rate elasticity of 0.5 induces enough export

TABLE 4.8

Effects of a Devaluation by Fifteen Percent

A. Prices and Quantities

	Base Run	No Export Response	Export Response Elast = 0.5	Export Response Elast = 2.0
P_1	1	0.9994	1.1245	1.2052
P_2	1	0.9994	1.1014	1.1593
P_3	1	1.0189	1.0629	1.0922
P_4	1	1.0061	1.0303	1.0465
P_5	1	1.0052	1.0394	1.0632
X_3	9.5712	9.5283	9.6598	9.7748
X_4	1.0262	1.0190	1.0350	1.0520
X_5	6.5749	6.5246	6.6034	6.6658

B. Savings and Investment

	Base Run	No Export Response	Export Response Elast = 0.5	Export Response Elast = 2.0
Agr. sav.	0.5373	0.5364	0.6060	0.6485
Wage sav.	0.6414	0.6460	0.6603	0.6709
Prof. sav.	0.5325	0.5344	0.5780	0.6120
Trade def.	0.1800	0.1539	0.1516	0.1392
Gov. sav.	0.1357	0.2247	0.2300	0.2431
Deprec.	0.7148	0.7148	0.7148	0.7148
Total:	2.7417	2.8102	2.9407	3.0285
Dom. inv.	2.3186	2.3625	2.4644	2.5325
Imp. inv.	0.1211	0.1393	0.1393	0.1393
Pr. stocks	0.4048	0.4113	0.4399	0.4596
Gov. stocks	−0.1028	−0.1028	−0.1028	−0.1028
Total:	2.7417	2.8102	2.9408	3.0285

C. Trade Balance

	Base Run	No Export Response	Export Response Elast = 0.5	Export Response Elast = 2.0
Compet. imp.	0.3782	0.3853	0.4021	0.4133
Imp. inv.	0.1211	0.1393	0.1393	0.1393
Imp. fertilizer	0.0588	0.0672	0.0677	0.0677
Imp. intermed.	0.5719	0.6547	0.6638	0.6717
Total:	1.1300	1.2464	1.2728	1.2919
Total exports	0.7100	0.8165	0.8452	0.8767
Remittances	0.2400	0.2760	0.2760	0.2760
Trade def.	0.1800	0.1539	0.1516	0.1392

D. Income Shares

	Base Run	No Export Response	Export Response Elast = 0.5	Export Response Elast = 2.0
Agr. income	0.3895	0.3878	0.4065	0.4150
Wage income	0.3765	0.3781	0.3586	0.3476
Profit income	0.2340	0.2341	0.2350	0.2374
Total:	1.0000	1.0000	1.0000	1.0000

demand to produce expansion in the nonagricultural sectors. However, there is also demand pressure on agriculture, which as usual must be met by rising prices. With an export elasticity of 2.0, this inflationary effect is quite strong. The rise of the agricultural income share by 2.5 percentage points is part and parcel of the food price inflation.

Effects of changes in the level of foodgrain supply from sector one are summarized in table 4.9. Note the price decreases that accompany higher cereal production. As discussed in sections 3.1 and 3.2, a fall in the food-

TABLE 4.9

Food Procurement Policy

A. Prices and Quantities

	Base Run	Output 3.6% Up Sector 1	+ Procur. Increase	Output 6.6% Up Sector 1	+ Procur. Increase
P_1	1	0.8309	0.99727	0.7303	0.9912
P_2	1	0.9769	1.0846	0.9654	1.1539
P_3	1	0.9821	1.0298	0.9721	1.0541
P_4	1	0.9864	1.0138	0.9786	1.0249
P_5	1	0.9844	1.0225	0.9756	1.0407
X_3	9.5712	9.5468	9.6726	9.5316	9.7524
X_4	1.0216	1.0201	1.0343	1.0193	1.0445
X_5	6.5387	6.5446	6.6249	6.5494	6.6943

B. Savings and Investment

	Base Run	Output 3.6% Up Sector 1	+ Procur. Increase	Output 6.6% Up Sector 1	+ Procur. Increase
Agr. sav.	0.5373	0.4821	0.5690	0.4494	0.5941
Wage sav.	0.6414	0.6347	0.6503	0.6308	0.6575
Prof. sav.	0.5324	0.5209	0.5666	0.5145	0.5948
Trade def.	0.1800	0.1828	0.2084	0.1873	0.2320
Gov. sav.	0.1357	0.1432	0.1439	0.1471	0.1511
Deprec.	0.7148	0.7148	0.7148	0.7148	0.7148
Total	2.7417	2.6785	2.8529	2.6439	2.9442
Total inv.	2.7417	2.6785	2.8529	2.6439	2.9442

C. Income Shares

	Base Run	Output 3.6% Up Sector 1	+ Procur. Increase	Output 6.6% Up Sector 1	+ Procur. Increase
Agr. income	0.3895	0.3675	0.3954	0.3533	0.3995
Wage income	0.3765	0.3918	0.3659	0.4015	0.3577
Profit income	0.2340	0.2407	0.2387	0.2452	0.2428
Total:	1.0000	1.0000	1.0000	1.0000	1.0000

grain price resulting from higher output can either stimulate or cut back on demand for nonagricultural products. Farmers' income drops as their output price declines sharply in the face of increased supply, while the real purchasing power of incomes generated in nonagricultural sectors goes up. Demand for nonagricultural products will rise or fall, depending on how these opposing income changes balance out.

In the India model, falling cereal prices slightly retard demand for sector three products (industry) and stimulate it for sector five products (services). At the same time, the income distribution swings against agriculture and in favor of wages and profits. All prices fall as foodgrain output rises, due to consumer demand and input-output linkages in the system.

The policy variable that the Indian government uses to stabilize the economy against food output shifts is procurement. The government has to honor the procurement price, which, with its initial value of one, lies above the market price in both cases of output increase shown in table 4.9. The "procurement increase" columns show what happens when the government buys enough grain to hold the market price steady at its initial (normalized) value of one. There is overall expansion, and government saving increases in nominal terms despite its outlays to buy grain.

Varying procurement to stabilize prices makes GP_1 almost an endogenous policy variable. When procurement is treated in this fashion, it is natural to ask about trade-offs between the amount of government purchases required to hold market food prices constant and the level of production. Figure 4.2 depicts the iso-price relationship between GP_1 and output X_1. The graph is essentially linear, and shows that a procurement increase of about three billion rupees' worth of grain will counteract a production increase of ten billion. Procurement appears to be an effective price stabilization instrument in India.[18]

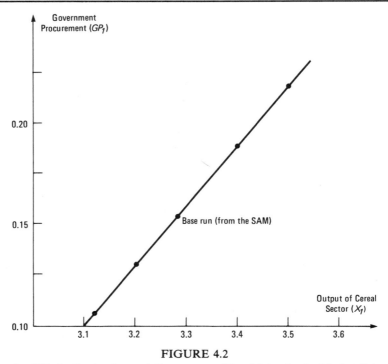

FIGURE 4.2

Levels of Grain Production and Procurement That Maintain the Market Price at Its Initial Level

4.6 Conclusions

The foregoing exercise shows in a near-practical context how price and quantity adjustments enter a macro model constructed along lines suggested in the previous two chapters. In most cases, the reactions of the adjusting variables to shifts in parameters or endogenous variables have "correct" signs, but some may be too large in magnitude to make sense.

Since the model is aggregated, it leaves out enormous detail regarding the Indian economy—demand-supply adjustment mechanisms for specific agricultural crops, regional variation, time lags achieving sectoral balance—a host of complications.

To point out the major features of adjustment, it makes sense to leave these complexities out. In applied policy analysis, it would be better to incorporate them insofar as possible, or change the specification to smooth them away. One obvious trick is to make agricultural supply dependent on the current period's price level, as in table 4.7. Equally, saving rates could be made dependent on income levels, or real investment might be assumed to fall if prices go up (on the hypothesis that investment outlays are planned in nominal, not real, terms).[19] Some of these changes would make the specification more neoclassical, as discussed in section 2.3; others would depend on policy judgment. But all of them amount to ways of sweeping innumerable microeconomic feedbacks to the macro system into a tidy pile; they add little to our understanding of how the system operates in the first place.

5

Money and Other Assets in the Short Run

THE DISCUSSION now shifts toward the finances of the economy, under simplifying assumptions about the real side. All intersectoral and trade balance considerations are dropped, to put emphasis on how the general price level may respond to financial perturbations in a short run during which the money wage, price expectations, and the capital stock and capacity utilization are all fixed. In chapter 6, these restrictions are lifted in a full monetary growth model.

The chief innovation in the discussion is inclusion of interest payments on working capital in variable cost. This specification reflects the fact that with poor articulation of both transport and financial systems in developing countries, entrepreneurs typically have to make large advances for working capital in the form of labor and intermediate goods; interest on these advances looms large in their statements of profit and loss. A reduction in the money supply drives up interest rates and can thus increase the price level from the side of cost. At the same time, higher interest rates will reduce investment demand. To see how these two effects can lead to stagflation—simultaneously rising prices and falling levels of economic activity—we begin the discussion with a simple short-run model in section 5.1. Since the emphasis is on inflationary processes, full capacity use and a variable price level are assumed, as in chapter 2.

In section 5.2, the financial side of the economy is described. Households hold three kinds of wealth: bank deposits, loans to firms, and a group of nonproductive assets called "gold." Excess demand functions for loans and gold are derived, with the interest rate and gold price as market-clearing variables. Demand and supply of bank deposits come into balance by Walras's law, although all three asset-market excess-demand functions may be shifted by a change in an exogenously specified deposit interest rate.

Section 5.3 describes short-run equilibrium in a two-asset model without gold. Depending on whether cost-push from working capital or demand reduction from less investment is more important, a rise in the interest rate can either drive up or reduce the price level. Comparative statics depend on which effect dominates. When working-capital costs are more important, it is shown that monetary contraction can lead to stagflation in the short run. Similar problems arise in section 5.4, with all three assets. An increase in the deposit rate can lead to stagflation unless it strongly shifts asset preferences away from gold, as opposed to productive loans from the household sector to firms.

The final section of the chapter is an empirical illustration of how stagflation can be induced by monetary contraction in a version of the India model of chapter 4 extended to include a money market. Monetary repercussions of currency devaluation are also assessed.[1]

5.1 The Real Side of the Economy

Since the emphasis in this chapter is on price instead of output changes, it is simplest to assume full utilization of capacity. Excess demand will adjust toward zero by forced saving in the short run, as described in chapter 2. The markup rate is an endogenous macro variable, while output is determined by available fixed capital,

$$X = aK \qquad (5.1)$$

where X is output, K is capital stock, and a is the output-capital ratio. An alternative, somewhat richer model would result if (5.1) were replaced by a rule such as $\tau = \tau\,(X/aK)$. As discussed in section 2.3, an increase in aggregate demand would then be associated with forced saving from the rising markup rate τ as well as output expansion. Without algebraic detail, how this more "neoclassical" model would behave is pointed out from time to time in the following discussion.

An extension beyond chapter 2 is consideration of demand for working capital by firms. The assumption is that entrepreneurs must have money on hand to pay in advance for the services of current inputs into the production process. In a poor, inflationary economy, suppliers of inputs are too financially constrained to allow their payments to wait.[2]

There has been substantial debate in the literature as to whether working-capital costs should be measured by the nominal interest rate i or a "real" rate defined as $i - \pi$, where π is the expected rate of price inflation. The choice really hinges in what one considers to be the "short run." Assume, for example, that production takes place during a period of T days, during which employment stays fixed at L. Workers have to be paid in advance, so working-capital expenses are given by borrowing costs at time t, when production is initiated, less the labor content of sales at time $t + T$,

$$\text{Cost} = L[w_t(1 + iT) - w_{t+T}]$$

in which i is the daily interest rate, and w_t and w_{t+T} are wages at the beginning and end of the period. If the money wage stays constant ($w_{t+T} = w_t$), then evidently $\text{Cost} = Lw_t iT$. Alternately, if the wage is perfectly indexed to expected inflation and the nominal interest rate is equal to some real rate j plus inflation ($i = j + \pi$), then we have:

$$\text{Cost} = L[w_t(1 + (j + \pi)T) - w_t(1 + \pi T)] = Lw_j T$$

so the real interest rate would be the appropriate concept of cost.

In reality, of course, time profiles of input use vary widely across production processes—ships and houses tie up streams of raw materials and intermediates over extended periods, while crude oil feedstocks for refineries may be in tankers or storage for a few weeks or even days. In the formal model discussed here, continuous flow input of labor is assumed, while excess macro demand is driven to zero during a period (implicitly of days or weeks) during which the money wage does not change. On these assumptions, working-capital costs should be measured by the nominal interest rate, so that the payment flows that exhaust the value of output are given by:

$$PX = (1 + i)wL + rPK \qquad (5.2)$$

The income decomposition underlying this equation is threefold—workers get a wage bill wL, firms receive a return rPK on their fixed capital (r is the profit rate, as usual), and banks get interest payments iwL on their working capital advances for employment of labor.[3] As just discussed, the labor input flow is proportional to the flow of output,

$$L = bx = baK \tag{5.3}$$

Substitution of (5.3) into (5.2) gives an expression for the profit rate as:

$$r = a\left[1 - \frac{(1 + i)\,wb}{P}\right] \tag{5.4}$$

Evidently, r rises with the price level but falls with both the interest rate and the money wage. Inverting (5.4) gives:

$$P = \frac{aw(1 + i)b}{(a - r)} \tag{5.5}$$

so that the maximum profit rate is the output-capital ratio a, reached when the real wage falls to zero.

Equilibrium excess demand for output must be zero:

$$C + I + G - X = 0$$

where C is household consumption, I is investment, and G is government consumption demand. As usual, we assume that there is no saving from wage income, and that the share of total profits rPK that is saved is a constant, s. This parameter captures saving from both firms (retained earnings) and personal incomes (dividends). The same sort of decomposition should apply to saving from interest income iwL, except that retained earnings of banks and especially moneylenders may be small, while interest recipients such as the traditional "widows and orphans" may not save much either. To save a parenthesis or two under these circumstances, it is simplest to assume that interest income is entirely consumed.[4] The value of private consumption thus becomes:

$$PC = (1 + i)wL + (1 - s)rPK$$

Substitution of this expression into the excess demand equation and manipulations such as those in chapter 2 give the investment-saving balance as:

$$g + \gamma a - sr = 0 \tag{5.6}$$

where $g = I/K$ is the growth rate of capital stock (and output) and $\gamma = G/X$ is the share of government demand in output.

Together with (5.4), equation (5.6) determines the equilibrium price level P. To get a final expression for P, a theory of investment must be added to the demand side. As before, returns to investment are measured by the profit rate r. A new feature is the cost of tying up resources in physical capital measured by the alternative uses to which they could be put. Since capital formation is a long-term process, the real interest rate $i - \pi$ is the appropriate cost concept. The simplest formulation makes the growth rate of capital depend on the difference between profit and real interest rates, or[5]

$$g = g_0 + h[r - (i - \pi)] \tag{5.7}$$

Solving (5.4) (5.6) and (5.7) together for P gives:

$$P = \frac{(s - h)aw(1 + i)b}{[s - (h + \gamma)]a - g_0 + h(i - \pi)} \tag{5.8}$$

Forced saving is built into (5.8) since an upward shift in autonomous investment g_0 drives up the price level relative to the money wage w. The consequent distributional shift toward profits generates the saving counterpart of the higher investment demand. An increase in i has an ambiguous effect on P. A rising interest rate may push up the price level by increasing working-capital costs or reduce it by cutting back on investment demand. To check the conditions under which one or the other effect dominates, one can differentiate (5.8). The sign of $\partial P/\partial i$ depends on the quantity:

$$[s - (h + \gamma)]a - g_0 - h(1 + \pi)$$

For given values of the other parameters, this expression shows that working-capital cost-push makes $\partial P/\partial i$ positive when the expected inflation rate π is relatively low. With more inflation, forced (dis) saving from reduced investment demand may come into play strongly enough to make the derivative negative. For future reference, note that simple manipulation makes the condition $(s - h)abw > Ph$ a requirement for working-capital cost-push to dominate.[6]

Before going on to discuss money and finance, we can derive two additional results from the saving-investment balance. First, P is a function of i and π from (5.8), and the profit rate r follows from (5.5). From (5.7), investment demand thus depends only on $i - \pi$. Going through the algebra shows that the growth rate is given by the expression:

$$g = \frac{sg_0 + h\gamma a - sh(i - \pi)}{s - h} \tag{5.9}$$

So long as $s > h$ (the effect on saving of profit rate increases exceeds the effect on investment—the standard stability condition), then an interest rate increase unambiguously reduces the rate of growth.

The second result is simply a closed form expression for commodity excess demand, which is:

$$\frac{(s - h)a(1 + i)wb}{P} - h(i - \pi)$$
$$+ g_0 - [s - (\gamma + h)]a = 0 \tag{5.10}$$

Excess demand on the left side of the equality is a falling function of *P*. This effect represents the forced saving adjustment mechanism. Discussion of how excess demand responds to interest rate changes can safely be postponed until after details of the financial market are set out.

5.2 Money and Other Assets

The ultimate holders of wealth in a country are its citizens. It is customary in macro models to treat them as being homogeneous in their choices regarding assets in which to store their patrimony, though, of course, rich and poor people behave entirely differently in this regard. However, the rich hold the preponderance of assets in capitalist economies. Data are hard to come by, but in England and the United States even the top 1 percent of wealth-holders own respectively 30 and 20 percent of financial assets.[7] Corresponding figures cannot be much lower (and may well be higher) in the Third World. Given such concentration in the control of wealth, assuming uniform behavior on the part of its owners may be an acceptable first approximation.

A second question is how to describe wealth. In any functioning economy, there are numerous formal financial instruments, informal debt and credit relationships in both urban and rural areas, productive economic assets such as physical capital, livestock and land, and unproductive ones like antique weapons and gold that are held for sentiment or speculative thrill. The usual models are based on the assumption that all assets must be held by someone, with their returns adjusting accordingly. The "adding-up" restriction that the value of assets should equal wealth puts strong restrictions on portfolio choice, as we will see later on in this chapter. Hence, selection of assets to be included in a formal model is not trivial, even if one residual, such as the "bond" of traditional macro theory, is included to absorb all the slack.

For the present, we will distinguish three sorts of assets held by persons. The first is money, conventionally held in the form of deposits with banks. The second takes the form of loans to firms, which in turn borrow from both banks and the public to finance fixed and working capital needs. (Firms are assumed not to sell equity, for the simple reason that stock markets are at best a decoration in most poor lands). Finally, the public is assumed to hold a congeries of assets such as currency, precious objects, and land and real estate, which we call "gold." This gold has its price fixed by simple market clearing and has no value in use. This asset specification is set up to emphasize the differences between wealth held with banks, or the formal financial system, and that held (perhaps with some sacrifice of liquidity) beyond the bankers' and tax collectors' view. Of our three assets, deposits are fully "monetized" or "intermediated" and gold is not. Loans to firms are somewhere in the middle. Informal credit markets are widespread in most countries, are often competitive and agile, and provide an area in which to hold resources besides a mattress or a hole in the ground or the banks. They also play an important macroeconomic role, as we will see shortly.

The balance sheets for the assumed financial system appear in table 5.1.[8] At the bottom, the public holds its wealth in the form of bank deposits D_P, loans to firms L_P, and gold. The fixed gold stock is Z, its price is P_z and the value of gold holdings is $P_z Z$. At the top of the table, the central bank holds government fiscal debt F as its only asset. The corresponding liability is commercial bank reserves H, which in the table's simplified accounting scheme are equivalent to the money base, or high-powered money.

The commercial banks have as assets their reserves, plus loans or net credit to the private sector. For simplicity, all credit is assumed to go to firms (in volume L_b). Bank liabilities are deposits held by the public and firms (respectively D_P and D_f). Firms receive loans both from banks and the public, while their assets are their bank deposits and the value of their fixed capital PK. After cancellation of all items entering on both sides of the accounts, wealth W turns out to be equal to $H + PK + P_z Z$, or the sum of the money base and the values of capital and gold. Consolidation of the bank's account shows that $H + L_b = D_p + D_f$, or outstanding credit to the government and firms just equals the money supply. These

TABLE 5.1

Financial Balance Sheets

Assets		Liabilities	
Central Bank			
Government debt	F	Bank reserves	H
Commercial Banks			
Bank reserves	H	Deposits from firms	D_f
Loans to firms	L_b	Deposits from the public	D_p
Firms			
Physical capital	PK	Loans from banks	L_b
Loans for working capital ($=$ deposits)	D_f	Loans from the public	L_p
Public			
Deposits with banks	D_p		
Loans to firms	L_p	Wealth	W
Gold	P_zZ		

Wealth identity: $W = H + PK + P_zZ$
Banking balance sheet: $H + L_b = D_p + D_f$

wealth and banking system "identities" of course hold when everyone's portfolio adjustment has arrived at an equilibrium.

What about working capital? Firms require advances in the amount $wL = wabK$ to pay the wage bill. If workers' own money holdings are small, which seems likely, they will respend their advances on consumption. In turn, firms will use these receipts to buy intermediate inputs and pay their own workers. In practice, then, working capital will mostly be held by enterprises and not the public. The simple hypothesis is that firm deposits are equal to working capital, or:

$$D_f = wbaK = H + L_b - D_P$$

where the second equality follows from the consolidated balance sheet of the banking system.

The next assumption is that banks don't hold excess reserves and that the banking authorities enforce a reserve requirement of the form $H = \mu(D_f + D_p)$, with $\mu < 1$. (We could alternately—and realistically—assume that the authorities restrict bank credit L_b to a given level and get essentially the same results.) Finally, assume that the public's demand for deposits takes the form $D_P = \psi(i, i_d, \pi, \pi_z)W$, where W is total wealth and the arguments of the function ψ are discussed in more detail below. In effect, the public is assumed to keep a fraction $\psi = D_P/W$ of its wealth in the form of bank deposits, providing liabilities for the banking system to transform into loans to firms. From the equation for D_f just above, excess demand equilibrium for these loans becomes:

$$wbaK - \left(\frac{H}{\mu}\right) + \psi(i, i_d, \pi, \pi_z)(H + PK + P_zZ) = 0 \quad (5.11)$$

The interest rate i is supposed to vary rapidly to drive excess demand to zero in the market for loans. This assumption marks a dramatic simplification of reality, but it seems best to adopt it for analytical purposes here.[9]

To close out the description of the asset market, only one additional excess demand function must be specified (with the wealth identity taking care of market clearing for the third asset.) Note first that real returns to the three assets are as follows:

$$\text{Deposits } D_P: \quad i_d - \pi$$
$$\text{Loans to firms } L_P: \quad i - \pi$$
$$\text{Gold } Z: \quad \pi_z - \pi$$

A controlled interest rate i_d is assumed to be paid on bank deposits—the real deposit rate is then $i_d - \pi$. Firms pay the rate i to both banks and the public for their loans, if market segmentation between lenders (or a controlled bank lending rate) is assumed away for simplicity. The real return on such loans is $i - \pi$. Finally, the only pecuniary reason to hold gold is in anticipation of capital gains. If the expected rate of growth of the price of gold is π_z, then real expected capital gains are $\pi_z - \pi$.

In the short run, gold is assumed to have a market-clearing price. If the public wants to hold a fraction ξ of its wealth as gold, then the short run condition for the excess demand to equal zero is:

$$\xi(i, i_d, \pi, \pi_z)\frac{W}{P_z} - Z = 0 \quad\quad\quad (5.12)$$

The gold price P_z varies to clear this market.

To summarize, the expected inflation rates π and π_z are given at any moment, so that the interest rate and gold price adjust to bring demands in line with supply. The excess demand balances (5.11) and (5.12) are brought into equilibrium in markets for loans and gold. When excess demands for these two assets are zero, then excess demand for money (by Walras's Law) will be as well.

5.3 The Model Without Gold—Short Run

The sensible way to figure out how a model with three assets works is to attack it by stages. In this section, we follow this strategy by leaving gold out. The relevant equations are commodity excess demand (5.10) and loan market excess demand (5.11), dropping the terms π_z, P_z and Z. For a fixed nominal wage w these equations constitute an equilibrium system for the commodity price level P and nominal interest rate i. The growth rate g follows as a dependent variable from (5.9). For the moment the hypothesis of static expectations is maintained, so that expected inflation π is a predetermined variable.

The Jacobian for (5.10) and (5.11) takes the form:

$$\begin{bmatrix} \dfrac{-\alpha}{P} & \dfrac{(s - h)awb}{P} - h \\ \psi K & \psi_i W \end{bmatrix}$$

where:

$$\alpha = [s - (\gamma + h)]a - g_0 + h(i - \pi) \qquad (5.13)$$

This long expression represents the excess of saving over investment when the profit rate takes its maximum value a, and in practice will be positive. Along with the condition $\psi_i < 0$ (demand for deposits declines when the interest rate on loans rises), $\alpha > 0$ assures that the trace of the Jacobian will be negative.

The determinant is:

$$\Delta = \left(\frac{1}{P}\right)\{-W\psi_i\alpha - K\psi[(s - h)awb - hP]\} \qquad (5.14)$$

To check the stability condition $\Delta > 0$, observe that the slopes of the excess demand functions for commodities and loans respectively are:

$$\left. \frac{dP}{di} \right]_P = \frac{(s - h)awb - hP}{\alpha}$$

$$= \frac{(s - h)awb}{\alpha} \{[s - (h + \gamma)]a - h(1 + \pi)\} \quad (5.15)$$

and

$$\left. \frac{dP}{di} \right]_i = -\frac{\psi_i W}{\psi K} \quad (5.16)$$

Since $\psi_i < 0$, the loan market equilibrium derivative is positive. The detailed explanation depends on the peculiarities of the asset structure set out in table 5.1, but would go through in its essentials under other specifications. In the present model, the immediate impact of an increase in the price level is to raise the value of firms' physical capital PK. With an agile equity market, this capital gain would soon pass through into an increase in price/earnings ratios on common stock. When equities are not widely traded (the assumption underlying table 5.1, and the truth in most poor countries), the assumption has to be that sooner or later firms will put their windfall gains to use by demanding more loans. Bank lending is limited by the reserve requirement; hence, public lending L_P must rise. The requisite resources are drawn into the loan market by an increase in the interest rate and a reduction in bank deposits as determined by ψ_i.

In macro equilibrium, comparison of (5.15) and (5.16) with (5.14) shows that the determinant Δ will be positive when the slope of the loan market schedule from (5.16) exceeds the commodity market slope (5.15). In connection with (5.8) it was already noted that this latter relationship between P and i can have either a positive or negative slope, depending on whether cost pressure or investment demand reduction from a rising interest rate is stronger. Macro instability occurs when working-capital cost-push is forceful enough (or expected inflation π low enough) to make the curve representing commodity market equilibrium steeper than the curve for the market for loans.

Figure 5.1 illustrates determination of short-run equilibrium, when the price level rises in response to higher interest costs. Adjustment dynamics are shown by the small arrows. In the upper quadrant, output is in excess demand below the commodity market curve and loans are in excess demand to the left of the loan market schedule.

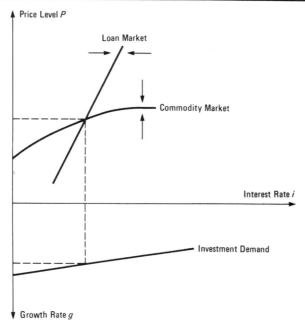

FIGURE 5.1

Determination of Short-Run Equilibrium When the Only Assets Held by the Public Are Bank Deposits and Loans to Firms

NOTE: There is assumed to be a strong effect of the interest rate on the price level via working-capital costs.

The main comparative static result is that the loan market curve will shift to the right either when there is monetary contraction or when the money demand function ψ shifts autonomously upward.[10] The outcome will be a rise in the interest rate i and declines in investment demand and the growth rate g. In a more complete model with variable capacity utilization, the story would be similar but slightly more complex. A rising interest rate would reduce investment demand through (5.9). At the same time, it would be reasonable to postulate an aggregate supply function of the form

$$X = X[P/(1 + i)w)]$$

At the initial price level P, an increased i would lead to cost pressures that would induce producers to reduce their output X. If supply went down more than demand, the resulting aggregate excess demand would lead to a rising price along the lines of figure 5.1. Thus, monetary contraction would not only slow growth and drive up prices, but also reduce output and employment in the short run. The possibility that stagflation may result

from economic stabilization policies that restrict the money supply has been
heavily emphasized in macro-policy literature in developing countries in
recent years.[11]

A second comparative static exercise of interest has to do with changes
in the expected inflation rate π. In equation (5.8) an increase in π will
reduce the real interest rate and stimulate investment demand, shifting up
the commodity market market curve in figure 5.1. For a given price level,
the loan market curve has to shift to the right, with a higher value of i
countering the increase in π to maintain equilibrium in (5.11). The outcome
is a higher level of P—an increase in inflationary expectations drives up
aggregate demand and the current output price. A similar linkage will turn
out to be important in the long-run stability analysis under rational (not
static) expectations about inflation that appear in chapter 6. But before
going on to ask how well short-run results carry over into longer periods,
we turn to the next section for a description of the macro system when there
are assets besides money and loans to firms.

5.4 The Macro System with Gold

One standard recommendation of orthodox experts from institutions like
the World Bank or International Monetary Fund when they visit poor
countries is that the local banking authorities should raise deposit rates.
Such a move is supposed to increase saving as well as lead to an influx of
deposits into commercial banks. Under full employment of capacity, the
rise in saving will lead to faster growth. Higher bank deposits in principle
expand ". . . the real size of the banking system and hence the net flow of
real bank credit to finance investment."[12] More bank lending capacity
should stimulate long-term growth, as well as help satisfy working capital
needs and thus reduce inflationary pressure at a given level of aggregate
demand.

It is interesting to give these ideas about financial liberalization a run for
their money in a full capacity model like the one in this chapter, where the
positive effect of a higher saving rate on the growth rate is a foregone
conclusion. (Things would, of course, go differently under excess capacity,
as discussed at length in chapter 2.) The main conclusion is that an increase
in the deposit rate may *not* lead to more overall credit to firms with
associated benefits. The key question is whether the new deposits are drawn
from existing productive loans from the public to firms or from other assets

such as "gold." In the former case, the deposit rate strategy could easily backfire, as we demonstrate shortly. This possibility perhaps explains why generously offered advice from flying experts about interest rate policy in the Third World has been almost universally declined.[13]

The model with gold is based on the three excess demand functions (5.10)–(5.12). For the record, one can write out the comparative statics of a change in the deposit rate in the following matrix equation form:

$$
\begin{bmatrix}
-\dfrac{\alpha}{P} & \dfrac{B}{P} & 0 \\[2ex]
\psi K & \psi_i W & \psi Z \\[2ex]
\dfrac{\xi K}{P_z} & \dfrac{\xi_i W}{P_z} & -\dfrac{(1-\xi)Z}{P_z}
\end{bmatrix}
\begin{bmatrix}
dP \\[2ex]
di \\[2ex]
dP_z
\end{bmatrix}
+
\begin{bmatrix}
0 \\[2ex]
W\psi_d \\[2ex]
\dfrac{W\xi_d}{P_z}
\end{bmatrix}
di_d
=
\begin{bmatrix}
0 \\[2ex]
0 \\[2ex]
0
\end{bmatrix}
\qquad (5.17)
$$

The symbol α has been defined in (5.13), B stands for $(s - h)awb - Ph$, and the subscripts i and d respectively denote partial derivatives with respect to the interest rate on loans to firms and the deposit rate.

The standard conditions for stability of a three-dimensional system like (5.17) are that the trace of the Jacobian should be negative, the sum of the three second-order principal minors (or 2×2 determinants linking each possible pair of excess demand functions) should be positive, and the third-order determinant should be negative. Both trace and second-order conditions follow easily when $\psi_i < 0$ and $\xi_i < 0$, or an increase in the interest rate on loans pulls wealth holding away from both bank deposits and gold. After some manipulation, the third-order determinant can be written as:

$$
\Gamma = \frac{Z}{P_z P}[\alpha W(\psi_i(1 - \xi) + \psi\xi_i) + B\psi K] \qquad (5.18)
$$

It is easy to see that Γ will be negative so long as B is not too large. A positive value of B occurs when a rise in the interest rate leads to a price increase due to cost pressure instead of a price reduction due to reduced investment demand. As in the model without gold, the stability condition is that the working-capital cost-push cannot be "too strong."

The derivative of the interest rate on loans with respect to the deposit rate is:

$$
\frac{di}{di_d} = -\frac{\alpha Z W}{\Gamma P_z P}[(1 - \xi)\psi_d + \psi\xi_d] \qquad (5.19)
$$

Note that the partial derivative ψ_d is positive since an increase in the deposit rate i_d presumably leads people to hold more deposits. By contrast, ξ_d is negative and the sign of the derivative in (5.19) is unclear. A negative sign for di/di_d occurs when the absolute values of both ξ and ξ_d are relatively large—the share of wealth held in the form of gold (ξ) and the willingness of the public to shift out of gold toward bank deposits (ξ_d) both have to be high. Under these circumstances, raising the deposit rate will pull money into banks for relending to firms, drive down the loan rate i, and lead to faster growth from the investment demand function (5.9). An added benefit will be a reduction in the price level when it responds positively to the interest rate from working-capital costs.

The economics behind these pleasant events can be illustrated further by manipulating the identities that link the different assets. It is straightforward to show that $di/di_d < 0$ when the following condition holds:

$$- \frac{\psi_d}{\xi_d} < \frac{(H/\mu) - wbaK}{L_P + D_P}$$

This condition is more difficult to satisfy when the absolute value of ξ_d is small, as just noted. It is also more likely to be violated when the commercial bank reserve requirement is large. Thus as μ approaches zero (and banks generate pure "inside" money by credit expansion), any ratio of deposit rate derivatives on the left side will satisfy the inequality. On the other hand, when μ is one (100 percent reserves and pure "outside" money) the condition becomes:

$$- \frac{\psi_d}{\xi_d} < \frac{H - wbaK}{H + PK}$$

in which the right side is certain to be less than one. Under these circumstances, financial liberalization will not bring good results, at least under the standard assumption that financial assets are gross substitutes, or $\psi_d > -\xi_d$.

The difference between the two extremes hinges on the degree of financial intermediation that the commercial banks can legally provide. The informal market operates with no reserve requirement, channeling resources toward firms with great efficiency. By contrast, a fraction of each new deposit in the commercial banks goes to reserves and cannot be loaned out. Thus, unless banks largely draw hoarded assets into deposits when i_d goes up, the overall effect of reform can be stagflationary.[14]

These effects can be illustrated in a diagram if we first solve for the price of gold by eliminating the wealth variable ($W = H + PK + P_zZ$) from (5.11) and (5.12):

$$P_z = \frac{\xi}{\psi}\left[\frac{(H/\mu) - wbak}{Z}\right] \tag{5.20}$$

Clearly, P_z falls as Z rises with unit elasticity. But the sign of its response to interest rate changes is ambiguous since both ξ_i and ψ_i are negative. If $|\xi_i/\xi| > |\psi_i/\psi|$, then the derivative dP_z/di will be negative. Again, the assumption is that the public is loath to hold gold when returns to alternative assets rise.

Plugging P_zZ from (5.20) back into (5.11) allows a solution of the system in the variables i and P alone. For the case of a positive response of the price level to the interest rate due to working capital cost, the comparative statics are shown in figure 5.2.

FIGURE 5.2

Effects of an Increase in the Deposit Rate When Increased Deposits Come Mainly from Gold Holdings and a Rise in the Interest Rate Drives Up the Price Level by Working-Capital Cost

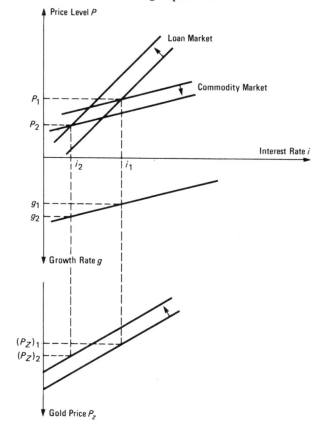

The deposit rate increase pulls resources into the banking system, having the same impact as an increase in the money supply. The loan market schedule shifts to the left. At the same time, if the saving rate goes up in response to a rise in i_d, there will be less demand pressure at a given interest rate and the commodity market schedule shifts down. The outcome will be lower prices and interest rates, coupled with faster growth. The financial reform package works well, with the only untoward consequence being a possible rise in the price of gold in response to the interest rate changes. Gold speculation resulting from strong expectations about a rise in its price could be destabilizing in the medium run, as discussed further on.

If the loan market curve in figure 5.2 were shifted to the right instead of to the left, it would correspond to a situation in which the deposit rate increase mostly pulls asset demand from loans to firms. If, in addition, the saving rate response to i_d is weak (a small downward shift in the commodity market schedule), the outcome would be a higher price level and slower growth. In this case, as in the monetary contraction discussed in connection with figure 5.1, orthodoxy gives rise to stagflation in the short run.

Finally, figure 5.3 illustrates monetary contraction, or a deposit rate

FIGURE 5.3

Effects of an Increase in the Deposit Rate When Increased Deposits Come Mainly from the Public's Loans to Firms and a Rise in the Interest Rate Reduces the Price Level by Decreasing Investment Demand

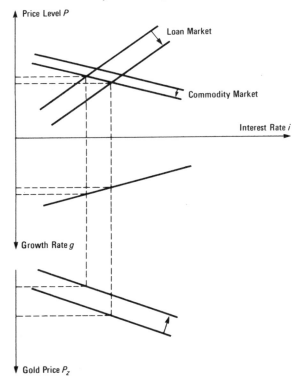

increase with stable gold demand in the case when the price level responds negatively to the interest rate. The result is more traditional in that growth slows and prices fall.

These outcomes suggest that simple pronouncements about financial policy don't make much sense, even in poor countries where financial markets are not notably complex.

Moreover, it is easy to spin out disquieting medium-run asset market scenarios set off by short-run events such as depicted in figure 5.2. For example, an increase in the deposit leads the interest rate i and output price P to fall and the gold price P_z to rise. Suppose that expected price changes π and π_z follow in the same direction. Then the returns to holding deposits and gold (respectively $i_d - \pi$ and $\pi_z - \pi$) will rise relative to the return to loans ($i - \pi$). The corresponding attempts to shift portfolios toward money and gold could lead to an accelerating gold price increase and shifts away from loans and (perhaps later) money. The final outcome could be rising interest rates and finally economic collapse as working capital finance dried up. Such unstable expectational bubbles are not easily ruled out when there are three assets on the scene.[15]

Even leaving aside unstable dynamic stories, there is quite a lot else that can happen in the economy as the results of these last two sections are extended toward the medium run. But the lesson remains that if assets held as gold, land, or other hoards are not easily relinquished when bank deposit rates go up, then aggressive interest rate policy will do little good for the economy in the short to medium run.

5.5 Money in the India Model

Some of the effects just discussed can be illustrated in practice by adding a demand-supply balance for money to the model for India from chapter 4. Both for simplicity and because of lack of data we eschew an extra asset in the system such as gold.

Tables 5.2 and 5.3 set out changes and additions to the model's original equations from table 4.2. Three major modifications are included:

1. Working-capital cost-push is assumed to be present in the industrial sector (number three). Thus the cost equation (4.16) is modified to include the interest rate i in nominal costs. Total working capital demanded by the sector is $k_{wc}B_3X_3$, where X_3 is the output level, B_3 is variable cost per unit output, and k_{wc} is a stock-flow conversion factor that relates the sector's stock of outstanding credit (estimated in practice from flow-of-funds data) to its flow of outlays for current production costs. The same factor k_{wc} enters, multiplying the interest rate in the new version of (4.16).

TABLE 5.2

Equations to Put Money in the India Model

I. Working-Capital Markup in Sector 3 [New Version of (4.16)]

$$P_3 = \frac{(1 + t_3)(1 + \tau_3)(1 + k_{wc}i)}{1 - (1 + t_3)(1 + \tau_3)(1 + k_{wc}i)a_{33}(1 - sub_3)}[\sum_{i=1}^{2} a_{i3}P_i + \sum_{i=4}^{5} a_{i3}P_i$$

$$+ w_3b_3 + a_{03}eP_{03}(1 - t_{03})] \tag{4.16}$$

II. Investment Demand

$$I_3 = I_3^\circ + h(i - i^\circ) \tag{4.49}$$

III. The Money Market

$$GBANK = GEXP + GINV + P_1(GP_1 - FA_1 - FN_1) + NA - GREV$$
$$- GBFOR - GBDOM - OTD \tag{4.50}$$

$$DRES = GBFOR + CBFOR - DEF - OTA \tag{4.51}$$

$$CURR_1 = CURR_0 + CURR \tag{4.52}$$

$$GBANK_1 = GBANK_0 + GBANK \tag{4.53}$$

$$DRES_1 = DRES_0 + DRES \tag{4.54}$$

$$CBANK_1 = k_{wc}B_3X_3 \tag{4.55}$$

$$CBANK = CBANK_1 - CBANK_0 \tag{4.56}$$

$$RLIAB_1 = RLIAB_0 + RLIAB \tag{4.57}$$

$$BLIAB_1 = BLIAB_0 + BLIAB \tag{4.58}$$

$$MDEM = \frac{1}{v_0 + v_1i}(Y_w + Y_a + Y_z + \sum_{i=3}^{5} GR_i) \tag{4.59}$$

IV. Demand-Supply Balance for Money

$$MDEM - (GBANK_1 + CURR_1 + DRES_1$$
$$+ CBANK_1 - BLIAB_1 - RLIAB_1) = 0 \tag{4.60}$$

---

2. Investment demand is assumed to respond to the nominal interest rate in (4.49). The coefficient h was assigned a value of 0.7, in line with econometric and Indian economists' intuitive assessments of investment demand responsiveness in the economy.
3. The demand-supply balance for money is tied back to variables generated on the real side of the system, with the interest rate acting as the corresponding adjusting variable.

The details of calculating money supply appear in equations (4.50) through (4.58). It is assumed that changes in *flows* such as government borrowing from the banking system or the balance of payments surplus affect the money *stock* within the model's solution period of one year. This treatment differs from the formal models of this and following chapters, where flows affect the time derivatives of stocks at "the present moment" and only cumulate into stock changes over time. The distinction arises because the formal models work with differential equations for mathematical tractability, whereas an applied model based on annual data has to take into account such banalities as the fact that the government spreads its borrowing from the banking system over the national accounts year instead of waiting to do it all at 11:59 P.M. on March 31.

The components of the money supply are shown in the term in parentheses in (4.60). The stock of bank credit outstanding to the government is $GBANK_1$; its change during the year is $GBANK$ from (4.50). The government's borrowing from the banking system rises with its current spending *GEXP*, investment *GINV*, foodstock accumulation $P_1(GP_1 - FA_1 - FN_1)$, and items that are not otherwise accounted (NA) for. Its sources of funds are current revenue *GREV* and loans from nonbank sources both home and abroad. For historical reasons the government of India (not the banks) has small currency liabilities to the public, accounted as $CURR_1$ at the end of the period. Foreign assets of the banking system (4.60) are $DRES_1$—their change *DRES* is defined in (4.51). *DRES* is the difference between government and commercial borrowing from abroad (*GBFOR* and *CBFOR*, respectively) and the current deficit *DEF* and other transactions.

The third main component of the money supply is credit to the private sector $CBANK_1$, which is related to flow demand for working capital in (4.55). The items $BLIAB_1$ and $RLIAB_1$ are nonmonetary liabilities of the commercial banks and the Reserve Bank of India. They can be varied to reflect monetary policy changes, as in the simulations that follow.

The entire equation (4.60) sets demand minus supply of money (or excess demand) equal to zero as an equilibrium condition. Money demand itself is *MDEM,* and is given as a function of the interest rate and total value-added in the economy in (4.59). The particular functional form assumed states that money velocity (or value-added divided by the money stock) is an increasing function of the interest rate; people hold less money as i goes up. The parameter values are $v_0 = 1.5215$ and $v_1 = 5.0$, in line with empirical estimates for India.

Table 5.4 shows results from two simulations with this extended version of the model. In the first, a monetary contraction is induced by reducing

TABLE 5.3

New Symbols for Putting Money in the India Model

I. Endogenous variables

I_3 — investment demand for sector 3 products (exogenous in chapter 4 model)
GBANK — within-period net government borrowing from the banking system
$GBANK_1$ — end-of-period government debt to the banking system
DRES — change in foreign asset holdings of the banking system
$DRES_1$ — end-of-period foreign asset holdings of the banking system
CBANK — within-period change in net bank credit to the commercial sector
$CBANK_1$ — end-of-period net bank outstanding credit to the commercial sector
$CURR_1$ — end-of-period government of India currency liabilities to the public
$RLIAB_1$ — end-of-period nonmonetary liabilities of Reserve Bank of India
$BLIAB_1$ — end-of-period nonmonetary liabilities of commercial banks
MDEM — demand for money
i — nominal interest rate

II. Exogenous variables

I_3° — autonomous investment demand for sector 3 products
GINV — value of government investment spending
GBFOR — government borrowing from abroad (rupees)
GBDOM — government borrowing from nonbank financial sector and the public
CBFOR — commercial sector borrowing from abroad (rupees)
CURR — within-period change in government currency liabilities to the public
BLIAB — within-period change of nonmonetary liabilities of commercial banks
RLIAB — within-period change of nonmonetary liabilities, Reserve Bank of India
NA — government current expenditures, not accounted otherwise
OTU — other government domestic transactions, from "statutary liquidity ratio"
OTA — other foreign transactions

III. Parameters

---

v_0, v_1 — money demand parameters
h — interest rate parameter for investment demand
k_{wc} — stock-flow coefficient between working capital demand and sector 3 output level

---

IV. Initial values

$CURR_0$ — initial government currency liabilities to the public
$GBANK_0$ — initial government debt to the banking system
$DRES_0$ — initial foreign assets of banking system
$RLIAB_0$ — initial nonmonetary liabilities, Reserve Bank of India
$BLIAB_0$ — initial nonmonetary liabilities, commercial banks
$CBANK_0$ — initial stock of bank credit to the commercial sector
i_0 — beginning-of-period nominal interest rate

TABLE 5.4

Effects of Contractionary Monetary Policy and Devaluation in the India Model Incorporating Money

A. *Prices and Quantities*

	Base Run	Mon. Policy	Deval.		Base Run	Mon. Policy	Deval.
P_1	1	1.0665	1.0003	X_3	9.5712	9.5621	9.5253
P_2	1	1.0488	0.9997	X_4	1.0262	1.0254	1.0191
P_3	1	1.0446	1.0226	X_5	6.5749	6.5703	6.5276
P_4	1	1.0198	1.0075	I_3	2.3186	2.2974	2.3168
P_5	1	1.0244	1.0069	i	0.1200	0.1503	0.1229

B. *Savings and Investment*

	Base Run	Mon. Policy	Deval.		Base Run	Mon. Policy	Deval.
Agr. sav.	0.5373	0.5723	0.5370	Dom. inv.	2.3186	2.3998	2.3692
Wage sav.	0.6414	0.6478	0.6463	Imp. inv.	0.1211	0.1211	0.1393
Prof sav.	0.5325	0.5773	0.5388	Pr. stocks	0.4048	0.4272	0.4127
Trade def.	0.1800	0.1962	0.1554	Gov. stocks	−0.1028	−0.1028	−0.1028
Gov. sav.	0.1357	0.1368	0.2260				
Deprec.	0.7148	0.7148	0.7148				
Total:	2.7417	2.8421	2.8183	Total:	2.7417	2.8421	2.8183

C. *Income Shares*

	Base Run	Mon. Policy	Deval.
Agr. income	0.3895	0.3956	0.3881
Wage income	0.3765	0.3626	0.3774
Profit income	0.2340	0.2418	0.2345
Total	1.0000	1.0000	1.0000

nonmonetary liabilities of the Reserve Bank of India to give a drop in money supply of 4 percent. The simulation is done with wage-indexation, foodstock speculation, and rising markups all incorporated in the model, along the lines of table 4.7.

The impact effect of the monetary contraction is to increase the interest rate, which leads in turn to cost-push in sector three and a decline in investment demand. With our assumptions regarding parameters, the outcomes include price increases in all sectors, output decreases in the nonagricultural sectors, and a shift in the income distribution from wages toward agriculture and profits. It seems reasonable to characterize the monetary contraction as stagflationary.

Somewhat similar results come from a 15-percent devaluation when exports are assumed not to respond to a higher exchange rate. As noted in connection with the discussion of table 4.8, devaluation in the model without money leads to a decline in the total of bank credit expansion induced by government borrowing and the balance of payments—as a consequence the money supply drops. The interest rate rises, and as shown in table 5.4 the result is price pressure and a fall in investment demand. Hence, devaluation has contractionary effects through monetary as well as real channels.

Under other parameterizations of the model, these results reverse themselves—they should not be taken as predictions about what will happen in India. Rather, they are presented here to illustrate the fact that stagflation from devaluation or contractionary monetary policy is by no means excluded as an outcome of a plausible general equilibrium model of an actual economy. Under certain circumstances, stagflation occurs in the real world as well as the model.

6

Money, Inflation, and Growth

THE ANALYSIS in chapter 5 was strictly for the short run. Now it is time to see how well it extends to a longer period of time. The "medium run" is considered here for an economy in steady state, with all real variables growing at a constant rate, and the growth rates of output and the price level summing to the rate of growth of money supply. One question asked regards the effect of changing the growth rate of money on other variables, across distinct steady states. A second question is whether or not the adjustment process between steady states will be stable. The answers are that slowing the growth of the money supply from an initial steady state can in certain circumstances lead to faster inflation, slower output growth, and a lower real wage at a new steady state. Moreover, the transition between trajectories can be stable under quite orthodox assumptions about the dynamics of the system. The results suggest that monetary contraction can be stagflationary in the medium run in real economies. The finding is novel, but perhaps not so surprising in light of the important role played by working-capital cost-push in the models of chapter 5.

Causality in this chapter's model runs along Marxian lines, from conflict between workers and capitalists about the rate of increase of the money wage in a generally inflationary situation. Rules for indexing the wage to past inflation are assumed to be in place. However, if inflation accelerates, the real wage will fall due to lags in the indexing process. Workers will force an acceleration in the growth rate of the money wage to try to regain their real income, and as a consequence there will be a profit squeeze. How this process works in detail is described in section 6.2.

With the real wage (or, for analytical convenience, the price-wage ratio) given by such class interaction, the macro system in the short run must adjust to predetermined levels of the price-wage ratio and the money stock (or, again for convenience, the ratio of money to the value of capital). A change in the price-wage ratio will affect available saving by shifting the income distribution, and investment must in some way respond. We adopt the fashionable rational expectations notion that the rate of inflation $\hat{P}$ varies to alter the real interest rate $i - \hat{P}$ and drives investment to equality with saving. As in most Marxian models, investment is finally determined by saving, but with the particularly un-Marxian rationale, expectations twist. How this saving-investment adjustment is linked with financial markets is described in section 6.1.

With wage and inflation dynamics set up in the first two sections, the story about transitions between steady states is told in section 6.3, when money and loans by the public to firms are the only assets in the system. The possible role of "gold" and other extensions are briefly sketched in section 6.4, while an appendix contains the mathematical underpinnings of some of the analysis that is done graphically in the body of this chapter.[1]

6.1 Short-Run Adjustment under Rational Expectations

One of the standard tricks in working with growth models is to invent "state variables" that fit into tractable differential equations so that their trajectories can be studied over time. The model from the last chapter can be restated usefully if we define two new variables as $R = P/w$, or the price-wage ratio, and $V = H/PK$, or the ratio of the money supply to the value of the capital stock. The depth or degree of intermediation of the financial system is loosely indicated by V—a higher value means more intermediation.

In terms of R and V, the excess demand functions (5.10) and (5.11) for commodities and money can be restated as:

$$\frac{(s - h)(1 + i)ab}{R} - h(i - \hat{P}) + g_0 - [s - (\gamma + h)]a = 0 \qquad (6.1)$$

and

$$ba + \psi(i - \hat{P})(V + 1) - \left(\frac{R}{\mu}\right)V = 0 \qquad (6.2)$$

where the actual inflation rate $\hat{P}$ replaces the expected rate π in the investment demand term $h(i - \hat{P})$ and the money demand function $\psi(i - \hat{P})$.

Adjustment stories in perfect foresight models are often farfetched, perhaps justly so in light of the incredibility of the hypothesis itself. In the present model, R and V are given at any point of time from dynamic processes to be described below. Hence we need two variables to adjust "within the moment" to assure that (6.1) and (6.2) are satisfied.

Look first at the market for commodities. If the price-wage ratio R rises from an initial equilibrium level, the macroeconomic outcome is an incipient excess of saving over investment (given that capitalists' saving rates exceed those of workers). In an agile financial market, one might expect the real rate of interest to fall, to stimulate investment demand, and to restore equilibrium. This bit of entelechy can occur through either a decrease in the nominal interest rate i or an increase in the inflation rate $\hat{P}$. Assume the latter, that inflation accelerates when there is initial excess saving supply. Then if the interest rate goes up when there is excess demand for loans in (6.2), we have a locally stable short-run adjustment process. Financiers are assumed to sense potential imbalance in commodity markets and adjust their inflation expectations and thus the cost of borrowing rapidly enough to prevent disequilibrium from actually coming about.[2]

This short-run market balance can be perturbed by shifts in the state variables. To see the details, we ask how $\hat{P}$ and i respond to maintain equilibrium in (6.1) and (6.2). For the financial market, the answer is easy. Money demand depends on the real interest rate $i - \hat{P}$. To maintain balance, any change in i has to be matched by an equal change in $\hat{P}$—the two variables trade off along a 45-degree line.

In the commodity market, the story is a bit more complex. For a *given* value of the interest rate, an increase in the price-wage ratio R generates extra saving by moving the income distribution in favor of profits. As discussed above, financiers catch this shift in the wind and increase their expected inflation rate $\hat{P}$ in anticipation of an investment boom to come.

Now turn to interest rate reactions. In the last chapter it was shown that at a given inflation rate, the nominal interest rate can either rise with the price-wage ratio when working capital costs are important, or fall to stimulate investment even further when R goes up. The outcome is an ambiguous slope of the $(i,\hat{P})$ equilibrium relationship in the commodity market. With dominant working-capital effects, the slope is negative—both $\hat{P}$ and i rise with R and must trade off inversely to hold R constant. When investment demand effects are more important, the equilibrium $(i,\hat{P})$ locus will have a positive slope.

Comparative statics of the dominant working-capital case are shown in figure 6.1. In the upper diagram an increase in V, the ratio of money to

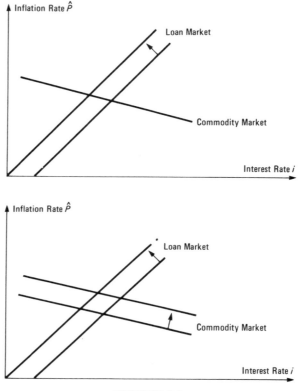

FIGURE 6.1

Comparative Statics of an Increase in the Money-Capital Ratio V (Upper Diagram) and Price-Wage Ratio R (Lower Diagram) When an Interest Rate Increase Drives Up the Price Level through Higher Working-Capital Costs in the Short Run

capital stock, requires a lower real interest rate to maintain money market balance; for a given $\hat{P}$, i must decrease. After commodity market reactions are taken into account, a rise in V is associated with a lower interest rate and a higher rate of inflation.

In the lower diagram of figure 6.1, we see that an increase in the price-wage ratio R is associated with a higher interest rate at a given inflation rate in the commodity market (as just discussed). In the loan market, an increase in R raises the value of the term $(R/\mu)V = H/\mu wK$ or the degree of monetization measured in wage units. Once again the real interest rate must fall, so the loan market curve shifts to the left. A higher price-wage ratio is associated with faster inflation, but an ambiguous shift in the rate of interest.

Figure 6.2 shows what happens when investment demand responses dom-

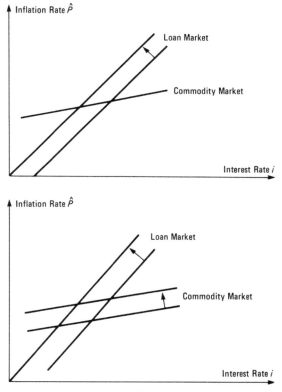

FIGURE 6.2

Comparative Statics of an Increase in the Money-Capital Ratio V *(Upper Diagram) and the Price-Wage Ratio* R *(Lower Diagram) When an Interest Rate Increase Reduces the Price Level by Cutting Back on Investment Demand*

inate the interest rate effect. In the upper diagram, an increase in the money-capital ratio reduces *both* the interest and inflation rates. The lower diagram shows an ambiguous response of both $\hat{P}$ and i to a higher price-wage ratio. However, $\hat{P}$ will rise if investment demand is insensitive to changes in the real interest rate and the commodity market curve is relatively flat.

6.2 Wage Dynamics in the Medium Run

To incorporate these comparative static responses into a growth model, the next task is to bring in wage and price changes. Assume that money wages are fully indexed to the rate of price inflation. However, even with full indexing, *lags* in the institutional adjustment process can lead to a loss in workers' purchasing power when the rate of price increase goes up. The time path of the real wage consistent with indexing rules will subsequently be taken as a standard around which actual wage inflation varies, but for the moment we concentrate on formulation of the standard itself.[3]

Suppose there is ongoing price inflation at the rate $\hat{P}$, where as usual the "hat" denotes a logarithimic time derivative: $\hat{P} = (dP/dt)/P$. Wages, however, are indexed only at discrete points in time, for instance, every year or every quarter. If λ stands for the indexing interval, then at times t, $t + \lambda$, and so forth, workers get a 100-percent adjustment in nominal wages to compensate for immediately past inflation, that is, $w_{t+\lambda}/w_t = e^{\hat{P}\lambda}$. At time $t + \lambda$, the real wage will satisfy a condition such as $w_{t+\lambda}/P_{t+\lambda} = w^*$, where the target real wage ω^* is assumed to be constant over time.

Figure 6.3 illustrates how the real wage changes between readjustments.

FIGURE 6.3

Variations in the Real Wage over Time When There Are Periodic Money Wage Adjustments with an Ongoing Price Inflation at Rate $\hat{P}$ and the Target Wage Is ω^*

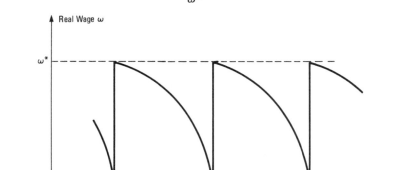

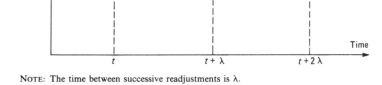

NOTE: The time between successive readjustments is λ.

There is a cycle between the values ω^* and $\omega^* e^{-\hat{P}\lambda}$, which is of course repetitive when the inflation rate stays constant.

Over time, the average real wage $\bar{\omega}$ is given by:

$$\bar{\omega} = \left(\frac{\omega^*}{\lambda}\right) \int_0^\lambda e^{-\hat{P}t} dt = \omega^* \left[\frac{1 - e^{-\hat{P}\lambda}}{\hat{P}\lambda}\right] \tag{6.3}$$

assuming $\hat{P}$ stays constant.

If we let $\hat{P}\lambda = \rho$, then from l'Hospital's rule one can easily show that $\bar{\omega}$ approaches ω^* as ρ approaches zero, that is, the average wage becomes the target either when inflation falls to zero or when there is instantaneous indexing. Similarly, one has:

$$\frac{\partial \bar{\omega}}{\partial \rho} = \frac{\omega^*}{\rho^2} \left\{ \left[\frac{1 + \rho}{e^\rho}\right] - 1 \right\}$$

But since $e^\rho = 1 + \rho + \rho^2/2 + \ldots$, this derivative is negative for $\rho > 0$. The real wage declines when either the inflation rate is higher or the indexing period gets longer. If the period is one year, the following numbers illustrate the impact of increases in the inflation rate on the real wage (and, for later reference, its inverse or the price-wage ratio):

Annual Inflation Rate	Real Wage	Price-Wage Ratio
0.0	1.0	1.0
0.10	0.952	1.051
0.25	0.885	1.130
0.50	0.787	1.271
0.75	0.704	1.422
1.00	0.632	1.582

With a fixed-period indexing scheme, an acceleration in inflation can cut back sharply on workers' real purchasing power.

To extend (6.3) to the macro system, one has to recognize that contracts are not all renegotiated or indexed on fixed calendar dates—there is likely to be some spread of wage bargaining over the year. If the time span between each group's readjustment is always λ, then it is easy to see intuitively (and can be verified formally) that (6.3) remains valid when readjustments occur uniformly over time. An example would be a yearly cycle in which $\frac{1}{12}$ of workers get readjustments at the end of January, $\frac{1}{12}$ at the end of February, and so on. In countries where 100-percent wage indexing has been applied, such uniformity is not observed.[4] However, we will assume that strictly uniform wage adjustment exists to make analytical discussion of the dynamics of inflation easier.

6.3 Inflation and Growth in the Medium Run (with no Gold)

Equation (6.3) is a relationship between the average real wage and inflation that would hold at all times if the economy's wage indexing rules were followed exactly. It summarizes institutional arrangements that give equilibrium on the supply side of the labor market (with "supply" referring not to the number of people seeking jobs, but rather to the real wage consistent with indexing rules when the inflation rate is $\hat{P}$). By inverting the equation, the supply side value of the price-wage ratio R_s can be written as:

$$R_s = \frac{\hat{P}\lambda}{\omega^*(1 - e^{-\hat{P}\lambda})} \qquad (6.4)$$

The derivative of R_s with respect to both the inflation rate $\hat{P}$ and the indexing period λ will be positive. The second derivative is also positive, or the impact of an increase in $\hat{P}$ on the equilibrium price-wage ratio strengthens as the inflation rate is higher.

Since it represents a bargained wage consistent with inflation in the medium run, R_s plays a role in the following analysis similar to the money wage of the short-run model—it provides a fixed magnitude against which the inflation rate can vary. At any time the observed ratio R can differ from R_s. The assumption is that the money wage will grow faster than inflation when the actual real wage is high relative to the institutionally warranted level from (6.4). In other words, a tight labor market leads to faster than normal money wage increases because the indexing rules get bent by wage drift, extra bonuses, and so on. This hypothesis amounts to a restatement in a model with inflation of the profit-squeeze cyclical adjustment outlined in section 2.4. Here, as in that model, stability will depend critically on shifts in the functional income distribution over time.

In formal terms, the money wage increases according to the equation:

$$\hat{w} = \hat{P} - \phi(R - R_s)$$

When the labor market is tight, R lies below R_s, and $\hat{w} > \hat{P}$. Restated in terms of R, this out-of-equilibrium adjustment rule becomes:

$$\hat{R} = \hat{P} - \hat{w} = \phi(R - R_s) \tag{6.5}$$

Note from (6.4) that R_s is a function of $\hat{P}$, while from (6.1) and (6.2) $\hat{P}$ is determined by R and V. Hence, (6.5) is a shorthand representation of how R evolves over time as a function of itself and V. We have one of the two differential equations for the state variables that we require.

The other equation can easily be written as:

$$\hat{V} = \hat{H} - \hat{P} - \hat{K} \tag{6.6}$$

For the moment, assume that the growth rate of the money base $(\hat{H})$ is exogenous. Equations (6.1) and (6.2) give $\hat{P}$ and i, while (5.9) gives $\hat{K}$ (or g) after the current inflation rate is substituted for the expected rate π. In effect, $\hat{V}$ becomes a function of R and V. Given equations (6.5) and (6.6), the next step is to consider their stability as represented by the Jacobian matrix:

$$\begin{bmatrix} \partial\hat{V}/\partial V & \partial\hat{V}/\partial R \\ \partial\hat{R}/\partial V & \partial\hat{R}/\partial R \end{bmatrix}$$

The sign pattern under appropriate assumptions takes the form:

$$\begin{bmatrix} - & - \\ - \text{ or } + & - \end{bmatrix}$$

so that stability occurs if the term in the southwest corner is not too strongly negative. The rationale goes as follows:

1. In the southeast of the Jacobian, begin by observing from figures 6.1 and 6.2 that a reduction in the price-wage ratio R pulls down the inflation rate in the short run, unless investment demand is highly sensitive to real interest rate changes. But then from (6.4) the price-wage ratio consistent with the wage indexing goes up. Workers' nominal wage demands moderate since the difference between the current real wage and the target declines (as also would the level of employment in a more realistic model with variable capacity utilization). If money wage growth slows sufficiently, $\hat{R} = \hat{P} - \hat{w}$ will rise. Hence, the derivative $\partial\hat{R}/\partial R$ takes a negative sign. From (6.5) it is clear that this result depends on a large

positive derivative of R_s with respect to $\hat{P}$ in (6.4), and of $\hat{P}$ with respect to R in (6.1) and (6.2). We assume that the derivatives are large enough for stability —an initial profit squeeze is followed by enough deflation to make the squeeze disappear. We have a restatement under inflation of the real-side dynamics of section 2.4, and the key adjustment mechanism in the present model.

2. The derivative $\partial\hat{R}/\partial V$ in the southwest corner of the Jacobian can take either sign. As argued in connection with figure 6.1, an increase in V lowers the interest rate and drives up the inflation rate in the short run when working capital dominates interest rate responses. The higher $\hat{P}$ raises the institutionally acceptable price-wage ratio R_s or lowers the indexed real wage. Workers' wage demands are animated as the indexing rules start to penalize them and money wage increases accelerate. As a consequence, the growth rate of the price-wage ratio slows, or $\partial\hat{R}/\partial V < 0$. The contrasting case is the reduction in the inflation rate resulting from a higher level of V in the upper diagram of figure 6.2 (referring to the case where investment demand effects dominate the interest rate response). The process just described is reversed, and $\partial\hat{R}/\partial V > 0$. The switch in signs of the partial derivative gives either a positive or negative slope to the locus of values of R and V, along which $\hat{R} = 0$. There is an exact parallel with the ambiguous slope of the commodity market relationship between P and i that was discussed in chapter 5, as is illustrated in figures 6.4 and 6.5.

3. The signs of the derivatives $\partial\hat{V}/\partial V$ and $\partial\hat{V}/\partial R$ depend on the effects of shifts in the state variables on inflation and the rate of capital growth, as can be seen from equation (6.6). If working-capital cost-push is the dominant effect of interest rate increases, figure 6.1 shows that $\hat{P}$ rises along with both V and R. When investment demand effects dominate as in figure 6.2, $\hat{P}$ may decline, but this response is likely to be weak. All the diagrams show that the real interest rate $i - \hat{P}$ declines when either V or R rises; from (5.9) the capital stock grows faster. The conclusion is that the growth rate $\hat{V}$ is likely to slow when either state variable gets bigger, that is, V and R trade off inversely to hold $\hat{V} = 0$.

The overall stability condition is that the slope of the locus of points along which $\hat{V} = 0$ should be less (more negative) than the locus along which $\hat{R} = 0$ in a diagram with V on the horizontal axis and R on the vertical. An increase in the rate of growth of the money supply $(\hat{H})$ shifts the $\hat{V} = 0$ locus to the right—either the inflation or growth rate has to rise to meet the steady growth condition $\hat{H} = \hat{P} + \hat{K}$, and either shift is associated with increased monetization V for a given price-wage ratio R.

If stability is assumed, figure 6.4 illustrates the dynamics in the dominant working-capital case. The adjustment involves a gradual increase in V and a *decline* in R from the model's initial equilibrium at A. Since at the new steady state at B the labor market will be in equilibrium, (6.4) shows that the inflation rate $\hat{P}$ will be lower. Also, since $\hat{H} = \hat{P} + \hat{K}$ the growth rate will be higher. Compared across steady states, faster money growth leads to lower inflation, more rapid capital stock growth, and a higher real wage when interest rate increases drive up working-capital costs. The faster

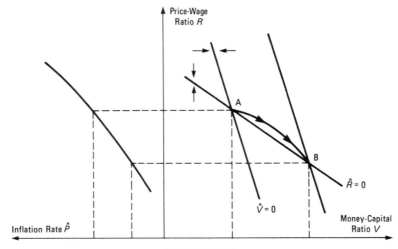

FIGURE 6.4

*Adjustment between Steady States under Rational Expectations in an Economy
Where an Interest Rate Increase Drives Up the Price-Wage Ratio from Working
Capital Cost-Push in the Short Run*

NOTE: Faster money growth gives lower inflation, an increased real wage, and faster output growth.

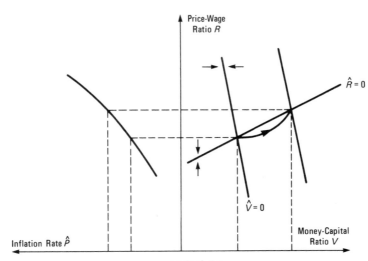

FIGURE 6.5

*Adjustment between Steady States in an Economy Where an Interest Rate
Increase Reduces the Price-Wage Ratio by Cutting Investment Demand*

NOTE: Faster money growth gives higher inflation, a reduced real wage, and faster output growth.

monetary expansion permits more rapid growth and less inflationary cost pressure in the long run.

Details of the transition between steady states depend on the specific dynamic assumptions of the model. In the case at hand, when money growth is jumped up from an initial steady state, V or H/PK will start to rise while R is momentarily stationary. The implication from figure 6.1 is that inflation will speed up. Thereafter, R will begin to fall (as it would with monetary expansion in the static expectations story of figure 5.1) and the inflation rate will follow. The adjustment pattern for "half-cycle" convergence as assumed in figure 6.4 will be initial acceleration and then deceleration of $\hat{P}$. There could be further oscillations with the adjustment trajectory spiraling in toward point B, but it is convenient to assume them away.

Adjustment in the alternative commodity market case in which an interest rate reduction drives up the price-wage ratio by increasing aggregate demand is shown in figure 6.5. As usual, the results are more traditional: an increase in the growth rate of money base leads to higher steady-state inflation by driving up the price-wage ratio R. The money-capital ratio V rises as well, so that the real interest rate $i - \hat{P}$ will fall. From (5.9) investment demand will be stimulated, so that the growth rate goes up in this case as well. There is not a sufficient fall in the interest rate to allow real wages to rise. Forced saving supports faster growth in the long run.

These results are fairly straightforward extensions of the short-run analysis of section 5.2, to a situation where plausible price and wage dynamics apply. With volatile rational expectations built into the specification, the model's stability properties are bound to be tenuous, as indeed they are. If there is stability, it comes from two linked relations. First, a rise in the price-wage ratio R (or a fall in the real wage) is linked to a faster inflation $\hat{P}$ through aggregate demand. Second, rising inflation pushes up the target price-wage ratio R_s (or reduces the target real wage) and thus slows the increase in R from (6.5). If these links are strong enough, stability can be observed; otherwise not. They could be strengthened by more wage lag, for example, less than complete indexation in (6.3) by reduction of the target real wage, lengthening of the adjustment period, or postponement of adjustment for last period's inflation until well into this period's calendar run. The fact that an institutional wage squeeze helps bring macro stability has not escaped the notice of monetarists. Their stabilization programs ostensibly (or ostentatiously) concentrate on reduced $\hat{H}$, but incomplete indexation of wages often also enters in. A dose of civil repression may be added to assure that workers stay in line.

A second observation is that so far $\hat{H}$ has been treated as exogenous. This hypothesis makes sense under the circumstances in which the central bank has both monetary and nonmonetary assets in its portfolio and can sell them back and forth (typically in open market or foreign exchange operations) with other agents in the system. Strictly speaking, such maneuvers are ruled out here by the balance sheets of table 5.1. Indeed, since there are no taxes in the model, monetary expansion is determined by the needs of government finance: $dH/dt = PG$. Plugging this expression in to the rest of the equations shows that the growth rate of money base is given by:

$$\hat{H} = \frac{1 - \psi\mu}{\mu} \cdot \frac{aR\gamma}{\psi R + ba} \tag{6.7}$$

Evidently, $\hat{H}$ depends on both i and $\hat{P}$ through the money demand function ψ and the markup R. The effects are ambiguous, but working through the algebra suggests that the negatively sloped equilibrium locus for $\hat{V}$ in figures 6.4 and 6.5 will remain. Money growth can be stimulated when (6.7) holds either by raising the government expenditure share γ or cutting the reserve requirement μ.

6.4 Gold and Other Matters

Bringing gold into the system means that another asset market and state variables have to be considered. Define the state variable as $U = P_z Z / PK$, or the value of gold holdings relative to the capital stock. The short-run equilibrium conditions incorporating gold become:

$$ba + \psi R(i - \hat{P}, i_d - \hat{P}, \hat{P}_z - \hat{P})(V + U + 1) - \frac{R}{\mu}V = 0 \tag{6.8}$$

for the loan market, and

$$\xi(i - \hat{P}, i_d - \hat{P}, \hat{P}_z - \hat{P})(V + U + 1) - U = 0 \tag{6.9}$$

for gold. Stability analysis could be done as before, by inverting (6.8) and (6.9) for $\hat{P}$ and $\hat{P}_z$ and then substituting the resulting expressions into differential equations for the state variables U and V. We forego the gory details and make only brief comments on the nature of steady-state equilibria.

First, the growth of money base must now be written as:

$$\hat{H} = \frac{(1 - \xi) - \psi\mu}{\mu} \frac{\gamma aR}{\psi R + (1 - \xi)ba}$$

Note that a rise in the deposit rate i_d increases ψ and reduces ξ, so that its effect on money growth is ambiguous. However, enthusiasts for financial liberalization presumably suppose that the effect of the change in ψ would be stronger, so that money growth falls. In the case where aggregate demand effects from interest rate changes dominate, figure 6.5 shows that inflation would drop off and the real wage would rise, but the growth rate would decline. A strong saving response to higher deposit rates could salvage the growth rate, although empirical evidence suggests little to hope for on this score. The story in figure 6.4 (dominant working-capital effects) is worse, for there the inflation rate would rise and real wage decline in the long run.

The conclusion is that unless coupled with expansionary monetary policy from some other source (perhaps a reduction in reserve requirements), financial liberalization will do little to benefit economic performance in the medium run. Moreover, it may not even lead to an increase in financial depth, as measured by the ratio H/PK. Simple manipulation of (6.8) and (6.9) shows that this variable can easily move in either direction across steady states.

A final question might be raised regarding the two aggregate demand cases so scrupulously distinguished in the analysis: Which one really matters in a given economy over a given time span? Regarding timing, investment demand responses to interest rate changes may take longer to build up than working-capital costs. The implication is that the effects shown in figure 6.5 (faster money expansion increases both inflation and growth) will hold in the longer run, although one could scarcely be sure. In any case, which effect dominates is an empirical matter that remains to be explored.

The evidence from a few econometric studies seems to show that the working-capital channel is the one that matters in the short run in developing economies, while traditionally Keynesian responses are more important in the longer run.[5] Proponents of deposit rate increases might draw support from these conclusions since their nostrum works better just under such circumstances. Nonetheless, the situation remains complex—too complex for any simple policy prescription along financial liberalization (or other) lines to be worth serious thought.

Appendix

A more formal stability analysis for the model of this chapter is straight-forward, but tedious to work out. A sketch begins with solving the commodity market demand-supply balance (6.1) for the interest rate,

$$i = \frac{\{[s - (\gamma + h)]a - g_0 - h\hat{P}\}R - (s - h)ab}{(s - h)ab - hR} \tag{6.10}$$

Note that this equation takes the form:

$$i = \frac{A_1 R - B}{B - A_2 R}$$

which will generate a positive value for i so long as both R and B are positive. The sign of the derivative depends on $A_1 - A_2$ or $[s - (\gamma + h)]$ $a - g_0 - h(1 + \hat{P})$, the criterion already discussed in connection with equation (5.8). For given values of the parameters, $di/dR > 0$ when the inflation rate is relatively low, from working-capital cost-push. For higher inflation rates, investment demand effects dominate and $di/dR < 0$. The expression $(s - h)ab - hR$ is positive when working-capital costs dominate and negative when investment demand is more important in determining price response. This distinction will be important in the stability analysis below.

A further step in solving (6.1) and (6.2) for i and $\hat{P}$ is to rewrite the latter equation as:

$$i - \hat{P} = \Lambda\left[\frac{RV/\mu - ba}{R(V + 1)}\right] \tag{6.11}$$

where Λ is the inverse function of ψ and has a negative first derivative. It is easy to show that the real interest rate $i - \hat{P}$ must fall in the loan market when either the price-wage ratio R or the degree of monetization V goes up. Let $\Lambda^* = \Lambda'/[R(V + 1)]^2 < 0$, where Λ' is the derivative of Λ. Then for reference the expressions for the partial derivatives of (6.11) are:

$$\frac{\partial \Lambda}{\partial V} = \Lambda^* R\left(\frac{1}{\mu} + ba\right) \tag{6.12}$$

and

$$\frac{\partial \Lambda}{\partial R} = \Lambda^* ba(V + 1) \qquad (6.13)$$

Solving (6.10) and (6.11) for i and $\hat{P}$ is straightforward. The results are:

$$i = \frac{\{[s - (\gamma + h)]a - g_0 + h\Lambda\}R}{(s - h)ab} - 1 \qquad (6.14)$$

and

$$\hat{P} = \frac{\{[s - (\gamma + h)]a - g_0\}R - \Lambda[(s - h)ab - hR]}{(s - h)ab} - 1 \qquad (6.15)$$

When both commodity and loan market equilibrium are taken into account as in these equations, $\partial i / \partial R$ still has an ambiguous sign. The positive effect comes from the bracketed term multiplying R in (6.14). Equation (5.13) shows that the bracket just equals $\alpha > 0$. The negative effect comes from the derivative of Λ with respect to R, as previously discussed. The corresponding partial derivative makes $\partial i / \partial V$ clearly negative.

Recall that the term $[(s - h)ab - hR]$ in (6.15) is positive when an increase in the interest rate drives up prices, and negative otherwise. Under rational expectations, $\partial \hat{P} / \partial V$ exceeds zero under dominant working-capital effects and is less than zero when the interest effect on investment demand is more important. The same effects go into $\partial \hat{P} / \partial R$, for which the formal expression is:

$$\frac{\partial \hat{P}}{\partial R} = \frac{1}{(s - h)ab}[\alpha - \delta \Lambda^* ba(V + 1)] \qquad (6.16)$$

where:

$$\delta = (s - h)ab - hR$$
$$= \frac{(s - h)ab}{\alpha}\{[s - (h + \gamma)]a - g_0 - h(1 + \hat{P})\} \qquad (6.17)$$

Since δ can be negative (when under high inflation investment demand effects dominate the interest rate response), $\partial \hat{P} / \partial R$ can in principle take either sign. However, a positive derivative will soon show up as a partial sufficient condition for stability of R and V in economic growth.

We are finally ready to deal with dynamics. The state variables change according to the rules:

$$\hat{V} = \left(\frac{sh}{s-h} + 1\right) \Lambda \left[\frac{RV/\mu - ba}{R(V+1)}\right] - i(V,R)$$
$$-\frac{sg_0 + h\gamma a}{s-h} + \hat{H} \tag{6.18}$$

and

$$\hat{R} = \phi\{R - R_s[\hat{P}(V,R)]\} \tag{6.19}$$

Equations (6.18) and (6.19) are unpleasantly nonlinear in V and R. For that reason, we will be content with stability analysis around a steady-state growth path where both variables are constant. One implication is that the value of capital stock grows at the same rate as money base, or $\hat{P} + \hat{K} = \hat{H}$. Secondly, there will be equilibrium in the labor market at steady state, or $R = R_s$.

At an initial steady state, the Jacobian of (6.18) and (6.19) is proportional to the matrix:

$$\begin{bmatrix} (shab + \delta)\Lambda^* R \left(\frac{1}{\mu} + ba\right) & (shab + \delta) \cdot \Lambda^* Rba(V+1) - \alpha \\ \phi \frac{\partial R_s}{\partial \hat{P}} \cdot \delta\Lambda^* R \left(\frac{1}{\lambda} + ba\right) & \phi\left\{1 - \frac{\partial R_s}{\partial \hat{P}}[\alpha - \delta\Delta^* Rba(V+1)]\right\} \end{bmatrix}$$

When $\delta > 0$ and working capital cost-push is the dominant interest rate effect, the northwest term will be negative. Since $\partial R_s/\partial \hat{P} > 0$, the southwest term will be negative when $\alpha - \delta\Lambda^* Rba(V+1)$ is strongly positive. But from (6.16) this condition just means that $\partial \hat{P}/\partial R$ should be large. The trace condition for stability will be satisfied for $\delta > 0$ under these conditions. Higher inflation or stronger investment demand would make $\delta < 0$, but by continuity of the functions stability should still be observed for values of δ not far below zero.

The determinant of the Jacobian is proportional to the quantity:

$$\Lambda^* R \left(\frac{1}{\mu} + ba\right) \phi\left[shab\left(1 - \frac{\partial R_s}{\partial \hat{P}}\right) + \delta\right]$$

Since $\Lambda^* < 0$, a positive determinant is more likely when $\delta < 0$ and investment demand effects dominate the macro response to interest rate changes. When $\delta > 0$ the condition:

$$1 - \frac{\partial R_s}{\partial \hat{P}} \alpha < 0$$

is required for stability. After a bit of manipulation, the relevant partial derivative can be written as:

$$\frac{\partial R_s}{\partial \hat{P}} = R_s \left[\frac{1}{\hat{P}} - \frac{\lambda}{e^{\hat{P}\lambda} - 1} \right]$$

Since α is a fraction, $\partial R_s / \partial \hat{P}$ will have to be substantially greater than one to make the determinant positive. If the zero-inflation value of R_s is set to unity by choice of units, then the numerical illustrations of section 6.2 suggest that with inflation, R_s will take a value between one and two. A bit of additional computation reveals that the derivative will be large only when the indexing period λ is longer than one unit of time in the model. A question of choice of time units is clearly involved, but with monthly inflation rates of, for example, 10 percent, relatively infrequent annual indexing might be required to assure macro stability when working-capital cost-push is the main channel for interest rate effects on the system. The situation is, of course, better when investment demand effects dominate.

7

Trade Balance
Complications

QUITE A LOT has already been said about the commodity trade entry in the balance of payments. Recall the contractionary devaluation tale of chapter 2, the travails of agriculture and mineral exporters in chapter 3, and the empirical wrinkles of chapter 4.

Perhaps surprisingly, trade poses still more riddles, especially about directions of causality in the macro economy. There are two key equations for what orthodox theorists call internal and external balance, but about a half dozen potentially endogenous variables enter into them. Hence, information beyond the equations must be used to specify chains of economic causes and the corresponding adjustment processes. There is no reason to expect the model to be the same for all countries or all times.

Section 7.1 sets up internal and external balance equations, or the saving gap and trade gap as they are known in the development literature. Section 7.2 explains the disequilibrium two-gap planning model interpretation of the balances, as well as two equilibrium adjustment processes for the rate of growth. The first has investment determined from saving, while competitive imports vary to close the balance of trade. The second, more realistic for application in poor countries, has growth fixed by available capital goods imports, while the income distribution changes to equilibrate saving supply with investment demand. Two additional pairs of adjusting variables are discussed in section 7.3. The exchange rate and capacity utilization as endogenous variables give a model resembling the mineral exporter of chapter 3, while endogenous capacity utilization and trade deficit comprise a system to be used in chapter 8 for analysis of macro stabilization policy.

Detailed though they are, these trade models say nothing about the capital account of the balance of payments. This omission begins to be remedied in section 7.4, where interest-bearing capital inflows to a sovereign borrowing country are analyzed in a two-gap framework. The chapter closes in section 7.5 with brief observations on the role of exports in trade models and their possible effects on economic growth.

7.1 Internal and External Balance

To keep the discussion within bounds, we will work with a one-sector economy, leaving out the interesting interindustry complications of chapter 3. The balance between supply and demand of a nationally produced good can be written as:

$$PX = PC + P\Theta I + [\epsilon_0 + \epsilon_1(eP^*/P)]PX \qquad (7.1)$$

As in the mineral exporting country of section 3.3, only a fraction Θ of total investment demand I is produced at home. The remainder, $(1 - \Theta)I$, must be imported. Roughly speaking, the home country is assumed to produce construction and unsophisticated equipment, while more elaborate capital goods come from abroad. Secondly, (7.1) incorporates the chapter 3 specification for the share of national production that is exported: $E/X = \epsilon_0 + \epsilon_1(eP^*/P)$. As usual, e stands for the exchange rate and P^* for the world price of goods similar to home exports. The export share will have an elasticity greater than one with respect to profitability eP^*/P when ϵ_0 is negative. Also, the world price of "our" exports is P/e, which is essentially determined by internal factors. For this reason, the models of this chapter can best be interpreted as referring to a semi-industrialized country. A pure primary product exporter would have its export price determined from abroad.

To (7.1) we add a hypothesis of markup pricing,

$$P = (1 + \tau)(wz + eP_0^* a_0) \qquad (7.2)$$

where P^*_0 is the world price of intermediate imports and a_0 is the corresponding input-output coefficient. The money wage is w and the labor-output ratio is z. All wage income is consumed, and a share s of profits is saved, so that the value of consumption is given by:

$$PC = wzX + (1 - s)\tau(wz + eP^*_0a_0)X \qquad (7.3)$$

Note that there is consumption only of the nationally produced good. Imports of consumer goods could be considered, but except for one point raised in the next section they just complicate the presentation. For that reason—and also because most poor countries ban almost all direct consumption imports by quantitative restriction—they are left out.

After all this preparation, it is simple to set down the value in domestic currency of the deficit on commodity trade as:

$$eB = eP^*_0a_0X + eP^*_i(1 - \Theta)I - [\epsilon_0 + \epsilon_1(eP^*/P)]PX \qquad (7.4)$$

where B is the deficit in dollars.[1] Insertion of (7.2), (7.3), and (7.4) into (7.1) gives a condition for zero excess demand of the nationally produced good:

$$[P\Theta + eP^*_i(1 - \Theta)]I - s\tau(wz + eP^*_0a_0)X - eB = 0 \qquad (7.5)$$

Unsurprisingly, this equation states that in equilibrium, the value of investment is equal to national saving (from profits) plus the deficit on current account.[2] Excess demand for foreign exchange (times the exchange rate) can be expressed as:

$$[eP^*_0a_0 - \epsilon_1eP^* - \epsilon_0P]X + eP^*_i(1 - \Theta)I - eB = 0 \qquad (7.6)$$

Equations (7.5) and (7.6) represent internal and external balance of the economy, respectively. Two variables must adjust to assure the balances hold in equilibrium. Various stable marriages are discussed in the following two sections. In preparation, we follow our usual strategy of dividing (7.5) and (7.6) by the value of capital stock, PK, to restate them as:

$$[\Theta + (1 - \Theta)qP^*_i]g - \frac{s\tau}{1 + \tau}u - qb = 0 \qquad (7.7)$$

and

$$[q(P^*_0a_0 - \epsilon_1P^*) - \epsilon_0]u + qP^*_i(1 - \Theta)g - qb = 0 \qquad (7.8)$$

where $g = I/K$ is the rate of growth of capital stock and $u = X/K$ measures capacity utilization. On the trade side, the current account deficit relative to capital stock is $b = B/K$, and $q = e/P$ is the ratio of the nominal exchange rate to the domestic output price. We follow the convention of calling q the "real exchange rate," though at times in the literature this label is applied to P/e, or q's inverse.

There are five possible variables to adjust in these two equations, viz g, u, and b on the quantity side and τ and q (or P and e) in terms of prices. The mechanisms can be described more easily if we adopt the "export optimist" assumption that $\epsilon_0 < 0$, or the export share of national output has a greater than unitary elasticity with respect to the real exchange rate. Also note that the quantity:

$$h = q[(1 - \Theta)P_i^* g - b] \tag{7.9}$$

is almost always positive for poor countries: net capital inflow (or the trade deficit) is less than the value of capital goods imports.[3] From (7.8) the condition $h > 0$ implies that $[q(P_0^* a_0 - \epsilon_1 P^*) - \epsilon_0]u < 0$. The interpretation is that exports exceed intermediate imports, or that the country runs a surplus on *current* trade to pay for the portion of its investment imports not financed from abroad. This sort of trade surplus strongly influences external adjustment in a semi-industrial country, as will be discussed in detail shortly.

7.2 The Two Gaps

One useful way of looking at (7.7) and (7.8) is in disequilibrium terms. To that end, assume provisionally that capacity utilization u, the real exchange rate q, and the markup τ are fixed. What then are the trade-off relationships between the trade deficit and growth? The relevant derivatives are

$$\left. \frac{dg}{db} \right]_{\text{Int}} = \frac{q}{\Theta + q(1 - \Theta)P_i^*}$$

from the internal balance condition (7.7) and

$$\left. \frac{dg}{db} \right]_{\text{Ext}} = \frac{q}{qP_i^*(1 - \Theta)}$$

from (7.8).

The internal balance slope is less than the one for external balance. A unit increase in b permits g to go up by more along (7.8) than (7.7) because only a portion of the commodities required for capital formation is supplied from foreign trade. This distinction is illustrated by figure 7.1.[4]

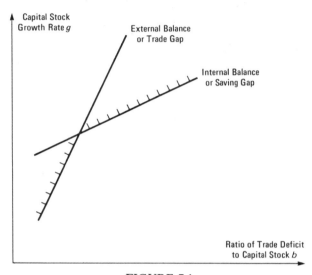

FIGURE 7.1

External Balance (Trade Gap) and Internal Balance (Saving Gap) Trade-Offs between the Trade Deficit and Capital Stock Growth

In a planning exercise, the diagram shows that an increase in the trade deficit will generate more growth if (7.8) is the constraining relationship between b and g than if (7.7) applies. Moreover, "something" must adjust to assure equality in the nonbinding constraint. As will be discussed shortly, if the external balance relationship or trade gap binds, then either the markup rate or capacity utilization could vary to assure the equals sign in (7.7). If the saving gap binds, an extra import term could bring balance in (7.8).

Many planning and development programming models have been based on this setup since it was proposed in the early 1960s—the simplest variant is outlined in section 8.4.[5] Usually, the models are set up to calculate feasible levels of investment for given capital inflows. The diagnosis of the "binding gap" required for such an assessment comes informally from what is happening in the macro economy. Domestic saving may constrain the system if central bank reserves or consumption imports are on the rise, while foreign exchange may be in short supply if capacity utilization is low or investment falling off.

These quick looks at the system replace specification of adjustment mechanisms in the two-gap approach. This absence of rules about what closes the "gap between the gaps" by driving left-hand sides of both (7.7) and (7.8) to zero has often been criticized. To illustrate the conclusions to which the criticisms lead, two formal processes are set out here.

First suppose that the saving gap binds, so that capital stock growth g increases when there is "excess supply" of saving. This is the same as writing the left side of (7.7) with the sign reversed:

$$\frac{dg}{dt} = F_g\{(1 + \tau)^{-1}s\tau u + qb - [\Theta + (1 - \Theta)qP_i^*]g\} \quad (7.10)$$

Also allow competitive imports of nationally produced goods to enter the economy in volume M. These imports (*net* of local commodity exports) will be the variable that adjusts to bring external balance; hence, we ignore the export supply term $(q\epsilon_1 P^* + \epsilon_0)u$ for the moment. Let $m = M/K$ and assume that m rises when there is an excess of foreign exchange:

$$\frac{dm}{dt} = F_m\{qb - qP_i^*(1 - \Theta)g - qP_0^*a_0 u - m\} \quad (7.11)$$

The nominal exchange rate is assumed constant and since there is free foreign trade the law of one price applies: $P = eP^*$. The markup rate is determined from (7.2), and the economy is supposed to operate at full capacity so the u is fixed. (Flexible wages and free capital-labor substitution may be postulated to back this hypothesis up.) Finally, the allowable trade deficit b is set by capital market conditions from abroad.

Under all these assumptions, it is easy to see that (7.10) and (7.11) define a stably adjusting system in g and m. The economics is simple. A unit increase in b, the trade deficit relative to the capital stock, generates enough saving to raise the growth rate by $q/[\Theta + (1 - \Theta)qP_i^*]$, from (7.10). But from (7.11) the extra growth uses only $P_i^*(1 - \Theta)$ in imports of capital goods, and the rest of the increment in foreign resources can go to competitive imports m. What happens when b is reduced and m tends to fall below zero is left unexplained.

This story clearly focuses on the saving gap—conditions of productivity and thrift within a country and capital donors' largesse abroad provide the saving that determines g. Then competitive imports adjust to keep trade in balance. The two-gap dilemma is dissolved by free trade. Not surprisingly, neoclassical trade theorists are the principal exponents of the foregoing sort of model.[6]

The main objections center on institutions—few countries permit free imports, full employment of resources is rarely observed, and the law of one price is more often than not in abeyance. Moreover, trade flows need not adjust with much rapidity. If m in (7.11) is negative (or the country is a net exporter of competitive commodities—the likely case), then in fact it may be very difficult to raise exports in the short run. The country may well be quantity-constrained in world markets, and run straight into two-gap problems.[7] Under such circumstances, the natural approach is to take the trade gap as ultimately binding on the growth rate, and ask what adjustment mechanisms act to bring national saving in line. The obvious possibilities are forced saving and output changes. We illustrate the former in a model where the markup rate τ and the growth rate g are endogenous variables.

The differential equations for adjustment are most easily expressed after multiplying (7.7) and (7.8) by $1 + \tau$. With response functions $F_\tau(\ )$ and $F_g(\ )$ they are:

$$\frac{d\tau}{dt} = F_\tau\{(1 + \tau)\Theta g + \tilde{q}[g(1 - \Theta)P_i^* - b] - s\tau u\} \quad (7.12)$$

and

$$\frac{dg}{dt} = F_g\{\tilde{q}b - \tilde{q}P_i^*(1 - \Theta)g$$
$$- [\tilde{q}(P_0^*a_0 - \epsilon_1 P^*) - (1 + \tau)\epsilon_0]u\} \quad (7.13)$$

where $\tilde{q} = e/(wz + eP_0^*a_0)$, or the nominal exchange rate divided by variable cost. Along with capacity utilization u and the trade deficit b, $\tilde{q}$ is assumed exogenous. The adjustment story is that the trade deficit determines g from the external balance equation (7.13), while the income distribution shifts through changes in τ to satisfy internal balance in (7.12). An equilibrium can easily be seen to be locally stable when $\tilde{h} = \tilde{q}[(1 - \Theta) P_i^* g - b] > 0$ and $\epsilon_0 < 0$.

Figure 7.2 illustrates the model; the small arrows indicate the stable dynamics. The two-gap interpretation hinges on two observations. First, when the saving gap binds, a higher growth rate requires a higher markup τ to the left of the kink at point A. Second, when the trade gap binds to the right of A, the import content of higher investment provides enough extra saving to drive τ down. The dominance of the trade gap in the overall specification stems from the fact that an increase in the deficit b generates $\tilde{q}/\tilde{q}(1 - \Theta)P_i^*$ additional growth from (7.13). The higher growth rate requires $(1 + \tau)\Theta + \tilde{q}(1 - \Theta)P_i^*$ in saving from (7.12). The required extra

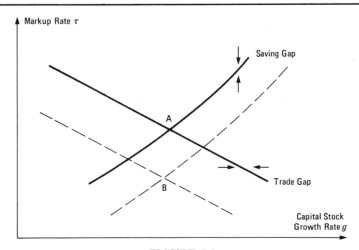

FIGURE 7.2

Adjustment of the Trade Gap by the Growth Rate and the Saving Gap by the Markup Rate

NOTE: The dashed lines show the effect of an increase in the intermediate import price, or an "oil shock."

saving exceeds that provided by a higher deficit alone, and τ must rise. In an alternative specification with capacity utilization as the adjusting variable, a larger deficit would permit both higher output and faster growth.

As a final exercise, consider what happens under an "oil shock" or increase in the intermediate import price P_0^* in the two specifications. When growth is saving-determined in (7.10) and (7.11), it is easy to see that a rise in P_0^* will cut back on both g and competitive imports m. Figure 7.2 shows what happens in the forced saving model. The higher import bill represents additional savings so that for a given τ, growth will be slowed from the trade gap, or that schedule shifts leftward. The outcome is a lower markup and (from arguments similar to those above) slower growth. In an output-adjusting model, capacity utilization would decline from lower aggregate demand, as in the model of contractionary devaluation of chapter 2. A lower markup is how the system adapts to fixed capacity utilization.

Regrettably, taxonomy runs rampant in this discussion of the two-gap model; it often does when foreign trade is the subject at hand. The differences in response are substantial enough to suggest that one should be quite clear about causal linkages in the system before jumping into policy advice. From a structuralist perspective, a model on which income distribution or level of output bears the brunt of adjustment looks decidedly more relevant than one in which freely adjusting foreign trade smooths all external shocks away. But as we see in the following section, there are further possibilities.

Balance equations alone cannot define what is happening in an economy; information outside the models has to say what is pushing the algebra around.

7.3 Exchange Rate and Output Adjustments

Why can't the exchange rate vary to smooth the two-gap kink away? If not constrained by the asset market (see chapter 8), in principle it can bear some part of macro adjustment. But even in commodity markets there are limits—no plausible exchange appreciation is going to turn Kuwait into a net importer. Moreover, the macro correlates of exchange rate adjustment may not be pleasing. To see why, consider a model in which capacity utilization rises in response to excess commodity demand in (7.7) and the exchange rate goes up when there is excess demand for dollars (a positive left-hand side) in (7.8). The growth rate, the markup, and the trade deficit are assumed to be fixed. This specification is not greatly different from that of the mineral-exporter model of chapter 3, and addresses the same issues discussed there.

The details of this model closure show up in the total differentials of equations (7.7) and (7.8):

$$
\begin{bmatrix} -\dfrac{s\tau}{1+\tau} & \dfrac{h}{q} \\[2em] -\dfrac{h}{u} & \dfrac{u\epsilon_0}{q} \end{bmatrix}
\begin{bmatrix} du \\[2em] dq \end{bmatrix}
+
\begin{bmatrix} -q(1+\tau)a_0 h \\[2em] qa_0 u[1 - \epsilon_0(1+\tau)] \end{bmatrix} dP_0^*
$$

$$
+ \begin{bmatrix} \Theta + q(1-\Theta)P_i^* \\[2em] q(1-\Theta)P_i^* \end{bmatrix} dg
- \begin{bmatrix} g \\[2em] q \end{bmatrix} db
= \begin{bmatrix} 0 \\[2em] 0 \end{bmatrix} \qquad (7.14)
$$

With $\epsilon_0 < 0$ (elastic exports, again) the trace of the Jacobian matrix multiplying du and dq will be safely negative. The same condition assures a positive determinant Δ:

$$
\Delta = \frac{h^2}{ug} - \frac{s\tau u \epsilon_0}{(1+\tau)q}
$$

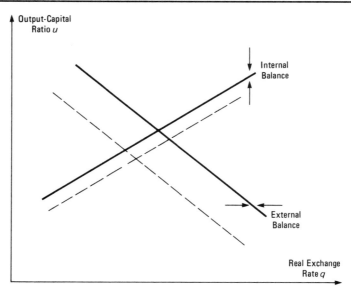

FIGURE 7.3

Adjustment of the Output-Capital Ratio or Capacity Utilization to Reach Internal Balance and the Real Exchange Rate to Reach External Balance

NOTE: The dashed lines show the effect of greater foreign exchange availability, as from foreign transfers or mineral exports.

The adjustment process is illustrated in figure 7.3. The output-capital ratio u responds stably to maintain internal balance and $\epsilon_0 < 0$ guarantees that the exchange rate does the same for foreign trade.[8]

An interesting comparative static exercise is an increase in the trade deficit b. More foreign aid or bigger mineral exports from a purely enclave sector could generate this pleasant macroeconomic shock. In the trade balance at a given capacity level, (7.14) shows that an increase in b reduces excess demand for dollars and consequently the real exchange rate q. Since a high trade deficit represents additional saving, capacity utilization u will also fall from reduced aggregate demand with a given q. As shown in figure 7.3, the external balance schedule shifts leftward, while internal balance moves down.

Clearly, output or capacity utilization drops due to a standard disincentive effect from additional foreign exchange. From (7.14), (7.7), and (7.9), the sign of the change in the real exchange rate depends on:

$$\frac{h}{u} - \frac{s\tau}{1 + \tau} = -\frac{\Theta g}{u} < 0$$

So long as there is some capital goods production at home, the extra resources brought in by an increase in the trade deficit exceed domestic use, and appreciation of the real exchange rate is an inevitable result.[9]

The extra foreign exchange turns out to be not so pleasant after all. National production declines in the short run, and in a dynamic model the lower real exchange rate would give scant incentive to investment demand. But then from (7.14) a lower growth rate would further reduce q, as both external and internal diversification declined. The long-term analog of our short-term formal results is a cumulative process in which freely available foreign resources reduce the real exchange rate, thereby cutting back investment and leading to internal stagnation in the long run. Gifts from the gods of politically determined foreign aid or bounteous exports are not without their sting.[10]

Even if these long-run difficulties don't arise, further problems can come from the asset market. In particular, if capital flows are not tightly controlled, they may influence the exchange rate, internal price level, or the interest rate via the capital account of the balance of payments. These responses depend greatly on institutions and modes of capital market intervention. Examples are given in chapter 8. In preparation for the analysis presented there, one more current account model is set out, in which the trade deficit instead of the real exchange rate varies to assure external balance. Also, the asset market may play a role in determining the price level. To capture this possibility, the markup expression $\tau/(1 + \tau)$ for profits per unit output in (7.7) is replaced by $(1 - \omega z - qP_0^* a_0)$ where $\omega = w/P$ is the real wage. The internal balance equation is thus rewritten as:

$$[\Theta + (1 - \Theta)qP_i^*]g - s[1 - \omega z - qP_0^* a_0]u - gb = 0 \quad (7.15)$$

The adjustment process is an increase in u when the left side of (7.15) exceeds zero, while b goes up in response to excess demand for foreign resources in (7.8). Foreign asset holders are ignored, so the higher trade deficit is financed by a reduction in national holdings of foreigners' liabilities —either central bank reserves or currency and other tradable wealth held in private hoards.

The total differentials of the balance equations resemble (7.14). The roles of dq and db are reversed, and dropping the markup term slightly alters the price responses. For the record, the expression is:

$$
\begin{bmatrix} -\dfrac{h + \Theta g}{u} & -q \\[2ex] -\dfrac{h}{u} & -q \end{bmatrix} \begin{bmatrix} du \\[2ex] db \end{bmatrix} =
$$

$$
\begin{bmatrix} -sP_0^* a_0 u + \dfrac{h}{q} \\[3ex] -\dfrac{\epsilon_0 u}{q} \end{bmatrix} dq \; - \; \begin{bmatrix} \Theta + qP_i^*(1 - \Theta) \\[3ex] qP_i^*(1 - \Theta) \end{bmatrix} dg \qquad (7.16)
$$

The determinant of the Jacobian is $\Theta qg/u$, safely positive.

For comparative statics, note first that (7.8) and (7.15) can be directly rewritten as equations in the ratios (u/g) and (b/g). An increase in g will raise u and b in the same proportion, or capacity utilization and the trade deficit are unit elastic functions of the growth rate. The same result of course can be verified from the heavier algebra of (7.16).

To check the effect of a shift in the real exchange rate, recall the assumption made in connection with (7.9) that $h > 0$, or the country has a surplus of exports over intermediate imports. The term $[q(P_0^* a_0 - \epsilon_1 P^*) - \epsilon_0]u$ in (7.8) must then be negative. Suppose further that $\epsilon_0 < 0$, or exports are more than unit elastic to exchange rate changes. The implication is that $q(\epsilon_1 P^* - P_0^* a_0) > 0$, or an increase in q drives up the difference between exports and imports. This healthy trade response raises capacity utilization since from (7.16):

$$
\frac{du}{dq} = \frac{u}{\Theta g}[(\epsilon_1 P^* u - P_0^* a_0 u) + sP_0^* a_0 u]
$$

In effect, the assumption that $\epsilon_0 < 0$ rules out contractionary devaluation of the type discussed in chapter 2. A positive value of ϵ_0—or a less than unit elasticity of exports to the exchange rate—would permit $(\epsilon_1 P^* - P_0^* a_0)$ to be negative, and perhaps du/dq would be less than zero as well. Determined to be sanguine about trade in the balance of payments analysis of chapter 8, we will there postulate contractionary devaluation away.

Responses are illustrated in figure 7.4. From (7.16), the slope du/db of

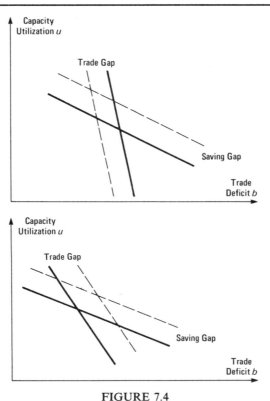

FIGURE 7.4

Effects of an Increase in the Real Exchange Rate q *on Capacity Utilization and the Trade Deficit When Devaluation Is Expansionary (Upper Diagram) or Contractionary (Lower Diagram)*

the internal balance or saving gap equation (7.15) will be less negative than that of the external balance or trade gap (7.8). In (7.15) an increase in q raises capacity utilization u at a given trade deficit b when $h > 0$. Under this condition, along with $\epsilon_0 < 0$, a higher q reduces the deficit for a given level of u in (7.8). The outcome is shown in the upper diagram of figure 7.4 —capacity utilization goes up and the deficit falls. For $\epsilon_0 > 0$, b can rise along with q, as shown in the lower diagram. Devaluation under such circumstances may worsen both the trade deficit and the level of economic activity.

If we banish the lower diagram by assumption, then this last model is quite standard—the exchange rate does the usual things and higher capital stock growth stimulates aggregate demand. Note, however, that from (7.15) the profit rate $(1 - \omega z - q P_0^* a_0)u$ initially falls when q goes up. Hence, capital stock growth might be expected to fall with devaluation or speed up when the exchange rate appreciates. How such an investment response complicates stabilization policy in an open economy is discussed informally in the following chapter.

7.4 Interest Costs and Export Performance

The foregoing models leave out an important contemporary item in the current account of developing countries—the interest cost on outstanding debt.[11] To see how debt and interest can influence trade behavior of developing countries, we can extend the accounting underlying (7.7) and (7.8) by letting F be the outstanding value of "our" country's foreign debt, and $f = F/K$. The definition of the current deficit in (7.4) has to be written as:

$$eB = eP_0^* a_0 X + eP_i^* (1 - \Theta)I - \left[\epsilon_0 + \epsilon_1 \left(\frac{eP^*}{P} \right) \right] PX + ieF \quad (7.17)$$

where i is the (real) interest rate on F. If reserve changes are zero, then in the overall balance of payments the current account B will have to be offset by increases in F, or capital inflows:

$$-B + \frac{dF}{dt} = -B + g_f F = 0 \quad (7.18)$$

where g_f is the growth rate of F. A higher current account deficit reduces foreign reserves, while a capital inflow (or an increase in foreign nonmonetary debt) adds to them. Finally, national saving decisions determine the level of consumption, so (7.3) has to be rewritten as:

$$PC = wzX + (1 - s)[\tau(wz + eP_0^* a_0)X - ieF] \quad (7.19)$$

Equations (7.17)–(7.19) can be combined with (7.1) and (7.2) to give new versions of the internal and external balance conditions (7.5) and (7.6). Assume that f is constant so that $g_f = g$, where g is the growth rate of capital stock. Division of these new balance equations by PK (the value of capital stock) then permits them to be stated as:

$$[\Theta + qP_i^* (1 - \Theta)]g - s(r - iqf) - qfg = 0 \quad (7.20)$$

and

$$-\epsilon u + qP_i^*(1 - \Theta)g + iqf - qfg = 0 \qquad (7.21)$$

where $r = \tau u/(1 + \tau)$ is the national profit rate and $\epsilon = q(\epsilon_1 P^* - P_0^* a_0) + \epsilon_0$ is the share of exports net of intermediate imports in total output. The internal balance equation (7.20) says that investment demand is met by national saving plus net capital inflows (per unit of capital stock) qfg. The external balance (7.21) shows that interest payments iqf plus investment imports $qP_i^*(1 - \Theta)g$ are balanced by capital inflows and net exports ϵu.

To illustrate these relationships, we can return to the planning approach of section 7.2, treating exports as a variable the country tries to control to determine its growth rate, *given* a level of the debt/capital ratio f. The export ratio can be manipulated by exchange rate policy, as well as tariffs, quotas, and nonmarket incentives. We do not go into the details of these interventions here. The fixed "debt-to-equity" ratio f is assumed to arise naturally from credit-rationing in international capital markets—lenders do not allow any nation's obligations to grow without bound.[12]

Equations (7.20) and (7.21) are illustrated in figure 7.5. In (7.20) for

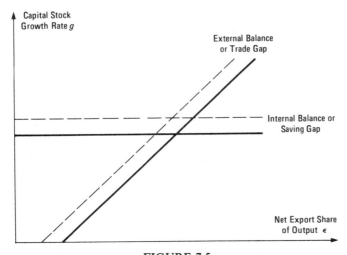

FIGURE 7.5

Effects of an Increase in the Debt/Capital Ratio f *on the Capital Stock Growth Rate* g *and and Net Export Share* ε

internal balance, the growth rate is independent of the export share, but its derivative with respect to f is given by:

$$\frac{dg}{df}\bigg]_{\text{Int}} = \frac{q(g - si)}{\Theta + qP_i^*(1 - \Theta) - qf} \qquad (7.22)$$

So long as si (the loss of national saving induced by net interest payments abroad) is small, an increase in capital inflows permits faster growth insofar as investment-saving balance is concerned.

In (7.21) for external balance, a higher export share ϵ permits higher capital goods imports and faster growth. The effect of more capital inflow is:

$$\frac{dg}{df}\bigg]_{\text{Ext}} = \frac{\epsilon u - iqP_i^*(1 - \Theta)}{[qP_i^*(1 - \Theta) - qf]^2} = \frac{q(g - i)}{q[P_i^*(1 - \Theta) - f]} \qquad (7.23)$$

The term in the numerator after the first equality is the difference between the ratio of net exports to capital stock and the interest costs on capital goods imports. This expression represents the recurring foreign exchange surplus that can be generated by putting foreign debt to use for capital formation. Countries without good export prospects could find this surplus negative; the implication is that they would be unlikely to have access to capital markets in the first place. For present purposes we assume the numerator positive so that an increase in debt permits faster growth along the trade gap, but bear in mind that some economies may not be so fortunate.[13] The expression after the second equality shows that having a growth rate less than the real interest rate on one's loans may be a sign of this sort of international impoverishment (under our standard assumption that financial capital inflows do not pay for physical capital imports: $P_i^*(1 - \Theta) > f$).

Suppose that the country passes this means test and is eligible for international loans. How does their presence affect the relative slopes of the trade and saving gaps? Recall from the discussion of figure 7.1 that the trade gap is usually assumed to be steeper, because the denominator in the term after the second equality in (7.23) is less than the denominator in (7.22). Note now, however, that if the interest rate i is high relative to the growth rate g, the usual condition can reverse and the derivative in (7.23) can be less than that in (7.22). The reason is that interest charges add to the current account deficit one-for-one, while they only reduce national saving by the fraction s. On a long-term basis, an increase in a country's creditworthiness as demonstrated by a rise in f may add more to its national saving than to its available foreign exchange. The effect on the economy would be contractionary—in a model with output adjusting to national excess demand, the outcome would be a lower level of capacity utilization, for example. While interest costs are probably not large enough in most practical cases to give such results, the possibility is worth bearing in mind.

Refer to figure 7.5. The growth rate is independent of net exports in (7.20), so this equation is represented by the horizontal line. There is a positive relationship between exports and growth in (7.21), as shown by the "External balance" schedule. A higher debt ratio f permits faster growth in both equations; both schedules shift up. How do net exports respond? The usual argument was already made in section 7.1 for the model with competitive imports. Extra foreign resources add more to growth through generating saving than through augmenting capital goods import capacity. There is spare foreign buying power, and net imports can rise or net exports fall. But once again, this result can reverse if international real interest rates are high. More capital flows may require a country to step up its export effort to meet payments on its foreign debt! Figure 7.5 shows this possibility through the ambiguous shift in ϵ as f goes up. In a diagram like figure 7.1, the induced rise in exports from higher foreign borrowing will occur precisely in the "perverse" case where the saving gap has a steeper schedule than the trade gap.

7.5 Exports and Growth

There is a final observation on the role of exports in all the models of this chapter: there is no very clear linkage between the net export share and other variables of interest, such as the rate of growth. A country at neoclassical full employment would demonstrate a negative relationship between exports as a fraction of potential output and the capital stock growth rate. Physical resources for higher investment would have to be diverted from net sales abroad, and the foreign deficit would have to increase to provide the saving counterpart of increased investment demand. If there is spare capacity, on the other hand, higher exports can stimulate growth, as in the Hobson-Luxemburg theory of imperialism discussed in chapter 10. And, of course, there may be shifts between regimes from time to time.

All this stands in sharp contrast to recent statistical exercises in which GNP growth is supposed to be monotonically related to the (average or marginal) export share or to the growth rate of exports.[14] First note that a positive relationship between GNP growth and the growth of exports would simply reflect a constant export share. The resulting regression coefficient is irrelevant to the question of how changes in the share might be associated with growth performance. Secondly, the models of this chapter strongly suggest a nonlinear relationship, shifting over time, between the two variables. Simple linear correlations fall well short of addressing the complex interactions between a country's balance of payments position and its rate of economic growth.

8

Foreign Assets and the
Balance of Payments

DETAILED though they are, last chapter's models say nothing about how private capital movements may affect the balance of payments. For developing countries, portfolio shifts between domestic and foreign assets can have important effects on the real exchange rate, and through it on inflation and output growth. A model based on recent stabilization attempts in several countries is developed in this chapter to address these issues. The specific policy question is the impact of a reduction in the rate at which the nominal exchange rate is depreciating, or what happens when a crawling peg is slowed. A three-asset model like the one in chapters 5 and 6 is developed to show that the "normal" financial market response to the slower crawl would be an upward shift in the schedule of bank lending to firms. A higher price level (or a lower real exchange rate) or a lower interest rate and faster growth would be the expected results, as shown in section 8.1. However, the opposite responses could also occur, for example, when a slower crawl leads wealth-holders to prefer nonmonetized assets (the "gold" of chapter 5) for purchase of which they can conveniently obtain bank loans. How these short-run stories work in steady state is sketched in section 8.2, and section 8.3 reviews in informal fashion several extensions to the basic model.

An additional point to note is that the crawling peg models really depend
on the two-gap (or internal and external balance) specification of chapter
7, plus the accounting identity for the banking system that says that the
money supply must equal the sum of banks' foreign assets and their domestic credit to the government and private sector. The two accounting gaps,
or balances, and the money identity also underlie other approaches to
macro analysis in the Third World. The practice of agencies such as the
World Bank and International Monetary Fund is discussed in section 8.4.

8.1 Asset Markets and the Capital Account

Few developing countries have a floating exchange rate. Several, however, revise their nominal rates regularly (every few weeks or months) in
a "crawling peg." This sort of policy was first used in Latin America in the
1960s. Its original purpose was to hold the real exchange rate steady in the
face of domestic inflation to maintain incentives for private sector exporters.
A second objective was to avoid the massive capital flows that a fixed rate
system stimulates when national prices keep going up. If the exchange rate
is held constant, exports might be expected to stagnate and imports stream
in. Sooner or later a maxidevaluation to restore the current account has to
occur. But before then, anyone with access to financial capital will send it
abroad, via legal channels, if they exist, and illegal ones like overinvoicing
of imports, underinvoicing of exports, and exaggerated interest payments
and royalties. Once the maxi occurs, capital comes back to reap its windfall
increase in local purchasing power. The sequence of minidevaluations that
makes up a crawling peg can substantially smooth these speculative ebbs
and flows.[1]

More recently, a third objective of a crawling peg has been enunciated
in the context of monetarist stabilization programs. The notion is that the
government should pre-announce the crawl at a rate lower than current
inflation. Inflationary expectations are supposed to be reduced, causing
actual price increases to decelerate after a time.

The policy of trying to wave down inflation with the exchange rate has
usually been applied in connection with the lifting of controls over capital
flows. The results were unexpected—capital came streaming in and led to
rapid accumulation of central bank reserves. Subsequent credit expansion
kicked off additional inflation, while the real exchange rate went down,
taking net exports with it. In other contexts the inflationary push was not

so overwhelming, but interest rates rose very high, leading to investment stagnation and slow growth.[2]

Both sorts of responses can be traced to asset-holders' reactions to the slower crawl. The return to retaining foreign assets is $i^* + \pi_e - \pi$, where i^* is the foreign interest rate (which we set to zero for convenience), π_e is the expected rate of devaluation, and π is the expected internal inflation. A slower crawl reduces π_e, leading those with wealth to try to shift their portfolios toward other assets. How the shift occurs and how much it is multiplied by credit creation in the banking system determine the macro-economic result. To begin to see the details, look at the balance sheets in table 8.1.[3]

Foreign exchange is assumed to be held by two parties—the central bank, which has dollar reserves in the quantity R (national value eR), and private individuals, who have quantity eJ.[4] Let $e(R + J) = eV$. Under a fixed exchange rate, in the short run V is constant. If the public wishes to hold fewer dollars, the central bank must absorb them at the given rate in

TABLE 8.1

Balance Sheets for the Open Economy Model

Assets		Liabilities	.
Central Bank			
Government fiscal debt	F	Bank reserves	H
Foreign reserves	eR		
Commercial Banks			
Bank reserves	H		
Loans to firms	L	Deposits from the public	D
Loans to public	$(1 - B)P_zZ$		
Firms			
Physical capital	PK	Loans from banks	L
		Net worth	N
Public			
Deposits with banks	D		
Foreign exchange	eJ	Wealth	W
Net gold	$B\,P_zZ$		

Banking balance sheet: $eR + [F + L + (1 - B)P_zZ] = D$
Foreign assets: $e(R + J) = eV$
Wealth with public: $W = D + eJ + BP_zZ$
Total wealth: $F + eV + PK + P_zZ = W + N$

exchange for domestic deposits. The total of bank and private holdings (or
V) can only change over time through a current account deficit or surplus.

As in table 5.1, the central bank also holds government debt F, which
sums with eR to give high-powered money H. Along with H, the assets of
the commercial banks are loans to firms L, and loans to the public $(1 - B)$
P_zZ. Regarding the latter, the hypothesis is that, as in chapter 5, the public
holds a nontradable asset, gold (or perhaps more realistically, "land").
Under existing financial customs, when people acquire Z, they finance a
fraction $(1 - B)$ of the purchase with bank loans. Think of mortgages.
Hence, bank assets include outstanding loans of this type, $(1 - B)P_zZ$. The
public holds the balance, BP_zZ. Individuals also have deposits D, a banking
system liability.

The consolidated balance sheet of the central and commercial banks takes
the form:

$$eR + F + [L + (1 - B)P_zZ] = D \qquad (8.1)$$

In words, money supply D is the sum of foreign assets of the banking system
(eR), bank credit to the government (F) and bank credit to the private
sector $[L + (1 - B)P_zZ]$. The definitional decomposition of money supply
into the credit items of the left-hand side of (8.1) is the basis of the "financial
programming" exercises of the International Monetary Fund, as discussed
in section 8.4.

The treatment of firms' assets differs somewhat from that in chapters 5
and 6. Working capital and associated cost-push are left out for simplicity.
Also, in the absence of an active equity market, firms are assumed to own
themselves. In practice, in poor countries a very restricted part of the
population plus the government will control most enterprises using large
amounts of physical capital, so this assumption is not so far-fetched as it
seems. Its implication is that PK—the value of capital stock—is the total
of firm assets, while their liabilities are loans from banks (L) and net worth
(N). The bank credit finances a fraction α of investment spending; hence,
in the notation of chapter 7, loan demand L^d is:

$$L^d = \alpha[\Theta P + (1 - \Theta)eP_i^*]I \qquad (8.2)$$

The public's wealth is W, the sum of bank deposits D, foreign exchange
eJ, and gold BP_zZ. Total primary wealth in the system includes physical
capital PK, total foreign assets $e(R + J)$, fiscal debt F, and gold P_zZ. It
is easy to see that these sum to $W + N$. The public's wealth W will shortly

be shown to be an endogenous variable with a changing value. Firms' net worth N is the residual that picks up the slack.

Public demand for assets is described by the equations:

$$D = \psi(i - \pi, \pi_e - \pi, \pi_z - \pi)W \tag{8.3}$$

$$eJ = \lambda(i - \pi, \pi_e - \pi, \pi_z - \pi)W \tag{8.4}$$

and

$$BP_zZ = \xi(i - \pi, \pi_e - \pi, \pi_z - \pi)W \tag{8.5}$$

where $\psi + \lambda + \xi = 1$. The real return to holding deposits is the interest rate i (very probably controlled by the authorities) less expected inflation π. Holdings of foreign exchange and gold respond respectively to net expected capital gains $\pi_e - \pi$ and $\pi_z - \pi$.

To demonstrate the endogeneity of the public's wealth, we can substitute equations (8.3)–(8.5) into the definition:

$$W = D + eJ + BP_zZ$$

If we follow the chapter 5 assumption that the authorities impose a reserve ratio μ on the commercial banking system so that $H = \mu D$ $(0 < \mu < 1)$, then wealth turns out to be:

$$W = \frac{eV + F}{\mu(1 - \xi) + \lambda(1 - \mu)} \tag{8.6}$$

Wealth is higher, the higher is the share of assets held in gold (ξ) and the lower in foreign exchange (λ). The impact of a rise in the reserve requirement μ is to reduce wealth by cutting banks' credit creation. If gold is ignored ($\xi = 0$) then (8.6) becomes:

$$W = \frac{eV + F}{1 - \psi(1 - \mu)} \tag{8.7}$$

which shows that W rises as more deposits are held (higher ψ) and as the reserve requirement is lower.

Using (8.6) and a bit more manipulation, one can derive an expression for loan supply to firms as:

$$L^s = \frac{B[1 - \mu(1 - \xi) - \lambda(1 - \mu)] - \xi}{B[\mu(1 - \xi) + \lambda(1 - \mu)]}(eV + F)$$

$$= \phi(i - \pi, \pi_e - \pi, \pi_z - \pi)(eV + F) \qquad (8.8)$$

Available loans rise along with the total primary financial assets ($eV + F$), but otherwise depend in a complex way on the workings of the financial system, as illustrated by the expression after the first equality. For future reference, all the interactions are boiled down into a single credit multiplier ϕ in the second expression.

When there is no gold, (8.8) simplifies dramatically to the equation:

$$L^s = \frac{\psi(1 - \mu)}{1 - \psi(1 - \mu)}(eV + F)$$

The arguments of ψ are $i - \pi$ and $\pi_e - \pi$, with positive and negative partial derivatives, respectively. Now suppose that the government promises to slow the crawling peg, and is believed. Then π_e will fall and ψ will rise as wealthholders shift toward domestic assets by trading in foreign currency at the bank. There is credit multiplication, and the loan supply to firms goes up. Our first conclusion is that in a very simple financial model, slowing the crawl with credibility will lead to domestic credit expansion.

When gold enters the picture, the wealthy have another option. After they convert their foreign holdings to national deposits, they can turn around and take out loans to finance gold purchases. If the initial deposits are relatively small (or are restricted by regulations on capital inflow) and the private loan demands large, then loans to firms will be cut back. Contraction of economically productive credit follows in wake of the slower crawl.

To see the details, assume that $d\xi = -\gamma d\lambda$, with $0 < \gamma < 1$. The new parameter γ is the fraction of their reduction in foreign exchange holdings that members of the public direct toward gold. Its magnitude will depend on both asset-holders' behavioral patterns and the institutional restrictions that the authorities place on the exchange market (for example, minimum maturity requirements on foreign loans, interest rate premia, and so forth). Differentiation of (8.8) shows that loan supply to firms will contract when the following condition is satisfied:

$$B < \frac{[\mu + \lambda(1 - \mu)]\gamma + \xi(1 - \mu)}{\mu\gamma + (1 - \mu)}$$

As γ approaches one, this expression simplifies to:

$$\mathbf{B} < \mu\psi + (\lambda + \xi)$$

so that an easily accessible mortgage market ($\mathbf{B} < 1$) and high reserve requirements (μ near one) go together with high gold or land demand (γ near one) to squeeze loans to firms.

The easiest way to check the macroeconomic consequences of these financial adjustments is to set excess demand for productive loans [the difference between (8.2) and (8.8)] to zero, after dividing by PK. The result is:

$$a[\Theta + (1 - \Theta)qP_i^*]g$$
$$- \phi(i - \pi, \pi_e - \pi, \pi_z - \pi)\frac{qV + (F/P)}{K} = 0 \qquad (8.9)$$

where ϕ is defined in (8.8). The foregoing arguments can be summarized by the observation that $\partial\phi/\partial\pi_e$ can have either sign.

The financial market model just sketched must be coupled with a description of the real side of the economy to say something about macro policy. We will use the second model of section 7.3 for this purpose. Its balance equations are (7.8) for the trade gap and (7.15) for the saving gap. Comparative static responses are summarized by equation (7.16) and figure 7.4, with the real exchange rate q and the capital stock growth rate g as shifting variables, and capacity utilization u and the current account deficit b endogenous. A credit market equation like (8.9) can be used to determine either g or q. A change in $q = e/P$ must take place via a change in P since at any moment the *level* of the nominal exchange rate e will be fixed, though of course e rises in a predetermined fashion over time according to the crawling peg. Also, real side macro adjustment occurs solely through changing capacity utilization, the real wage having been assumed fixed in (7.15). The underlying labor market story is that the money wage is instantaneously indexed to the price level.

There are two obvious possibilities for the adjusting variable in (8.9). One is the interest rate, which could rise in response to loan excess demand. The effects would be to increase bank deposits and thus loan supply through credit multiplication and to reduce investment demand g. Both responses would give a stable adjustment.

A second, more monetarist approach is to assume that the price level P is determined by money market conditions. This line of analysis presupposes that prices are determined neither from markup rules as in chapter 2 nor from trade arbitrage between domestic and competitively imported goods, which would enforce the Law of One Price. Under either hypothesis the price would be fixed in the short run, and changes in money or credit supply would spill over into the balance of payments, as in the International Monetary Fund financial programming models discussed in section 8.4. The IMF in fact follows what is usually called the monetarist approach to the balance of payments, and our determination of the price level here by *internal* monetary conditions would be considered heretical (but perhaps acceptable to monetarists if current account foreign transactions are assumed constricted by protection). Be that as it may, we are after a structuralist story under circumstances where money creation *may* be inflationary in any case.

With the price allowed to vary, it is reasonable to assume that it will increase when there is an excess *supply* of loans in (8.9), in a case of financial credit chasing producer's goods. With a pegged nominal exchange rate at any point in time, this adjustment amounts to postulating that the real exchange $q = e/P$ will rise with loan excess *demand*. The process will be locally stable when $\Theta > 0$, or some share of investment demand is satisfied with goods produced at home.[5]

Suppose that loan supply ϕ goes up with the slower crawl. Then the alternative adjustment mechanisms would lead to either lower interest rates and faster growth, or rapid price increases and exchange appreciation (lower q) after the policy shift. Alternatively, if loan supply goes down, the outcome could be high interest rates and investment stagnation, but a drop in inflation and real devaluation (with a consequent push to exports). Depending on interest rate restrictions, market dynamics, and other considerations, a combination of interest rate and price response could of course happen. By and large, the symptoms of credit expansion were observed during stabilization attempts in Argentina, Uruguay, Israel, and Spain in the late 1970s, but the reverse was true for Chile.

8.2 Dynamics of Exchange Adjustment

To tell a fully dynamic story about changes in foreign exchange holdings and the inflation rate over time, we have to settle on one of the two short-term adjustments just discussed—interest rate or price level variation. The analytics is easier and exchange rate dynamics more interesting with the latter, so assume that the price level (or real exchange rate) varies to assure loan market equilibrium in (8.9), while the interest rate is held constant by bank regulation. The capital stock growth rate g is supposed fixed for the moment, from singularly stable investment demand. Finally, the national component of the money base is ignored. In table 8.1 F is set to zero and the central bank's only assets are foreign reserves eR. Similarly, the term (F/P) disappears in (8.9).[6]

The second model closure in section 7.3 now comes into play since it shows how b (the trade deficit divided by the capital stock) is determined by g and the real exchange rate q. This information is of interest since total foreign assets held by the central bank or the public can only change from the trade account:

$$\frac{dV}{dt} = -bK$$

It was noted in connection with (7.16) that b is proportional to g in the model at hand. Set $b = \eta g$ and substitute in the above equation to get:

$$\frac{dV}{dt} = - \eta g K \qquad (8.10)$$

where

$$\eta = P_i^*(1 - \Theta) + \frac{\Theta[(P_0^* a_0 - \epsilon_1 P^*)q - \epsilon_0]}{q[s(1 - \omega b - q P_0^* a_0) + q(P_0^* a_0 - \epsilon_1 P^*) - \epsilon_0]}$$

This expression is dreadful enough to leave out of the following discussion, but do recall our foreign trade optimists' assumption that real devaluation helps the current account, or $\partial \eta / \partial q < 0$. This hypothesis is important since from the loan market balance (8.9), an increase in V lowers q. But then η will rise, and from (8.10) $dV/dt < 0$. Foreign assets demonstrate a stable adjustment around an equilibrium point.

The next step, routine in the circumstances, is to assume that the economy is initially in a steady state, $\hat{V} = \hat{K} = g$. Putting this condition together with (8.9) and (8.10) gives an expression in the real exchange rate,

$$-q\phi\eta = \alpha[\Theta + P_i^*(1 - \Theta)q]g \qquad (8.11)$$

which determines a $\bar{q}$ consistent with steady state. The minus sign on the left side implies that $\eta < 0$. Since the model omits foreign aid, emigrant remittances, and similar transfers from abroad, the only way the home country can maintain a growing money supply is to run a trade surplus.

Now add two more pretty incredible assumptions. First, expected inflation rates in the prices of commodities and gold (π and π_z) are static. Second, all agents really believe that the authorities will stick with their announced exchange rate crawl, so that $\pi_e = \hat{e}$ is given.

If $\hat{e}$ is reduced under these circumstances, the "normal" response in (8.9) is that ϕ should rise. Then the real exchange rate has to appreciate from (or drop below) its steady-state value $\bar{q}$ to maintain equilibrium in the loan market. Since $\partial\eta/\partial q < 0$, the trade surplus will diminish, and V/K will fall over time. The real exchange rate will gradually rise back toward $\bar{q}$, implying that price inflation $\hat{P}$ will be *slower* than the crawl rate $\hat{e}$. The dynamics are shown in figure 8.1. The "loan market" schedule in the

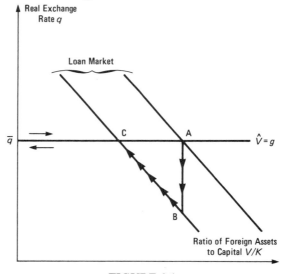

FIGURE 8.1

Adjustment of Foreign Asset Holdings to a More Slowly Crawling Peg under Static Expectations

NOTE: The supply of loans to firms rises when the crawl is slowed. When the policy shift is (credibly) announced, the real exchange rate jumps down from A to B, and than gradually rises from B to C as domestic inflation declines below the rate of crawl.

diagram corresponds to (8.9). The initial steady state is at point A, with the exchange rate $\bar{q}$ determined from the "$\hat{V} = g$" line corresponding to (8.11). A decline in the crawl rate $\hat{e}$ increases loan supply $\phi q V/K$. At the initially given level of V/K, the real exchange rate must shift down to maintain loan market equilibrium—q jumps from A to B as the loan market schedule adjusts. The trade deficit worsens, and q gradually rises back to $\bar{q}$ at point C, with a lower steady-state foreign exchange/capital ratio V/K.

To summarize, if everybody believes in it, a slower crawl will first kick off a price increase and real exchange appreciation, followed by a period of concomitant trade deficits, declining inflation, and persistent real devaluation, until a steady state is attained. In Argentine practice, at least, the first stage occurred, but citizens ceased to believe in the second-stage adjustment before it reached consummation. The Chilean mirror image—real devaluation followed by steady appreciation (mellowed for profit recipients by wage repression and unemployment)—may work better in practice, though it presupposes export optimism and (as shown shortly) unstable exchange dynamics in the long run.

Much the same occurs under other assumptions about expectation formation. For example, under fashionable rational expectations, $\pi_e = \hat{e}$, $\pi = \hat{P}$, and $\pi_z = \hat{P}_z$. If we ignore details of the gold market to keep the problem tractable, then we can look at dynamics in (8.9) with the arguments of ϕ restated as $i - \hat{e} + \hat{q}$, $\hat{q}$, and $\hat{P}_z - \hat{e} + \hat{q}$. These substitutions transform (8.9) into an implicit differential equation for $\hat{q}$ as a function of q, with $\hat{e}$ as a shift variable. In the case when a slower crawl boosts loan supply, the first partial derivative of ϕ will be positive and the second, negative (with absolute magnitude smaller than the first, from an assumption that assets are gross substitutes). An increase in $\hat{q}$ will drive up ϕ, and from (8.9) will reduce q. Inverting this relationship makes $\hat{q}$ a declining function of q, or (8.9) defines a locally stable adjustment process of adjustment for the real exchange rate.

The dynamics of adjustment for (V/K) and q are shown in figure 8.2.

FIGURE 8.2

Adjustment of Foreign Asset Holdings to a More Slowly Crawling Peg under Rational Expectations

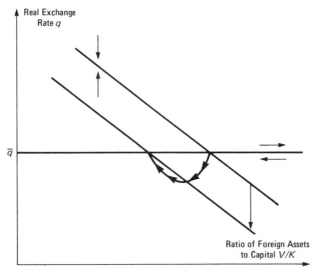

NOTE: The supply of loans to firms rises when the peg is slowed.

There could be oscillations, but if half-cycle convergence is assumed (as shown) there will be a spell of real exchange appreciation after the crawl is slowed, followed by depreciation back to the steady-state value $\bar{q}$ at which $\hat{q} = 0$. The country as a whole will shed foreign assets along the way, though central bank reserves may rise as individuals shift out of foreign exchange.

In the case where a slower crawl contracts loan supply, (8.9) makes $\hat{q}$ an increasing function of q. The outcome is saddlepoint dynamic instability, as shown in figure 8.3. All trajectories share rational expectations, but only

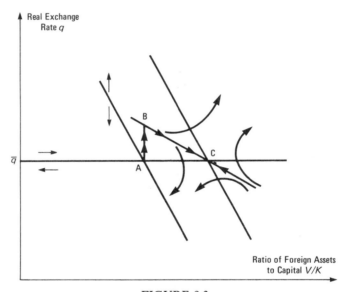

FIGURE 8.3

Adjustment of Foreign Asset Holdings to a More Slowly Crawling Peg under Rational Expectations When the Supply of Loans to Firms Rises

NOTE: The adjustment process demonstrates a saddlepoint instability. To reach the trajectory converging stably to C, the real exchange rate must jump from A to B immediately when the crawl is slowed.

the one linking points B and C converges to a steady state. The other paths diverge in a speculative bubble of some sort. If, after the crawl is slowed, the government, speculators, or the gods assure that the real rate jumps from A to B, then there will follow steady appreciation, trade surpluses, and convergence to point C in the long run. Otherwise, the clock just unwinds.

8.3 Extensions and Reality Checks

Like the analysis of chapter 6, figure 8.3 suggests that one should take long-run arguments involving formation of expectations with a grain of salt. Real people are always capable of changing their minds and mucking up the model makers' conceits. Even when they aren't supposed to be following acrobatic saddlepaths to steady state as in figure 8.3, sensible folk revise expectations in response to both economic and noneconomic information. Their changing opinions can substantially alter the policy regime. For example, politically powerful groups, such as Argentine exporters, found scant profits during the course of a stately real devaluation along the lines of figures 8.1 and 8.2. Use of an overvalued peso in an attempt to control inflation led inevitably to a squeeze on local industry. Capitalists revolted, there was a run on the peso, and a maxidevaluation was the final result. Monetarist rationalization of a slow crawling peg was faulty—it buckled under current account duress.

Besides these exchange rate effects, monetarist stabilization is prone to other ills. Working capital cost-push along the lines of chapters 5 and 6 could be added to the present analysis, with predictable but relevant results.[7] A more interesting twist can be based on the observation that in both Argentina and Uruguay a slower crawl was initially followed by an investment boom and a rapid approach to full employment. Thereafter, the economy went in a cyclical trough and recession accompanied the exporters' blues.[8]

The initial investment burst follows naturally from (7.15), where initial appreciation of the real exchange rate can be seen to lead to an increase in the profit rate $(1 - \omega z - qP_0^* a_0)$. Higher investment demand would be a natural consequence. Thereafter, profit squeeze along the lines of section 2.4 could set in, acting together with lagging exports to exacerbate a recession. The reader is encouraged to work out the details.

8.4 Real and Financial Programming

The final issue to be discussed in connection with the balance of payments is how the real hardhats go about their work of maintenance and repair. We refer, of course, to the operatives of the World Bank and International Monetary Fund, whose preferred tools are, respectively, the saving and trade gap equations (7.7) and (7.8), and the money supply decomposition

(8.1). Note that these equations are virtually accounting identities. Working with the simplest possible models is the professionals' stock in trade.

Most policy-related work with the balance or gap equations is based on using them independently to get alternative predictions of the trade deficit for a given rate of growth (or the other way round). The parameters in these computations are usually derived by a combination of guesswork and simple regression equations between such variables as intermediate imports and GDP. The regressions may be run over time spans of a very few years because those are the statistical degrees of freedom that the data permit.

If the two gaps or trade deficits come out about the same in the projections, then at least that bit of consistency is something to rely on. It can be tested by alternative specifications of input coefficients, saving rates (including that of the government, omitted for simplicity from the models here), capacity utilization, and the rate of capital stock growth. Evidently, (7.7) and (7.8) will yield determinate solutions for b and g. The question is whether these projections are consistent with available finance for the trade deficit, aspirations about growth and income distribution, anticipated changes in the real exchange rate, world prices, and the parameters. The equations are useful devices for organizing country experts' thoughts around these issues. The widely used RIMSIM, or Revised Minimum Standard Model of the World Bank (unfortunately undocumented in the academic literature), amounts to (7.7) and (7.8) programmed out in enormous national and capital payment (interest and amortization of loans) accounting detail. Its simulations often seem to call for cutting imports (and capacity utilization) or maintaining profits. But such results may not be surprising when coming from an institution that makes shibboleths of a virile balance of trade and fast growth.

The Fund and the central bank governors it monitors go through similar exercises on the basis of (8.1), but with conclusions even more predictable than those of planning ministers and the World Bank. The IMF model can be interpreted as an applied version of monetarist balance of payments theory (though chronologically it came well before the academic explosion of the 1970s) and as such is documented in the journals.[9]

Fund-style financial programming adds the familiar equation of exchange,

$$DV = PX \qquad (8.12)$$

to the accounting identity (8.1), slightly revised as:

$$eR + F + L_P = D \qquad (8.13)$$

in which L_P is total bank credit to the private sector. The other new symbol is V (redefined from last section), the velocity or turnover rate of money:

$$V = \frac{\text{Value of transactions}}{\text{Money stock}} = \frac{PX}{D}$$

In planning financial developments, an output projection (even the two gaps) will give X, and notions about cost-push or the Law of One Price give a number for P. Velocity is not supposed to change much from historical values; hence, one has a value for V. "Required" money supply follows directly from (8.12).

Now plug this value for D in the right side of (8.13). An improvement in the trade balance—the Fund's real concern—will show up as an increase in eR. How to accommodate this reserve increase within the projection for money demand? If credit to the private sector is maintained, then evidently bank credit to the government has to fall. If, for political reasons, it can't decline enough, then the public has to tighten its belt as well. Finance for working capital and investment is sacrificed to the projections for money demand and trade surplus.

A letter of intent from a country to the Fund (but more or less dictated by the latter) will contain specific limits on increases in F and L_P. Just to make sure that the trade balance gets better, a devaluation may be thrown in. And wage repression will help shift the income distribution toward capitalists, thus generating the saving that under the model's implicit assumption of stable capacity use will turn automatically into increased investment and growth.

As in all short descriptions, there is an element of caricature in what has just been said. The perceptive members of the Fund (and Bank) staff contribute more to policy than economic mystification based on accounting tricks. Nonetheless, the average mission falls well short of what might be desired. All the topics discussed in this book—contractionary devaluation, working-capital cost-push, unexpected asset market responses to exchange rate manipulation, interindustry transmission channels, and terms-of-trade changes—lead one to believe that trying to stabilize or regulate an economy by routine application of accounting identities is going to hurt more than it helps.

At least two problems arise with overly simplistic models. First, the formal analysis here suggests that orthodox policies all act the same way, and their simultaneous application amounts to overkill. A contractionary devaluation on top of stagflation from working-capital cost-push does not allow much room for keeping up investment, operating near full capacity, or reaching an equitable income distribution. Second, there are enough variables in the accounting equations to ensure that developments will never turn out as planned. The emphasis on different possible adjustment mechanisms in this chapter and elsewhere precisely underlines the uncertainty that policy makers always face.

Fund efforts at stabilization have not been remarkably successful—a point recognized even from within.[10] Less dogmatic and more elastic application of their accounting tools by staff members might help improve their performance in years to come.

9

Two-Sector Models of Inflation, Distribution, and Growth

THE MODELS of the last four chapters went into great detail regarding finance and the balance of payments but said nothing about how linkages between sectors may affect the pattern of economic growth. In this chapter, the emphasis switches to intersectoral complications, under the hypothesis that money and trade adjust to whatever happens in the real domestic economy. Postulating "passive money" under inflation has a long tradition in structuralist macroeconomics, and is adopted here to keep the discussion within bounds.[1] A foreign sector could be added to the chapter's two models without much difficulty, but again to keep things relatively simple this extension is left for the interested reader to pursue.

The first two sections are devoted to interactions between a food-producing sector and the rest of the economy, along the lines of chapter 3. In section 9.1, a model is set up to describe inflation resulting from conflicting claims to product between workers and profit recipients under conditions of lagging food supply. (The assumption of passive or accommodating monetary policy clearly underlies this approach.) Thereafter, section 9.2 contains an analysis of how food and nonfood sectors may expand together in the long run, as usual interpreted as a constant growth steady state.

The second model has two sectors with markup pricing and excess capacity, as opposed to the agriculture/nonagriculture dual system in which food price adjusts to clear its market. Demands for "wage" and "luxury" goods differ between classes, and the key question is how policies aimed at changing the income distribution would affect patterns of intersectoral resource allocation and growth. The short-run model appears in section 9.3, and the growth story follows in section 9.4, where it is shown that the growth rate can move either up or down after redistribution.

9.1 Inflation from Lagging Food Supply

As in chapter 3, suppose that there are two sectors in the economy, agriculture and nonagriculture. We are interested in how inflationary processes can be set off from lagging food supply. To that end, the price P_a for the agricultural sector is assumed to rise when there is excess demand:

$$\hat{P}_a = \mathbf{B}_a [P_a (X_a^d - X_a)] \tag{9.1}$$

where X_a^d is the current level of demand for food, X_a is supply, and $\mathbf{B}_a$ is a constant describing speed of adjustment. Equation (9.1) says that the food price responds to the *value* of excess demand $P_a (X_a^d - X_a)$—little would change in the analysis if it were assumed to respond to demand volume $X_a^d - X_a$ instead. Finally, food supply X_a is assumed fixed, as in chapter 3.

The price P_n in the nonagriculture sector is determined by a markup

$$P_n = (1 + \tau) w b_n \tag{9.2}$$

where τ is the markup rate, w the money wage, and b_n the labor-output ratio. There is spare capacity, and output X_n rises to meet excess demand:

$$\hat{X}_n = \mathbf{B}_n [P_n (X_n^d - X_n)] \tag{9.3}$$

Again, the demand level X_n^d follows from aggregate income and prices.

And, as usual, the difference between investment and saving $(I - S)$ is equal to the sum of excess demands in the economy:

$$I - S = P_a(X_a^d - X_a) + P_n(X_n^d - X_n) \qquad (9.4)$$

The key factor in inflation dynamics is the response of wage-earners to a fall in real income caused by a rise in food prices. For rigor, their real purchasing power should be defined in terms of the true cost of living index associated with the utility function underlying their demand equations for food and nonfood.[2] For present purposes such sophistication is pretentious; we simply assume that workers react to a price index of P of the form:

$$P = P_a{}^\alpha P_n{}^{1-\alpha} \qquad (9.5)$$

The weighting parameter α is usually taken as the food share in the consumption budget in some base year.

To make use of (9.5), add a definition of the agriculture/nonagriculture terms of trade ϕ:

$$\phi = \frac{P_a}{P_n} \qquad (9.6)$$

Then if the real wage is defined as $\omega = w/P$, it is easy to show that

$$\omega = [\phi^\alpha(1 + \tau)b_n]^{-1} \qquad (9.7)$$

In words, the real wage is a decreasing function of the terms of trade ϕ, the markup rate τ, and the labor-output ratio (inverse of productivity) b_n.

The next step is to build this trade-off between the real wage and terms of trade into a model of inflation when claims to food output exceed the available supply. The approach here differs somewhat from the profit-squeeze dynamics of chapters 2 and 6, which amount to a fairly complex (though realistic) theory of how worker-capitalist conflict can underlie a cyclical approach to steady-state growth under inflationary conditions. Here the emphasis is on inflation resulting from workers' attempts to maintain their real consumption standards when food is a major component of their expenditure basket. The appropriate hypothesis is that if the real wage falls below some target level ω^*, then workers push for increases in the only price over which they have any influence, the money wage. But from (9.7) the real wage target ω^*, can be used to define a target terms of trade, ϕ^*.

Hence, the equation for changes in the money wage becomes:

$$\hat{w} = \hat{P}_n = B_w(\phi - \phi^*) \qquad (9.8)$$

where price inflation $\hat{P}_n$ follows from (9.2). This equation asserts that wage
and price inflation are more severe when the terms of trade shift in favor
of agriculture. For many developing countries, (9.8) appears to be an accu-
rate rule.[3] Putting it together with the rest of the model leads to an expression for the change in the terms of trade, $\hat{\phi} = \hat{P}_a - \hat{P}_n$:

$$\hat{\phi} = B_a[(I - S) - P_n(X_n^d - X_n)] - B_w(\phi - \phi^*) \qquad (9.9)$$

The inflationary process can easily be illustrated as in figure 9.1. The
"$I - S$" schedule shows levels of output X_n and terms of trade ϕ consistent
with macro equilibrium in which $I - S = 0$ in (9.4). At a given level of
ϕ, investment exceeds saving below this line (under the standard stability
condition that an increase in X_n stimulates saving supply more strongly
than investment demand). Similarly, the "$\hat{X}_n = 0$" locus shows equilibrium
in the nonagricultural market. From the discussion in chapter 3, this curve
can slope either way and demonstrates a low income elasticity for food
demand in figure 9.1. As the arrows show, output X_n falls when supply

FIGURE 9.1

*Determination of the Equilibrium Nonagricultural Output Level and Terms of
Trade in a Model Where Inflationary Pressure Arises from a Low Real Wage*

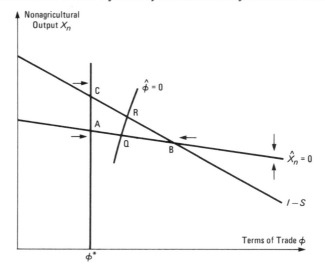

exceeds demand above the market equilibrium line. Finally, the vertical line at ϕ^* indicates the level of terms of trade at which there is no wage inflation.

The next step is to characterize the locus "$\hat{\phi} = 0$," along which the terms of trade stay constant. To begin, suppose the economy is at point A, where $\phi = \phi^*$ and $X_n^d = X_n$. However, investment exceeds saving, so that from (9.9), the terms of trade will rise (as illustrated by the arrow). At B, by contrast, $\hat{\phi} < 0$ since investment equals saving and the nonagricultural market is in equilibrium, but $\phi > \phi^*$.

With opposite directions of motion for ϕ established at A and B, it is easy to imagine moving along the line between them to some intermediate point Q at which $\hat{\phi} = 0$. Here the wage push from high terms of trade is just offset by excess demand for food and ϕ stays constant.

Much the same analysis can be applied along the "$I - S$" locus to get another stationary point for ϕ. At C, ϕ is rising since there is excess food demand (which follows from (9.4), where $I - S = 0$ and there is excess nonagricultural supply). Hence, there will be a point R between B and C at which ϕ is constant. Connecting Q and R is the curve "$\hat{\phi} = 0$" for stable terms of trade. To its left ϕ rises and to its right ϕ falls.[4]

Given this adjustment dynamics, it is clear that there is a stable equilibrium at Q, with the nonagricultural commodity market in balance and unchanging terms of trade. However, as argued above, there will be excess food demand, and from (9.1) the food price P_a will rise at a constant rate. Given the constant terms of trade, w and P_n will increase at the same speed as well.

The model thus generates persistent inflation. Of course, if workers were willing to accept a lower target wage, the rate of price increase would be reduced. In figure 9.1 ϕ^* would rise and Q would shift to the right, lowering excess demand. For typical levels of living in poor countries, such meekness on the part of labor is improbable, unless imposed. Without wage repression, a more promising policy is to increase food supply. The impact would be to shift the "$I - S$" locus down and B to the left. Point Q would also shift left, lowering the rate of wage inflation. Extra food could come from imports or (better) more efficient agriculture. Land reform has often been proposed to this end.[5]

Finally, note that the present model at best applies to the short run since it generates persistent macro disequilibrium. In any functioning economy, the observed market responses would be reductions in food stocks and queues. The latter might persist, but stock reduction, imports, and similar adjustments guarantee that the national accounts will never register an item for "excess demand." If only for this trite statistical reason, the model would be difficult to fit to data. In practice one would have to assume that the food price responds much more rapidly to excess demand than does the money wage to shortfalls of the real wage below its target. In symbols, B_a would be much larger than B_w and the stable inflation point Q would be close to the macro equilibrium B in figure 9.1. Having gone this far, it is simpler to assume that the food price varies to clear the market in the very short run (say a period of days), while wage inflation persists until the real income shortfall is closed, as in (9.8). With a homogeneous model like the one developed in chapter 3, prices would also increase at the same rate as the wage. Long-run policies that may affect rates of both price and output increase are discussed in the following section.

9.2 Growth in an Economy with an Important Food Sector

To set out the details of growth in a food-producing economy, a precise description of short-run excess demand patterns in required. Since it is ready at hand, we use the model of sections 3.1 and 3.2 here. The two relevant equations are the investment-saving balance (3.8) and the market equilibrium condition for food (3.10). The nonagricultural output level X_n and the food price P_a are supposed to vary to assure both macro and food market equilibrium in the short run.

To study economic expansion, it is useful to rewrite these equations in terms of growth and profit rates. Let $g_n = I_n/K_n$ and $g_a = I_a/K_a$ be growth rates of capital stocks in the two sectors (where the investment levels I_n and I_a sum to I in (3.8)). Profit rates in the N-sector and A-sector, respectively, are:

$$r_n = \frac{\tau}{1 + \tau}\left(\frac{X_n}{K_n}\right)$$

and

$$r_a = \frac{P_a X_a}{P_n K_a} = \frac{P_a}{P_n}a = a\phi$$

In the definition of r_a the assumption that labor and capital incomes are not separated in agriculture is maintained, so that the profit rate can be determined on the basis of the total value of output $P_a X_a$. With a fixed output-capital ratio a in the food sector, r_a turns out to be proportional to the terms of trade ϕ. As we will see shortly, high agriculture profits and inflation go hand in hand.[6]

With this much notation set out, the investment-saving and food market balances can be written as:

$$\lambda g_a + g_n - \lambda r_a [s_a - (\epsilon/a)] - s_n r_n = 0 \qquad (9.10)$$

and

$$\frac{1 + \tau}{\tau} \alpha \gamma_n r_n + \lambda r_a \left[\frac{\Theta/K_a}{a} + \frac{\epsilon}{a} - (1 - \alpha \gamma_a) \right] = 0 \qquad (9.11)$$

Besides the N-sector markup rate τ, the parameters carried over to these equations from chapter 3 include α and Θ from the demand functions (3.4) and (3.5), and the consumption propensities γ_a and γ_n defined in connection with (3.3). Two new symbols are $\lambda = K_a/K_n$ and $\epsilon = E/K_a$. The first measures the relative size of the two sectors, while ϵ indicates the importance of agricultural exports relative to the sector's capital stock.

Equations (9.10) and (9.11) almost describe a tractable growth model, but two simplifications are still required. First note that if Θ is constant, then the ratio Θ/K_a will steadily decline as the economy expands. Since $\Theta > 0$ when food demand is income inelastic, a decreasing ratio of Θ to K_a means that Engel effects become less important as growth proceeds. On the other hand, a steady state can never be reached so long as Θ/K_a is changing. For that reason, it is simplest to set Θ to zero and assume that demands for both goods have unit income elasticities. This is standard practice in growth models. A more realistic alternative (which the reader might want to pursue) would be to assume that Θ grows at a constant rate to represent population pressure.

The second simplification is to set the two sectoral saving rates equal: $s_a = s_n = s$. This assumption is mostly adopted to shorten lengthy algebraic expressions and could be relaxed.

We first describe how the economy behaves in steady growth, and then briefly discuss stability. At the steady state, set $g_a = g_n = \bar{g}$. Then (9.10) and (9.11) can be solved to get the two sectoral profit rates as:

$$r_a = \frac{1 + \lambda}{\lambda} \frac{\alpha[1 + (1 - s)\tau]}{\Delta} \bar{g} \qquad (9.12)$$

and

$$r_n = (1 + \lambda)\frac{\tau[1 - \alpha(1 - s) - (\epsilon/a)]}{\Delta}\bar{g} \qquad (9.13)$$

where

$$\Delta = s(\tau + \alpha) - (\epsilon/a)[\alpha(1 + (1 - s)\tau) + s\tau] \qquad (9.14)$$

Note that r_a declines and r_n rises as λ (or K_a/K_n) goes up. A shift in capital stock toward agriculture lowers the profit rate there and raises returns in the nonagriculture sector. We will shortly specify an investment function that responds to a difference between the two profit rates strongly enough to drive them to equality. When $r_a = r_n = \bar{r}$ at steady state, the corresponding value of λ is given by:

$$\bar{\lambda} = \frac{\alpha[1 + (1 - s)\tau]}{\tau[1 + \alpha(1 - s) - (\epsilon/a)]} \qquad (9.15)$$

Contemplation (or differentiation) of (9.15) shows that the steady-state capital stock in agriculture will be relatively large when α is high (a large consumer budget share for food), ϵ/a is high (large agricultural exports), s is low and τ is high. Both supply and demand factors enter into the latter two results. Finally, $\bar{\lambda}$ is independent of the steady-state growth rate $\bar{g}$, though from (9.12) and (9.13) it is clear that profit rates increase along with growth.

The equilibrium is shown in diagrammatic form in figure 9.2. Its stability follows if we postulate that the agricultural growth rate is fixed at $\bar{g}$ from technical considerations—food supply is the limiting restriction on expansion of the economy. Under such circumstances, a plausible investment function for nonagriculture would take the form:

$$g_n = \bar{g} + z(r_n - r_a) \qquad (9.16)$$

N-sector entrepreneurs are assumed to aim for balanced expansion of their capital stock at rate $\bar{g}$ to maintain a normal level of capacity utilization. However, extra high profits r_n (relative to agricultural profits r_a) will stimulate investment demand.

The growth rate of the capital stock ratio is $\hat{\lambda} = g_a - g_n = \bar{g} - g_n$. Substitution from (9.16) gives the equation:

$$\hat{\lambda} = z(r_a - r_n) \qquad (9.17)$$

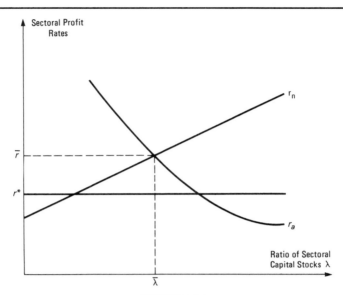

FIGURE 9.2

Determination of Steady-State Values of the Profit Rate r̄ and Capital Stock Ratio λ̄ for a Given Food Sector Growth Rate ḡ

NOTE: There will be wage inflation from low real purchasing power of workers when *r* lies above *r**.

to describe medium-run adjustment around the steady-state growth path. From figure 9.2, when λ exceeds the steady-state value λ̄, then $r_a < r_n$ and $\hat{\lambda} < 0$. Thus λ̄ represents a stable equilibrium. At an initial steady state, an increase in the agricultural budget share α, for example, will raise r_a and lower r_n from (9.12) and (9.13). From (9.16) investment demand will shift away from the N-sector until a new steady state with a higher value of λ̄ is reached.

Now consider inflation. From (9.8) money wages will increase so long as the current terms of trade φ lie above a critical value φ*. But since r_a is proportional to φ, there will also be inflation when the steady-state profit rate r̄ lies above some value *r**. Figure 9.2 depicts such a situation. To ask how the inflation problem might be resolved, it is useful to look at an explicit solution for r̄, as follows:

$$\bar{r} = \frac{\tau[1 - (\epsilon/a)] + \alpha}{\Delta}\bar{g} \qquad (9.18)$$

Note that when $\epsilon/a = 0$ (no food exports), then $\bar{r} = \bar{g}/s$. More generally, (9.18) is a standard formula for forced saving models, showing here that the profit rate must rise to generate additional saving when investment demand to support faster agricultural growth goes up. This result carries directly over to steady-state growth from the short-run models of chapter 2.

The lesson of (9.18) is that an increase in the saving rate s will permit a lower long-run profit rate and less inflation when the economy is limited by growth (and investment requirements) in one sector. Public sector investment financed by taxes on profits could do the trick. More rapid agricultural expansion, on the other hand, would worsen inflation by putting pressure on profits and the terms of trade. The profit rate would fall with faster food supply growth only if it came from an increase in agriculture's output-capital ratio when exports were positive. Under the circumstances, the export effort would be less costly in terms of domestic resources and inflation would drop off.

A final policy to be considered is reduction of the markup rate τ, for instance, from industrial price controls. From (9.7), any target real wage would be consistent with higher terms of trade, hence r^* in figure 9.2 would shift up. This change might or might not be offset by other macro impacts of a change in τ. In section 3.2, it was observed that the agricultural price P_a can respond either way to a higher markup in the short run. Differentiation of (9.18) shows that the same conclusion carries over to the steady-state profit rate. With high enough saving rates, a fall in τ will reduce $\bar{r}$. If agriculturalists and profit recipients save a lot, then a reduction in the markup that the latter receive will permit a lower profit rate and less inflation in a resource-limited long run. A plausible justification for urban price controls could be developed along these lines.

9.3 Effects of Income Redistribution in an Industrial Economy

Results of the same type as those just developed carry over into other models with one fixed-price and another flexible-price sector. For example, one can extend the analysis of internal and external diversification of the mineral exporting economy of chapter 3 in fairly straightforward fashion to the long run. This story is not pursued here to save space. Rather, the discussion in section 2.2 of the possible expansionary effects of income redistribution is extended to an economy with two sectors, respectively producing wage (subscript w) and profit recipients' (subscript p) goods.[7]

A system in which food or intermediate input shortages are not restrictive is assumed; hence, there is excess capacity and markup pricing in the two sectors according to the rules:

$$P_w = (1 + \tau_w)wb_w \tag{9.19}$$

and

$$P_p = (1 + \tau_p)wb_p \tag{9.20}$$

For simplicity, workers in both sectors are assumed to receive the same wage w. However, markup rates and labor-output ratios can differ. As discussed below, employment and distributional impacts of policy changes depend crucially on intersectoral variation in these parameters.

All wage income goes to consumption, while a proportion s of profits (from both sectors) is saved. Workers devote a fraction α_w of their consumption spending to the wage good and $(1 - \alpha_w)$ to the more luxurious commodity; profit recipients follow the same pattern but with a parameter α_p. The names of the sectors already imply that $\alpha_w > \alpha_p$. Finally, the P-sector is the only one to produce capital goods. The W-sector can be imagined as making food products, clothing, and so forth, while the P-sector provides cars, consumer and producer durables, and services catering to high-income tastes. (In a poor country, the latter would range from domestic servants to good restaurants to high tech health care supply.)

To set out balance equations, let λ now stand for the ratio of W-sector to P-sector capital ($\lambda = K_w/K_p$) and define sectoral profit rates as:

$$r_p = \frac{\tau_p}{1 + \tau_p} \frac{X_p}{K_p} \tag{9.21}$$

and

$$r_w = \frac{\tau_w}{1 + \tau_w} \frac{P_w}{P_p} \frac{X_w}{K_w} \tag{9.22}$$

The price ratio P_w/P_p in (9.22) is required to put profit rates on a common base. As discussed in chapter 4, one can always measure quantities of goods in such units as to set base year prices to one. We assume therefore that $P_w/P_p = 1$.

With this notation, one can immediately set down the saving-investment balance as

$$\lambda g_w + g_p - s(r_w\lambda + r_p) = 0 \tag{9.23}$$

where g_w and g_p are growth rates of capital stocks in the two sectors. The condition that excess demand for the wage good is equal to zero takes the form:

$$(1/\tau_w)[\alpha_w + \alpha_p(1 - s)\tau_w - (1 + \tau_w)]r_w\lambda$$
$$+ (1/\tau_p)[\alpha_w + \alpha_p(1 - s)\tau_p]r_p + (\alpha_w - \alpha_p)(T/P_pK_p) = 0 \qquad (9.24)$$

The last term introduces a tax/transfer policy variable that can be used to redistribute income. A nominal amount T is taken from profit recipients' *consumption* spending (as by a consumption tax) and transferred to wage-earners. The equation shows that as T rises in relation to the P-sector capital stock, then demand for wage goods will go up.

In the very short run, sectoral capital stocks are fixed and λ is predetermined. If, for simplicity, we assume that investment demand levels g_w and g_p are constant, then (9.23) and (9.24) can be solved for r_w and r_p. Sectoral outputs will, of course, be proportional to the profit rates, from (9.21) and (9.22). After the algebraic dust settles, the solutions turn out to be:

$$r_p = \frac{1}{1 + \Delta}\left[\frac{g_w\lambda + g_p}{s}\Delta - \xi\right] \qquad (9.25)$$

and

$$r_w = \frac{1}{\lambda(1 + \Delta)}\left[\frac{g_w\lambda + g_p}{s} + \xi\right] \qquad (9.26)$$

where

$$\Delta = \frac{\tau_p}{\alpha_w + \alpha_p(1 - s)\tau_p}\frac{(1 + \tau_w) - [\alpha_w + \alpha_p(1 - s)\tau_w]}{\tau_w} \qquad (9.27)$$

and

$$\xi = (\alpha_w - \alpha_p)(T/P_pK_p) \qquad (9.28)$$

The coefficient Δ amounts to a profit rate multiplier. For plausible values of the parameters, it will have a value close to (perhaps a fraction greater than) one. Equations (9.25) and (9.26) show that profit rates and output levels in both sectors respond to increased investment demand. When there is an income transfer from profit recipients to wage earners (an increase in

T and ξ), r_p will fall and r_w will rise. If L is total employment, one can write out an expression for its level as:

$$L = b_w K_w \frac{1 + \tau_w}{\tau_w} r_w + b_p K_p \frac{1 + \tau_p}{\tau_p} r_p$$

If b_w and K_w are small in comparison to b_p and K_p, it is clear that employment may fall as a consequence of an income transfer toward wage-earners.

During the 1970s many input-output calculations of possible impacts of redistribution on output patterns, employment, foreign exchange use, and so forth, were made using blown-up versions of the present model (with tens of sectors, classes of income recipients and so on). The results usually gave changes on the order of a percent or so in sectoral outputs in response, for example, to an income redistribution involving 5 or 10 percent of GNP. Employment sometimes fell in the experiments, basically as a consequence of a high service component in the consumption basket of the well-to-do.[8]

In retrospect, these "small" changes in the production structure after redistribution should not be too surprising. After all, they depend on differences in income elasticities and budget shares between classes, such as the ($\alpha_w - \alpha_p$) term in (9.28). For empirically estimated parameters, these differentials are usually quite small.

A more interesting question, which the empirical studies did not address, is how initial distributional realignments might cumulate into growth patterns in the longer run. An attempt at an answer requires specification of investment functions, as in the following section.

9.4 Income Distribution and Patterns of Growth

To take up the longer term impacts of redistribution, it makes sense to work with fairly general investment functions such as those specified in chapter 2. Following equation (2.7), investment demand by capitalists in the wage goods sector can be written as:

$$
\begin{aligned}
g_w &= z_{0w} + z_{1w} r_w + z_{2w}(X_w/K_w) \\
&= z_{0w} + \left[z_{1w} + z_{2w} \frac{1 + \tau_w}{\tau_w} \right] r_w \\
&= z_{0w} + \phi_w r_w
\end{aligned}
\tag{9.29}
$$

Here, z_{0w} is a base rate of growth for which entrepreneurs aim. They respond to higher profits with a coefficient z_{1w} and to capacity utilization according to z_{2w}. As noted with chapter 2, the capacity utilization effect amounts to an accelerator term in investment demand. Econometrics suggests that $z_{2w} > z_{1w}$.

Capitalists making luxury goods follow basically the same pattern; hence, their investment demand is:

$$g_p = z_{0p} + \left[z_{1p} + z_{2p} \frac{1 + \tau_p}{\tau_p} \right] r_p = z_{0p} + \phi_p r_p \qquad (9.30)$$

As it turns out, most of the action in the model depends on the difference between ϕ_w and ϕ_p, which empirically likely sectoral distinctions in markup rates (or shares of profits in value-added) will make nonzero even if all investment demand parameters are the same. To save space, we thus set $z_{0w} = z_{0p} = z_0$ in what follows.

It is easy to solve (9.29) and (9.30) for profit rates in terms of growth rates. Substitution into (9.25) and (9.26) then gives expressions for growth rates only:

$$g_w - z_0 = \frac{\phi_w}{(1 + \Delta)\lambda} \left(\frac{g_w \lambda + g_p}{s} + \xi \right) \qquad (9.31)$$

and

$$g_p - z_0 = \frac{\phi_p}{1 + \Delta} \left(\frac{g_w \lambda + g_p}{s} \Delta - \xi \right) \qquad (9.32)$$

Consider a steady state in which $g_w = g_p = \bar{g}$, and the transfer term ξ is equal to zero initially. Then it is easy to see from (9.31) and (9.32) that the value of the steady-state capital stock ratio is:

$$\bar{\lambda} = \frac{\phi_w}{\phi_p \Delta} \qquad (9.33)$$

Routine differentiation shows that $\bar{\lambda}$ will rise when α_w or α_p goes up, or s falls. These are the responses one might expect. The effects on $\bar{\lambda}$ due to changes in the markup rates are ambiguous since the investment parameters and Δ move in opposite directions.

Now suppose that ξ rises from zero as an income transfer is attempted.

Even at steady state, (9.31) and (9.32) form a nonlinear system in $\bar{g}$, $\bar{\lambda}$, and ξ. Resorting to total differentiation shows that $\bar{\lambda}$ will rise in response to an increase in ξ. Across steady states, a transfer from profit to wage incomes will shift the structure of production toward wage goods. This is a direct analog of the short-term result in the last section.

Regarding growth, the situation is more complex. One can show that the derivative of the steady-state growth rate is:

$$\frac{d\bar{g}}{d\xi} = \frac{\bar{g}\bar{\lambda}\phi_p\Delta}{z_0(1 + \bar{\lambda})(1 + \Delta)}\left(1 - \frac{\phi_p\Delta}{\phi_w}\right)$$

Clearly, $d\bar{g}/d\xi$ can have either sign. From (9.33) it will be negative when the existing steady-state capital stock ratio K_w/K_p is less than one. A relatively small W-sector (in these terms) will occur if Δ is larger than one and the investment response of P-sector captitalists to higher profits is as strong as the response of their colleagues in the W-sector. The implication is that an income transfer toward wage recipients will make the growth rate *fall.* Or, the other way round, policies aimed at worsening the income distribution might stimulate long-run growth.

Evidently, a serious empirical question is involved in these results. It was already noted in chapter 2 that Indian economists, in particular, have argued that stagnation can result from an unequal income distribution. By contrast, one can find Latin Americans asserting that deteriorating equity goes hand in hand with faster growth.[9] Cumulative processes of the type illustrated here clearly underlie these judgments, and it would be interesting to explore empirically whether they are valid or not. Unfortunately, this task would not be easy since specification and estimation of investment functions at a sectoral level is very hard to do.

The final matter to be discussed is stability of the steady state. Again setting ξ to zero for simplicity, one can solve (9.31) and (9.32) for the growth rates. Since $\hat{\lambda} = g_w - g_p$, substitution shows that the growth of the captial stock ratio (around an initial steady state) is

$$\hat{\lambda} = \frac{z_0}{\Gamma}\left\{\frac{\phi_w}{(1 + \Delta)s}[(1/\bar{\lambda}) + 1] - \frac{\phi_p\Delta}{(1 + \Delta)s}(1 + \bar{\lambda})\right\}$$

where

$$\Gamma = 1 - (1/s)\left(\frac{\Delta}{1 + \Delta}\phi_p + \frac{1}{1 + \Delta}\phi_w\right) \qquad (9.34)$$

is the determinant of the equation system. For stability, the derivative of $\hat{\lambda}$ with respect to $\bar{\lambda}$ must be negative. Such will be the case when Γ is positive. From (9.34) this condition requires that s—the saving response to profit rate increase—exceed a weighted average of the investment responses ϕ_w and ϕ_p. As usual in models without capacity limits, long-run macro stability occurs when savers respond more strongly than investors to profit rate shifts.

10

Trade Patterns and Southern Growth

THERE IS a long tradition of analysis in international trade theory that is based on the notion that countries are dissimilar—in particular, that developing economies in the "South" are shackled by trade patterns imposed by colonialism and their own lack of technical mastery when they were integrated into the world system in the nineteenth century. There are recent exceptions to this generalization—the large petroleum exporters and the so-called newly industrializing countries, or NICs. But by and large most underdeveloped countries remain in the position of being hewers of raw materials and drawers of oil for the industrialized world.[1] In this chapter, a simple formal model of such dependence in trade is presented. The key assumptions go as follows:

The industrialized countries of the "North" grow in Keynesian fashion, with excess capacity that can be reduced by brisker export sales to the South. Northern investment demand and saving supply both respond to the local rate of profit. When saving equals investment in macro equilibrium, the North's growth rate, profit rate, and output level are all determined. By contrast, investment and growth follow from available saving in the South, where output is constrained by supply conditions as opposed to demand in the North. Surplus labor fixes the South's real wage.

Consumption patterns differ in the two regions, but in the North the Engel elasticity for the South's export is less than one. The South is also dependent on the North for supply of its capital goods; that is, technology for production of commodities viable under the existing trade regime requires capital inputs traceable only to the North. The amount of Northern financial capital transferred to the South (that region's trade deficit) is assumed to be determined by political factors, and is fixed in the short run. (Alternately, capital flows responding positively to interest rate differences between the regions and negatively to their own volume, or "lender's risk," could be postulated without changing the model's basic results.)

Finally, there is a third region in the system selling an imported intermediate input to the North at a nominal price of its own choosing. Part of the proceeds from sales of the intermediate flow back to the North as export demand. A rise in this price is a stylized version of an oil shock.

All these assumptions go together to give conclusions that are very strong, viz

1. There are not enough degrees of freedom in the international system to allow the South to choose its own growth rate or terms of trade. Macro equilibrium is determined by saving and investment functions in the North, plus its determination of the magnitude of capital flows.
2. A productivity increase, or an oil shock by itself, will reduce aggregate demand in the North, leading to slower growth in both regions and a fall in the South's terms of trade. In the medium run, the nominal wage rate in the North might be expected to rise following either event, to restore aggregate demand. Any inflationary impact would be beneficial to the South.
3. Faster capital flows from North to South stimulate the latter's growth rate and terms of trade; however, the quantitative response may be small. Capital flows stimulate Northern capacity utilization and output growth. These responses follow from determination of output by aggregate demand in the North (the Hobson-Luxemburg theory of imperialism) and the role of surplus labor and capital inflows in shaping saving supply in the South.
4. Productivity increases in the South will reduce its terms of trade and growth rate so long as the North's Engel elasticity for consumption of Southern exports is less than one. Such impoverishing effects of technical change are often invoked in structuralist discussions of the terms of trade, as several authors have pointed out.[2]
5. In steady state, the Southern growth rate remains determined by the Northern rate, and the response coefficient is equal to one. A perturbation to steady state, such as an oil shock or a Northern productivity increase, will reduce the coefficient, so that Southern growth will lag. The South carries a major share of worldwide economic adjustment costs.

The reasons why these conclusions arise are singled out in the formal discussion, which begins in section 10.1 with a description of growth in the

North. Section 10.2 discusses growth in the South, and section 10.3 takes up interactions of the two regions in terms of the system's equations for excess demands. Section 10.4 is devoted to comparative dynamics, and section 10.5 concludes with a few additional observations and sketches directions for further research.

10.1 Growth in the North

The strategy will be to set up a model in which the North grows along lines sketched for the industrial economy in chapter 2, while surplus labor characterizes the South. In addition, the North purchases an intermediate imported input from a third party, "OPEC". The three countries are linked through trade and transfers and have their own behaviorally determined demand and supply patterns.

The natural way to describe the North is as a Keynesian economy in which firms are on their labor demand curve and labor can be hired as necessary at the current nominal wage (with workers drawing on knowledge that real wages have increased with productivity over time.) There is excess capacity and markup pricing according to the rule:

$$P_n = (1 + \tau)(w_n b_n + vm) \tag{10.1}$$

In this equation, the North's price P_n is determined by a markup over variable input costs. The markup rate is τ, and the inputs are labor and the imported intermediate—the wage is w_n, the labor-output ratio is b_n, the cost of the intermediate is v, and its input-output coefficient is m.

Income flows in the North come from wages and profits. If all wages are consumed and a share s_n of markup income is saved, then consumption demand from Northern incomes is:

$$[w_n b_n + (1 - s_n)\tau(w_n b_n + vm)]X_n = \gamma X_n$$

where X_n is the Northern output level. Total spending γX_n is devoted to purchases of Northern and Southern commodities. One key structuralist hypothesis is that the South's output has a low income, or Engel elasticity, in Northern markets. Following the model of chapter 3, the simplest way to capture this assumption formally is in the following expenditure equations:

$$\text{Spending on North's commodity} = (1 - B)\gamma X_n - \Theta P_s$$
$$\text{Spending on South's commodity} = B\gamma X_n + \Theta P_s$$

Here P_s is the price of the South's output. So long as the constant Θ is positive, the Engel elasticity for the South's commodity is less than one. The marginal propensity to spend on this commodity from total consumption in the North is B (and the propensity from output X_n is $B\gamma$). It is easy to verify that the sum of expenditures for the two goods is equal to γX_n.

Now we want to describe macroeconomic equilibrium in the North. Let the values of net exports to the South and OPEC be $P_n Z$ and $(1 - s_o)$ vmX_n, respectively. How real net exports to the South (Z) are determined is taken up later; OPEC is simply assumed to save a fraction s_o of its income vmX_n and redirect the balance to consumption imports of Northern goods. If the North's investment level is I_n, then its savings-investment balance takes the form:

$$(P_n - \gamma - vm)X_n + [vmX_n - P_nZ - (1 - s_o)vmX_n] = P_nI_n \quad (10.2)$$

The first term on the left of (10.2) is saving generated by Northern production, and the second term is the trade deficit. The two sources of saving sum to the value of investment, P_nI_n.

This expression can be simplified if we define r_n, the Northern profit rate on capital, as

$$r_n = \frac{P_nX_n - (w_nb_n + vm)X_n}{P_nK_n} = \frac{\tau}{1 + \tau}\frac{X_n}{K_n} = \frac{\tau}{1 + \tau}u \quad (10.3)$$

The interpretation of this string of equalities is the same as in chapter 2. Total profits are sales less costs, or the numerator in the expression after the first equality sign. As the volume of output X_n increases, then so do total profits and the rate of profit r_n on existing capital. The last equality shows that r_n is proportional to the output-capital ratio u.

Along with r_n and u, we define three other new symbols. The export to capital stock ratio Z/K_n is z; the share of intermediate imports in Northern variable cost $vm/(w_nb_n + vm)$ is ϕ; and the growth rate of Northern capital stock I_n/K_n is g_n. In this notation, the savings-investment balance (10.2) can be rewritten as:

$$(s_n + \tau^{-1}\phi s_o)r_n = z + g_n \quad (10.4)$$

Saving supply in the North is proportional to the profit rate r_n, with a coefficient determined by the North's saving rate s_n and net savings generated by imports from OPEC. The saving is used to finance growth of capital stock at rate g_n and also net exports to the South (measured relative to capital stock).

To determine macro equilibrium in the North, investment demand must balance with saving supply. If investment rises with the profit rate, then the demand function can take the form:

$$g_n = g_0 + hr_n \qquad (10.5)$$

Solving (10.4) and (10.5) together determines the growth and profit rates g_n and r_n. The resulting equilibrium will be stable under Keynesian output adjustment in the North if investment responds less strongly to the profit rate than saving, or $s_n + \tau^{-1}\phi s_o - h > 0$. A graphic presentation appears in the right-hand quadrants of figure 10.1. The northeast quadrant shows

FIGURE 10.1

Determination of Macroeconomic Equilibrium under Trade between the North and South

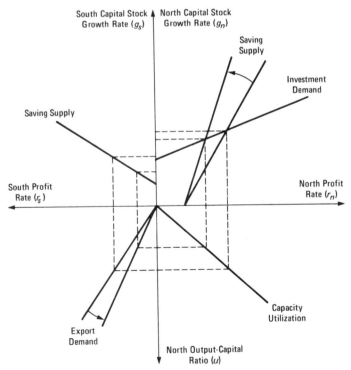

NOTE: The shifting schedules depict the response of the system to an "oil shock."

savings-investment equilibrium, and then the output-capital ratio u follows along the "Capacity utilization" schedule from the profit rate in the southeast quadrant.

Comparative statics are straightforward. We present three exercises here in preparation for later discussion. First, an increase in the price of the imported intermediate will raise ϕ, its share in variable cost. As imports become more costly to the North, potential saving goes up. From (10.4) the change takes the form of a rotation to the left of the savings schedule. The diagram shows that the Northern response to something like an oil shock will be slower growth, a lower profit rate, and less capacity utilization.

Second, ϕ will also rise when there is a reduction in the labor-output ratio b_n, that is, a productivity increase. Once again, there will be economic contraction. The cause this time is loss of jobs due to the productivity shift. In practice, one would expect increases in both productivity and the import price to be offset after a lag by a rise in the money wage w_n. The wage increase following a productivity gain is noninflationary and represents the normal way in which a capitalist economy responds to technical change. The increase after an oil shock of course adds to inflation but also stimulates aggregate demand. These dynamic responses are not our main concern here, but they illustrate the fact that the North possesses mechanisms to deal with deflationary shocks. The same is far less true of the South, as we will see.

Finally, consider an increase in the North's export surplus with the South, z. From (10.4) an upward shift in z slides the intercept of the saving schedule on the r_n-axis in figure 10.1 to the right. The outcome is faster growth, higher profits, and more capacity use. The Northern economy is stimulated by higher net exports, as stressed by John Hobson and Rosa Luxemburg long ago.[3]

10.2 Growth in the South

With its large subsistence sector, the South will have a labor supply function elastic to the real wage. Moreover, labor supply conditions will determine wages in the medium run, precisely because there is no history of rising real income to induce workers to be somewhat tolerant of employment lapses from time to time. To keep to simple formulations, we will assume that the South's real wage is constant in terms of its own product —there is an infinitely elastic labor supply.

To explore the implications of surplus labor, we must specify conditions of production in more detail. There are two key assumptions. First, capital scarcity is the rule in the South, so that there is full capacity utilization (as opposed to determination of output from the demand side in the North). That is, Southern output X_s is proportional to the capital stock, K_s:

$$X_s = aK_s \qquad (10.6)$$

The second assumption is that capital goods are imported. This polar case in effect amounts to saying that all capital takes the form of "machines" that are made only in the North. Our main results remain valid if part of capital ("construction") is Southern-made, but the algebra becomes cumbersome enough to be left out.

With a fixed real wage and capital valued at the Northern price P_n, the Southern profit rate r_s can be written as:

$$r_s = \frac{P_s X_s - P_s w_s b_s X_s}{P_n K_s} = \frac{P_s(1 - w_s b_s)a}{P_n} \qquad (10.7)$$

Here, w_s is the South's wage and b_s is its labor-output ratio.

Since real wages are fixed in terms of the South's product, it is natural to assume that all consumption demand from labor income is devoted to the home-produced good. Further suppose that profit recipients consume only imports. In our scheme of things, Southern capitalists (or landlords) form a "comprador" class living off local surplus extraction but focusing their demand pattern abroad. Equating the values of demand and supply for Southern output gives the equation:

$$(B\gamma X_n + \Theta P_s) + P_s w_s b_s X_s = P_s X_s \qquad (10.8)$$

The term in parentheses on the left of (10.8) is Northern demand for the South's exports, and the other term shows consumption from labor income. These two sources of demand exhaust the value of Southern output, $P_s X_s$. Equation (10.8) determines the South's price level (and its terms of trade P_s/P_n) from Northern aggregate demand, X_n. From (10.7) the South's profit rate becomes:

$$\begin{aligned} r_s &= \frac{(1 - w_s b_s)a}{(1 - w_s b_s)X_s - \Theta} \frac{B\gamma X_n}{P_n} \\ &= \frac{(1 - w_s b_s)X_s}{(1 - w_s b_s)X_s - \Theta} \frac{B\gamma u}{P_n}\lambda \qquad (10.9) \end{aligned}$$

where $\lambda = K_n/K_s$ is the ratio of capital stocks in the two regions.

Equation (10.9) is graphed as the "Export demand" schedule in the southwest quadrant of figure 10.1. The rightward rotation corresponds to an oil shock or a Northern productivity increase not offset by a wage change. The algebra becomes clear if we make the substitution:

$$\frac{\gamma}{P_n} = \frac{w_n b_n + (1 - s_n)\tau(w_n b_n + vm)}{(1 + \tau)(w_n b_n + vm)} \frac{(1 - \phi) + (1 - s_n)\tau}{1 + \tau}$$

into (10.9). A higher value of ϕ (the share of imports in Northern variable costs) reduces the slope of the schedule relating r_s to u. An increase in the Northern wage rate w_n following a rise in productivity or the price of oil will reduce ϕ and benefit the South. However, such a response in the North is always in danger of being cut off by anti-inflationary moves.

Perhaps surprisingly, an increase in Southern productivity also cuts back on the Southern profit level (and export terms of trade) for a given level of Northern capacity utilization u. This effect shows up algebraically in a positive derivative of the expressions for r_s in (10.9), with respect to the labor-output ratio b_s, when Θ is greater than zero. Inelastic Northern demand for the South's export leads to a fall in its profit rate when b_s declines due to a productivity gain. Adverse effects of technical progress on the South's terms of trade (and, as we shall see, growth) are a staple component of structuralist doctrine. They come out clearly from the demand conditions facing Southern exports in the model here.[4]

The final task is to determine the growth rate in the South. Sources of saving are from income of capitalists and the North's trade surplus $P_n Z$, which serves as a source of foreign saving for the rest of the world. We assume that only a fraction t of this capital inflow is in fact invested, the rest feeding into consumption imports from the North.[5] On these hypotheses, the South's saving-investment balance becomes:

$$s_s(1 - w_s b_s)P_s X_s + t P_n Z = P_n I_s$$

where I_s is the South's real investment level. Dividing this expression by $P_n K_s$ and substituting gives the relationship:

$$g_s = s_s r_s + t z \lambda \qquad (10.10)$$

where g_s is the growth rate of Southern capital stock (or I_s/K_s). This equation appears as the "Saving supply" curve in northwest quadrant of figure 10.1. It shows that Southern growth increases with the profit rate r_s and the Northern trade surplus z (though the quantitative importance of the latter is attenuated by the consumption leakage parameter t).

10.3 How the Regions Interact in the Short Run

To put the model together, observe that in equilibrium it reduces to three excess demand functions:

North Commodity Market

$$\frac{(1 - B)\gamma X_n}{P_n} - \frac{\Theta P_s}{P_n} + \frac{(1 - s_s)(1 - w_s b_s)P_s X_s}{P_n}$$
$$+ (1 - t)Z + \frac{(1 - s_o)vm X_n}{P_n} + I_n + I_s - X_n = 0 \quad (10.11)$$

South Commodity Market

$$\left(\frac{B\gamma X_n}{P_s} + \Theta \right) + w_s b_s X_s - X_s = 0 \quad (10.12)$$

South Saving Supply

$$s_s(1 - w_s b_s)P_s X_s + t P_n Z - P_n I_s = 0 \quad (10.13)$$

The market for the North's commodity is quantity-cleared; hence, the equilibrating variable is output X_n. The Southern commodity is sold in a price-clearing market, so that P_s (or the terms of trade P_s/P_n) adjusts. Finally, if the North's trade surplus (or the South's deficit) $P_n Z$ is fixed, then Southern investment I_s must be the endogenous variable in (10.13). Alternately, an independent investment function in the South would require the region's trade deficit to be endogenous. Essentially on political grounds, we rule this possibility out. The North determines its export surplus domestically (savings directed abroad cannot be used for public or private investment at home), and Southern investment accommodates to bring macro equilibrium about. An important aspect of dependence is the inability of a country to determine its own investment demand.

In equations (10.11)–(10.13), equilibrium is easy to find. Equation (10.12) makes P_s a function of X_n, so that from (10.13) I_s depends on X_n as well.

Substitution into (10.11) gives a solution. If the North's macro equilibrium is stable, then overall stability is assured when $(1 - w_s b_s)X_s - \Theta > 0$, that is, the South generates a surplus of product beyond its own worker's demand and the "floor" level of Northern imports, Θ.[6]

These equations also give rise to figure 10.1. The flow of causality in the model is clearly illustrated by the diagram. Macro equilibrium is determined by the North's saving and investment functions in the northeast quadrant. Northern output and capacity utilization follow in the southeast and determine real demand for the South's export. This demand determines the South's terms of trade and profit rate (the southwest quadrant), and its growth rate (the northwest quadrant). Growth in the South is ultimately determined only by what happens in the North and OPEC.

The main comparative static results that follow from figure 10.1 have already been derived, and can be summarized as follows:

1. When not offset by wage increases, Northern productivity growth or an oil shock will reduce growth and profit rates in the two regions, and the North's output-capital ratio will fall.
2. An increase in Northern net exports to the South raises output, growth, and the profit rate in the North. It also increases the South's terms of trade, profit rate, and growth rate, but the quantitative responses will depend on the North's marginal propensity to consume Southern goods (B) and the share of capital inflows to the South that is actually saved (t). Both parameters may be small.
3. A productivity increase in the South will reduce the region's terms of trade, profit rate, and growth.

Other exercises could be pursued, but these suffice to illustrate the short-run workings of the model. To close off the analysis, we turn to growth analysis in steady state.

10.4 Steady State

To illustrate how North and South grow together, it is simplest to impose balanced trade, or $z = 0$. Also, note from (10.9) that unless the North's floor level of consumption (Θ) increases over time, it becomes quantitatively unimportant in the determination of the profit rate r_s as X_s goes up. A time trend in Θ would probably be observed in the data (as is usually the case when the linear expenditure system is estimated econometrically), but for present purposes it is simplest to set Θ to zero, so that the Engel elasticity of demand for the South's commodity is equal to one. Under these assumptions we can solve (10.4) and (10.5) to get growth and profit rates in the North as:

$$g_n = \frac{(s_n + \tau^{-1}\phi s_o)g_0}{s_n + \tau^{-1}\phi s_o - h} \tag{10.14}$$

and

$$r_n = \frac{g_0}{s_n + \tau^{-1}\phi s_o - h} \tag{10.15}$$

From (10.9) and (10.3), the South's profit rate r_s is determined by r_n in the expression:

$$r_s = B\lambda[\tau^{-1}(1 - \phi) + (1 - s_n)]r_n \tag{10.16}$$

where it may be recalled that λ is the ratio of capital stocks, K_n/K_s. Finally, note that when there are no capital flows the growth rate in the South is given by:

$$g_s = s_s r_s = s_s B\lambda[\tau^{-1}(1 - \phi) + (1 - s_n)]r_n \tag{10.17}$$

The capital stock ratio λ is the variable that adjusts to generate steady states. It satisfies the simple differential equation:

$$\frac{d\lambda}{dt} = \lambda(g_n - g_s)$$

of the same general type as discussed in chapter 9. A steady state will be observed when the growth rates in North and South are equal, so that $d\lambda/dt = 0$. Such a growth path is locally stable since g_n is independent of λ, whereas g_s is an increasing function of λ from (10.17). Substitution shows that the standard stability condition is satisfied—$d\lambda/dt$ is a decreasing function of λ itself. For the geometry, look at figure 10.1, which is drawn with $g_n > g_s$. From this inequality, λ will increase, causing the South's schedule for export demand (southwest quadrant) and growth rate (northwest quadrant) to rotate clockwise. The Southern growth rate will increase until $g_s = g_n$ and the adjustment converges.

Equating g_n to g_s determines the steady-state value of λ as

$$\lambda^* = \frac{s_n + \tau^{-1}\phi s_o}{s_s B[\tau^{-1}(1 - \phi) + (1 - s_n)]} \tag{10.18}$$

With this expression in hand, it is easy to characterize the steady state. First insert (10.18) into (10.16) to get the South's steady-state profit rate:

$$r_s = \frac{s_n + \tau^{-1}\phi s_o}{s_s} r_n$$

The implication is that profit rates are not equalized. Rather, if the Northern saving rate s_n exceeds the Southern rate s_s, then the South's profit rate will be higher than the North's (even ignoring the saving generated from intermediate imports). This finding is generally in line with the stylized facts.

Second, from (10.4) and (10.17), the two growth rates are related as:

$$g_s = \frac{s_s B\lambda[\tau^{-1}(1 - \phi) + (1 - s_n)]}{s_n + \tau^{-1}\phi s_o} g_n \qquad (10.19)$$

When λ takes its steady state value λ^*, this expression reduces to $g_s = g_n$. But suppose that the steady state is perturbed by an oil shock or a Northern productivity gain. The import cost ratio ϕ will rise, and from figure 10.1 or equation (10.14), the Northern growth rate g_n will fall. Since the coefficient in (10.19) tying g_s to g_n declines as well, Southern growth is doubly hurt in the short run. In the longer run, (10.18) shows that the steady-state capital stock ratio λ^* must rise in response to the lag in Southern growth. The final outcome is a new steady state at a lower growth rate, but with the South having carried the brunt of the adjustment cost.

The conclusion is that growth in the North serves as a locomotive for the South—equation (10.19) assures that fact. However, the locomotive loses traction whenever Northern productivity or the real cost of intermediate imports goes up. Any time either event occurs, the coefficient relating g_s to g_n becomes less than one. Even in terms of growth rates, conjunctural perturbations help assure that parity between the two regions is indefinitely postponed.

10.5 Final Observations

The foregoing results are quite striking, and should serve as a useful purgative for anyone who is sanguine about benefits to the South from the international economic system as presently arranged. Moreover, the analysis can be extended along several lines.

Can the framework here be broadened to deal with other issues in the international order? One possibility is to consider dualities within the dual regions of the present model. In the North, for example, a number of writers have pointed to an emerging dichotomy between human service and environmentally oriented sectors with high income elasticities of demand on the one hand, and the more traditional industrial sectors on the other. Within the South, this same sort of industry is dual to the rural/agricultural sector in ways that are illustrated in chapters 3 and 9. Addition of another commodity to each country (nontraded services in the North, industry in the South) would permit discussion within something like the present model of such issues as to how sectoral polarities within each country are (or are not) mutually reinforced through the system of international trade. Exploration of such dualities has long been the stock in trade of dependency theorists; there is no reason why mainline economists shouldn't learn something from it as well.

Finally, both the present model and dependency theory reach strong conclusions about what is in store for the South. It is caught in a web of economic restrictions from which the exits are difficult and few. Realignment of export patterns to more "modern" products, reduction of the need for imported capital goods, elimination of surplus labor—these changes are as difficult as they are essential to a more equable alignment of international growth. The North will not willingly yield the upper hand. Internally oriented policy and great self-reliance might enable the South to seize it in the fullness of time.

Policy Lessons

TWO MAJOR THEMES emerge from the model-building exercises in the previous chapters. The first is of a long-run nature and reflects the diversity of countries that make up the Third World. Each economy confronts a special set of structural constraints on its possible evolution, and these restrictions vary greatly from place to place and time to time. Resource-rich countries face different problems than do resource-poor ones; equal and unequal income distributions give rise to different patterns of demand and possibilities for growth; the relative importance of the agricultural sector strongly influences inflationary pressures and formation of aggregate demand. No single set of intuitions or equations can capture all this variety, but country-specific models taking into account the salient features of the economy at hand can say something about its medium- and long-term prospects. The details appear in the rest of the book, but the lessons for policy are spelled out in nonmathematical language in sections 11.9 through 11.13.

The second major theme is that standard short-run stabilization tools can easily have undesirable effects in the Third World, again because there are important structural features of poor economies that the usual models omit. This point is argued in sections 11.1 through 11.8, where first the orthodox stabilization package is described and then its weaknesses pointed out. Some suggestions are offered about more reasonable approaches to stabilization, but panaceas do not exist. There is ample room for innovation in the short-term macro policy field.

11.1 Orthodox Stabilization Ploys

Imagine a country facing balance of payments difficulties, accelerating inflation, and blatant mismanagement in key sectors of its economy. The latter problems may include huge purchases of military equipment by generals and admirals who happen to be running the political show, insatiable greed and speculative binges on the part of their military and civilian counterparts in charge of public enterprises, or the destabilizing impact of rapidly growing demands for money wage increases on the part of workers pushing for immediate and massive income redistribution. Compound all this with sudden reluctance on the part of foreign commercial bankers to increase their lending and possible political pressures from the superpowers. What is the economic policy team supposed to do?

In most capitalist or mixed economies (and increasingly even in socialist ones) there is a standard set of remedies that tends to be applied, often through the intermediation of the International Monetary Fund. One can distinguish at least seven distinct policies that go into orthodox packages. The first three in the following list are almost always recommended, and the other four show up frequently as well:

1. Monetary contraction, usually due to the imposition of separate ceilings on credit from the banking system to the private sector and the central government.
2. Devaluation, either explicit or in disguised fashion through cuts in quotas, higher prior deposits for imports and subsidies for exports, and general tightening of trade restrictions. In-country economists may prefer the latter package of indirect measures, while the IMF typically presses for a devaluation up front.
3. Abolition or reduction of government intervention in the price system, for example, consumer food subsidies.
4. Internal financial reform and liberalization, in particular, attempts to raise interest rates.
5. External liberalization in the form of reduction of barriers to trade and capital flows. Again, there may be strong differences of opinion as to whether these will be useful policies, but the consensus among the staffs of the Fund and the World Bank and many academic consultants is that liberalization is a good thing.
6. With or without discrete devaluation, there may be advice to slow the *rate* at which the local currency is devalued over time in a crawling peg. The slower crawl is supposed to dampen expectations and be an anti-inflationary force.
7. Freezing of wage demands is often recommended to cut inflationary pressure and perhaps shift the income distribution toward high-saving profit recipients and the upper middle class.

How is a specific package fashioned from these elements likely to work? The whole will certainly differ from the sum of the parts, a point taken up in section 11.8. But first we have to look at the components, specifically monetary contraction in section 11.2, exchange rate changes in section 11.3, effects of intervention in food and other markets in section 11.4, interest rate reform in section 11.5, foreign capital markets and the crawling peg in section 11.6, and attempts at income redistribution in section 11.7.

11.2 Monetary Contraction

There are two justifications for monetary contraction, which get muddled in minds of practitioners of applied orthodoxy who jet out to the Third World. The first is based on the hoary equation of exchange from the quantity theory of money, which states that the value (price times quantity) of transactions in the economy is proportional to the money supply. If the quantity of transactions or output stays constant, then a smaller money stock ought to be associated with a lower price level. On this rationale, cutting the money supply or at least its growth is a key anti-inflationary move.

Open economy monetarism retains the hypotheses of the equation of exchange and stable output (or, effectively, full employment) but adds the notion that the price level is determined in the short to medium run either from competition of imported goods or from labor and intermediate import costs, that is, the levels of the wage and exchange rate. The IMF couples these assumptions with the balance sheet identity for the banking system —any rise in the money supply (the banks' main liability item) must be balanced by increases in loans to the government or private firms, or else by higher foreign exchange reserves (banks' loans and foreign exchange holdings are their principal assets). Monetary restriction takes the form of ceilings on credit to the government and private sector; the main benefits are supposed to come in the form of higher foreign reserves, *not* lower prices.

To apply the open economy monetarist model in detail, first make projections of output and the price level; then you have money demand. Put limits on government and private borrowing from the banking system. From the banks' balance sheets, the change in foreign reserves "must" be determined as a residual item. Or, in other words, if domestic borrowing from the banking system is restricted, then the balance of payments will improve.

This reasoning persuades many, and is certainly neat—causality runs crisply from monetary restraint to lower prices and better external balance.[1] Doubts can be raised, but necessarily center on inelegant details such as the likely effects of monetary contraction in practice.

One objection—put forth as often by conservative businessmen as by progressive economists—is that tight money drives up interest rates on loans to firms for working capital and investment, and thus increases costs. The normal business response would be to cut back on activity and attempt to pass increased costs through to higher prices. Even if aggregate demand falls under monetary constraint, aggregate supply may fall by more, so that excess demand for commodities (demand minus supply) goes up. Further inflationary pressure results.

The implication, argued in chapter 5, is that monetary restraint may be stagflationary in the short run, increasing prices and causing output contraction if interest rate cost-push is strong enough. The first monetarist model—less money means lower prices—becomes insecure. The second model—less money improves the foreign balance—goes through because output contraction reduces intermediate imports. Can trade improvement be made less burdensome? In the orthodox script, devaluation now plays a central role.

11.3 Devaluation—Real Effects

There is little room in the monetarist model for devaluation. The exchange rate may enter into import costs and the price level, but otherwise is singularly absent from the accounting. To give devaluation a macro role, two additional relationships have to be considered: internal balance or the saving gap, and external balance or the trade gap. Details appear throughout this volume, especially in chapter 7.

Internal balance says that investment demand must be met by saving from the government, private citizens, and foreigners. Foreign saving is equivalent to a current account deficit, with the corresponding capital account surplus representing an increase in foreigners' saving in the form of claims on "our" national wealth. External balance says that the current account deficit is equal to imports of intermediate, capital, and consumer goods plus interest payments less exports and net foreign remittances.[2] These balances represent two restrictions on the macro system—there have to be two corresponding endogenous variables. Candidates on the side of real magnitudes include investment demand (or output growth), the level of economic activity as a determinant of intermediate imports and national saving, and the current account deficit itself. Possible endogenous prices are the exchange rate and the aggregate price level (and implicitly the distribution of income if the money wage is fixed). Different models follow from different hypotheses regarding which variables are exogenous and which are endogenous. In analyzing short-run stabilization, it is reasonable to take the exchange rate as a policy variable and investment as fixed. The level of output, the current account deficit, and the internal price level become endogenous if the latter is determined by producers' markups over intermediate import and wage costs.[3]

Devaluation or an increase in the local currency to dollar exchange rate has several effects. Prices will rise within the economy as intermediate input costs are driven up, even if the money wage stays fixed. The real wage will fall, and the income distribution may shift from low-saving workers toward high-saving capitalists or markup income recipients.

A second increase in potential saving is from the trade deficit if (as usual) devaluation is the last resort when there is an unfavorable foreign balance. The rise in local currency prices of traded goods gives an income gain to exporters with one hand but extracts a loss from importers with the other. The loss exceeds the gain when there is a trade deficit, and real demand for national products falls. Equivalently, foreign saving goes up.

The outcome from higher potential saving is bound to be economic contraction coupled with a worsening income distribution unless export volume responds smartly to the higher exchange rate. There is trade balance improvement through reduced intermediate imports, but it comes at high social cost.

Despite these ill effects, orthodox stabilizers see devaluation unambiguously as a useful thing. The reason is that the rise in domestic value of exports is supposed to stimulate their production and sale abroad and offset the contraction (though not the price increase nor the real wage decline). Is this a likely event? Results differ from model to model, but in the simplest cases of chapters 2 and 7 it can be shown that devaluation will be expansionary when the elasticity of export volume with respect to the exchange rate exceeds the ratio of exports to intermediate imports. Note from the external balance relationship that intermediate imports + capital goods imports = exports + deficit if minor items are omitted from the accounting. The stylized fact is that the trade deficit or financial capital flow toward a developing country is likely to be *less* than its capital goods imports.[4] Hence, exports must exceed intermediate imports, and the export elasticity that guarantees expansionary devaluation can be less than one.

An export elasticity near one with respect to the exchange rate is reasonable in most countries, but only in a "medium" run of more than a few quarters. Before then the export response will be weak, and devaluation stagflationary. If monetary restraint is also stagflationary, there is ample possibility of excessive contraction, or what has been called "overkill" by the standard package. We return to this point in section 11.8.

11.4 Intersectoral Complications

The effects of any macro policy are complicated by the fact that in many developing countries distributional and price interactions between sectors are complex. The paradigm case is an agricultural (or food) sector for which the market is cleared by a varying price coupled with a nonagricultural sector in which output responds to demand. We can begin to understand this system by looking at how income effects influence consumer decisions.

In the market for food, an increase in nonagricultural output and income will raise demand. If supply is fixed or not very price elastic, the incipient demand increase will have to be cut back by a higher price. Since demand for food consumption is not elastic, the increase may be sharp.

In the market for nonagricultural products, things are harder to figure out. A rise in the agricultural price, on the one hand, will increase farmers' incomes and their demand for industrial products. By hypothesis, for a generally oligopolistic industrial/service sector, the demand increase will be met by increased supply.

On the other hand, an increase in food prices will reduce real income elsewhere in the economy (bread or rice becomes more expensive and your overall purchasing power falls), leading to less buying of nonagricultural products by nonagriculturalists. Hence, demand for nonfood products can either rise or fall with the food price. Consider the two possibilities in an economy where policy is suddenly redirected toward an increase in agricultural exports.[5]

Farmers' income would rise with the policy change; it cuts internal supply and drives up agricultural prices. If demand for nonagricultural products is dominated by rural income, there would be an export-induced boom. By contrast, if the initial real income loss in the nonagricultural sector is the dominant effect, demand for industrial products would fall and recession would result. In the first case, the food price increase is likely to be large since demand is price inelastic; in the second case, the real nonagricultural output loss could be serious. Agricultural exporters are perched on a knife-edge. Devaluation or other stimuli to exports do not ease their balancing act.

The same line of reasoning applies to cutting food subsidies, another orthodox policy move. Demand for food products will fall, leading to a decline in either imports or the internal producer's price (or both). There may be a spillover into demand for nonagricultural goods, leading to overall output contraction. Once again, a foreign balance improvement is obtained at the cost of reduced economic activity and a price-induced shift in the income distribution against the poor, who devote a large share of their spending to food.

These two examples plus others presented in section 3.2 show that the terms of trade between the agricultural and nonagricultural sectors are in principle highly sensitive to attempted policy changes. Given that food products make up a large share of total production and consumption activity in poor countries, the consequent shifts in income distribution and resource allocation could be expected to be large. In practice, violent responses are not frequently observed. The reason is that governments almost always intervene in food markets, separating and stabilizing consumer, producer, and import prices to try to maintain or at most marginally alter the status quo among the interest groups involved.[6]

This policy stance responds to the structure of a poor economy in which price formation and output responses vary significantly across sectors. This sort of problem is less serious in a more homogeneous developed country. Simple attempts to alter the terms of trade by shifting food subsidy rates or enacting agricultural export promotion schemes are bound to have general equilibrium effects that will call forth reaction on the part of groups that get hurt. In some circumstances, such policy changes might be sensible; they are just extremely difficult to apply.[7]

11.5 Mongering Financial Reform

Monetary contraction, devaluation, and tinkering with the commodity price system represent the first line of orthodox stabilization policy. Now we turn to more subtle moves, for example, a recent thrust toward financial reform. This policy change is discussed in detail in chapters 5 and 6, but the main conclusions are summarized here.

In practice, the reform package for internal finance is constructed around an attempt to raise interest rates. Rates in "official" money markets (especially on bank deposits) are often controlled in developing countries as a natural counterpart to central bank regulation of the banking system through credit restrictions as opposed to rediscounting and open-market operations. These latter, market-based interventions are infeasible when the local financial system is not highly articulated, as is the case in much of the Third World.

The fixed interest rates are often negative in real terms, that is, the nominal rate less the observed rate of inflation is less than zero. Negative real rates are common in advanced economies, but have been pointed to as a "distortion" ripe for liquidation in the Third World. The current rate of inflation provides a convenient benchmark against which to measure what the nominal interest rate "should" be.

What are higher interest rates supposed to achieve? One benefit, long term at best, would be increased use of the banking system and greater financial intermediation. More financial depth would permit open-market operations and other flexible regulation policies and undoubtedly is a goal to be pursued, but is not relevant in a stabilization context. What *is* relevant is the notion that interest rate increases will raise saving rates and available deposits in the banking system. If, as in neoclassical growth theory, the extra saving gets translated automatically into higher investment, the economy can be boosted painlessly onto a faster growth path.

It is argued in chapter 2 that the world probably does not operate neoclassically—an *ex ante* increase in saving is more likely to lead to economic contraction than a sudden investment spurt. Nonetheless, let us assume for discussion that saving does rise with increases in bank interest rates, but that investment demand is interest-sensitive as well. The question becomes: sensitive to *what* interest rates? In many countries, the relevant rates would appear to be the ones ruling in informal financial markets. Except for the largest, both industrial and agricultural firms have recourse to informal lenders instead of the banking system for their finance. Curb and village credit markets are often efficient and well tailored to the needs of small borrowers. Not surprisingly, the interest they charge is also quite high.

Now assume that bank deposit rates are increased, and in fact more deposits come in. What is their origin? One possibility is a reduction in informal lending, and a second is a drawing-down of hoards of gold, idle balances, and sales of real estate and similar goods. If the latter occurs, there will be a transfer from productively useless to useful assets. Bank lending can increase, investment demand be stimulated, and working-capital costs fall—all in all a favorable outcome.

The other story is more grim. If higher deposit rates induce moneylenders or their backers to pull resources out of informal markets and put them in banks, there can easily be an overall credit contraction because reserve requirements or credit ceilings in official institutions are bound to be more strict than those along the curb. The outcome could be working-capital cost-push and a decline in investment demand and the level of economic activity—stagflation once again. Under these circumstances, the increase in *ex ante* saving would only make things worse.

Which outcome is more likely can only be judged by informed observers in a specific country; broad generalizations are beside the point. The important conclusion is that the existing financial structure can frustrate simplistic attempts at reform by "getting the interest rate right." A second observation is that even if the policy is successful it will work only by getting the financial system tail to wag the capital formation dog. Directly stimulating investment and technical progress would be a straighter route to sustained economic growth.

11.6 Crawling Pegs and External Financial Reform

Besides revising interest rates, recent orthodoxy has focused its attention on the market in foreign assets and the role of the exchange rate in influencing portfolio choice. To set the stage, consider an economy where the authorities have been steadily devaluing the nominal exchange rate in a "crawling peg" at a rate more or less equal to the difference between the domestic and foreign rates of inflation.

Such policies were first introduced in Latin America in the 1960s. As discussed in chapter 8, their rationale was to keep the real return to export activities stable, and to preclude speculation against a maxidevaluation such as occurs in a fixed-rate exchange regime.[8]

More recently, a third justification for a crawling peg has been proposed. If the crawl is slower than the actual rate of inflation, it can dampen expectations and gradually direct the economy toward an equilibrium with stabler prices.

When crawling pegs were slowed in practice during the 1970s, the shift came as part of a package involving reduction of restrictions on both foreign trade *and* international capital flows. The results were unexpected.

First, foreign-held capital came streaming toward the domestic banking system, which at any time had to trade national currency for dollars at the ruling exchange rate. Slowing the speed at which the local exchange rate was raised in periodic minidevaluations reduced the short-term return to holding assets abroad, which can be written as foreign interest rate + expected depreciation of national currency − expected foreign inflation rate. So long as asset-holders continued to believe that the slower crawl would be followed, they had strong incentives to repatriate wealth held in dollars.

Second, the capital inflow led to substantial credit expansion by the banking system as new deposits were lent out. The jump in money and credit in the system led to a burst of inflation and instant appreciation or a fall in value of the real exchange rate (defined as the nominal rate divided by the national price level).

Third, there was an investment boom, easily explicable by euphoria in the capitalist system and the increase in the profit rate entailed by lower real import costs.

Now come the difficulties. After the initial exchange appreciation, there was supposed to be a period during which the real exchange rate gradually rose (or depreciated) toward a long-term level consistent with equilibrium in the balance of payments. The rate of change of the real rate is the speed at which the nominal rate is rising *minus* price inflation. If the real rate is to rise, inflation must run slower than the crawling peg. The whole system was expected to proceed to a low-inflation, steady-state equilibrium.

Of course, this intricate minuet never was properly danced. The initial investment boom was followed by wage pressure, a profit squeeze, and a cyclical downturn in standard market economy fashion.[9] More seriously, the lagging real exchange rate held down exports and led to unrest on the part of businessmen in the export sector. Not willing to wait for slow, real depreciation and return to external balance, they put their money abroad in speculation against the nominal exchange rate. Meanwhile, export stagnation worsened the internal recession. All signs pointed toward a maxidevaluation with consequent inflationary burst, output shock, and balance of trade improvement, and that finally occurred. An elegantly contrived long-term stabilization scheme ran afoul of the short-run facts of life.

What one learns from these failures is that it is perilous to trust in things working without hitches in the medium to long run. Trying to wave down inflation with a stable exchange rate presupposes that people with access to wealth will behave the way you want them to. Such an assumption is dangerous, doubly so when financial liberalization removes most obstacles to capital flows. Too much was attempted with the slower crawling pegs because the models underlying the policy were too simple and their architects paid scant heed to the historical failure of such policies before. The fiasco of stabilization based on a slower crawl strongly suggests that the model results be taken with a grain of salt, especially in the long run.

11.7 Income Redistribution and the Export Push

Usually, income distribution against labor and the poor is implicit in stabilization attempts. Wages may be frozen, food subsidies cut, and exports stimulated, all with benefit to landlords and rentiers.

Justifications for these policies are diverse: to increase saving and "therefore" investment and growth (the neoclassical growth model again); to contract "excessive" aggregate demand; to impose greater discipline on the system, and so on.[10]

Progressive economists have not been much more coherent in their judgments about possible effects of redistribution. One strand—ranging from the Franco-Italian Sismondi early last century to the Russian *narodniki* to modern Indian scholars—argue that an income distribution *toward* the poor will stimulate aggregate demand, lead to an investment increase through accelerator effects, and raise the economy to higher growth. Alternatively, the Latin American structuralist school in the 1950s and 1960s explicitly stated that income concentration might be necessary to stimulate demand for "luxuries" such as consumer durables, which would be the basis for economic expansion after an "easy" phase of import-substituting industrialization had passed.[11]

In the context of stabilization policy, these long-run models suggest that the income concentration associated with most stabilization efforts may dampen aggregate demand overall and at best stimulate only certain sectors of the economy. The stimulation may or may not feed back into higher investment and more economic animation after the stabilization episode is over.

One particular issue that comes up repeatedly in both short- and medium-run contexts is the possible effect of an export push. A number of factors have to be considered:

First, is the economy at full employment of available capacity? If so, an export effort will divert resources from either investment or consumption. If growth is maintained, there would have to be income concentration to lower the aggregate propensity to consume and permit greater sales abroad. If the economy is not at full capacity, then exports add to aggregate demand and permit higher output and growth. The discussion of devaluation in section 11.3 presupposes excess capacity, but recall from there that the beneficial output effects may take some time to appear.

Second, intersectoral redistribution may be important. Do saving and/or consumption propensities differ across income flows generated by export and nonexport sectors? One example in which demand-composition effects matter is in mineral-exporting economies. The export revenues usually accrue to the government, which preferentially demands nontraded goods. The outcome is a higher home goods price, a lower real exchange rate, and a lack of stimulation for production of nonmineral tradable goods at home.[12] Other less extreme models can also be produced, suggesting that an export drive sets off general equilibrium effects that are not easy to trace. Like attempts to get one or another price right, efforts at stimulating particular sectors or activities can easily go awry.[13]

Finally, the models in section 7.4 show that high interest payments can skew relationships between internal and external balance sufficiently to make export expansion contractionary when there is less than full capacity and can also create other paradoxes. In part these results are *curiosa,* but approach reality in countries that borrowed heavily during the 1970s.

11.8 Summing-Up on Stabilization

Table 11.1 presents in summary form the judgments one can reach about the effects of orthodox stabilization policies taken one by one. The results are decidedly a mixed bag. Moreover, it is easy to show with simulation models, such as the one in chapter 4, that often unfavorable effects are

TABLE 11.1
Likely Effects of Orthodox Stabilization Policies

	Maintain Output	Improve Balance of Payments	Reduce Inflation	Improve Income Distribution
Monetary contraction				
a. Working capital important	−	+	−	−
b. Otherwise	−	+	+	+
Devaluation	− initially + later	+	−	−
Commodity price reform (especially food)	−	+	+	−
Higher interest rates				
a. Draw resources from idle balances	+	?	+	?
b. Otherwise	−	?	−	?
Slower crawling peg	+ initially − later	+ initially − later	−	?
Export push (at excess capacity)	+	+	−	−

strengthened when two policies are applied simultaneously. For example, devaluation coupled with monetary contraction can, under certain circumstances, lead to extreme output loss, higher inflation, and income concentration in the short run.

A second point is that the policy effects can differ, depending on conditions under which they are applied. If working-capital costs are important, monetary contraction can drive up prices; if it pulls resources from productive loans to the banking system, an interest rate increase will be counterproductive. But in other situations both policies could work well. Orthodox programs implicitly postulate favorable circumstances. Less adventurous packages can be based on the recognition that things are not necessarily going to be all right.

All these complications exist in real economies and are not put forward to argue that stabilization is not important or not necessary in some cases. Rather the structuralist view emphasizes complexity and the need for wisdom and receptiveness to how the economy at hand seems to work. A structuralist stabilization package would no doubt include many of the policies listed in table 11.1. Not many others are known. But it would not apply them all in the usual directions, and would also incorporate distributional considerations and nonmarket interventions explicitly. The basic question at hand is how best to avoid the ill effects of standard policy tools and to forge new ones. Structuralists have much work to do in these directions.

11.9 Toward the Long Run

Many of the factors that condition long-run change in developing countries have already been touched upon. Nonetheless, their secular influence merits restatement and emphasis. The main topics discussed in previous chapters are the following:

1. The terms of trade between agriculture and industry or (not the same thing) traded and nontraded goods are less free to vary in some structural situations than others, with consequent effects on sectoral growth and income distribution.
2. The income distribution itself may affect patterns of commodity demand, and through induced sectoral investment the long-term growth prospects of the economy.
3. The rate of inflation, rate of growth, and income distribution all interact in complex fashion under different monetary growth rules and fiscal policy regimes.

4. Poor countries as a group may find their possibilities for autonomous development circumscribed by their dependent position in the international system.

These four issues are taken up in the following sections.

11.10 Terms of Trade

A fair policy question to ask is how long-term developments may be altered by adjustments in key relative prices in the economy, for example, between agriculture and industry or traded and nontraded goods. The models in this book suggest that prospects for such changes are not always favorable.

The traded/nontraded price ratio, for example, is a measure of the real exchange rate. If it is low, there will be little stimulation for production of tradable goods. Consider a mineral-exporting country as a case in point. In the long run, world financial market conditions place an upper bound on the ratio of its feasible trade deficit to GDP.[14] To find the country's import capacity, its mineral export total should be added to the deficit since, with a typically low cost of extraction and weak linkages to the rest of the economy, the mineral sector essentially is a conduit for foreign exchange transfers from the rest of the world to the home country.

Few economies resist the temptation to use up the transfer, through imports, internal inflation, and capacity adjustment. Absorption of a large volume of tradable goods requires their prices to be relatively low. The productive structure is skewed toward nontradables, and both agriculture and industry lag. Nonmineral exports stagnate under the low real exchange rate, and both internal and external diversification of the economy decline.

The lack of diversification is rooted in the transfer; agricultural monoexporters do not face the same problems, for example, because much of their export revenue takes the form of generation of domestic value-added. If a broadly based economy is taken as a policy goal, then one has to ask what tools a mineral exporter can use to achieve it.

A frontal assault on the low real exchange rate through nominal devaluation seems unlikely to succeed. Traded goods prices will initially rise, but the pressures to import remain. The usual outcome is that wages and nontraded prices go up *pari passu,* and the real exchange rate is not altered.

More subtle strategies are piecemeal and dispersed: an export subsidy in one sector, making another sector effectively nontraded through protection, trying to cut back on imports by curtailing mineral production, or putting the proceeds in long-term assets abroad. Whether such ploys can be effective is open to question—it is easy to point to mineral-exporting countries around the world that have never effectively diversified. Their real terms of trade between traded and nontraded goods remain low because of the structure of their situation.

Somewhat similar issues arise between agriculture and industry, where policy and custom separate internal prices in the food sector from those in the world market.[15] The agriculture/nonagriculture terms of trade are determined by internal supply-demand balance. A particular problem is that a lagging agricultural sector can drive up the terms of trade and thereby severely constrict demand for industrial products. Demand-creating policies will not be useful in such a situation since much of their effect will be dissipated in rising food prices.[16]

Here, the structural bottlenecks can only be broken by secular increases in agricultural supply, or demand shifts away from food. New production techniques may help on one front; urbanization on the other. But once again, existing technology and demand patterns strongly limit variation in the intersectoral terms of trade and resource allocation.

11.11 Income Distribution and Patterns of Growth

Additional terms-of-trade issues could be mentioned; for example, the discussion in chapter 3 of the risk of high food prices, industrial stagnation, and adjustment instability in agricultural mono-exporters. But it makes sense to shift focus and inquire as to long-term prospects in economies where supply restrictions are not of overriding importance. In particular, how do the income distribution and patterns of demand and growth interact?

As already mentioned in section 11.7, underconsumptionist theories have a long tradition on the left. The theme is that shifting the income distribution toward workers and the poor will raise demand in the short run and stimulate growth over a longer period. A more recent variation is that demand-composition effects may preclude this happy result.

Theory does not take one very far in narrowing down the possibilities. An investment-driven model is presented in chapter 9 to show that things can go either way. An income redistribution toward labor could raise the growth rate if the wage-goods sector is initially large enough and if its entrepreneurs respond to increased demand with an investment push. supply-oriented models cited in this chapter give similarly ambiguc sults.

These exercises suggest that the feasibility of effective redistribution coupled with growth depends crucially on the institutions and detailed characteristics of the economy. It is very difficult to say whether (and under what circumstances) progressive redistributive policies will work.[17] Here—as in suggesting truly innovative stabilization measures—we have an area where structuralism is weak. The lacunae are more of fact than theory, but that does not mean they should not be filled.

11.12 Inflation, Class Struggle, and Growth

Inflation as a macroeconomic phenomenon is poorly understood—one need only contemplate the profusion of theories to recognize the point. Structuralist models are not complete but at least provide a consistent framework for understanding the phenomenon. Three mechanisms are important. First, in many economic systems conflicting claims between classes to the available product get translated into steadily rising prices. The classic example is the attempt by workers to maintain living standards when there is lagging agricultural supply. Food prices go up, and they bid up money wages in consequence. The higher wages are passed along into higher output prices, and a cumulative inflationary process (described in chapter 9) is set up. Were workers willing to accept a lower standard of living, the inflation would not occur. But the same can be said of capitalists, the people who mark up rising money wages into higher prices. Inflation is a sign that a capitalist economy is trying to sweep class conflict over distribution of product under the rug.

The second mechanism hinges on the observation that class power to enforce claims depends on the economic situation—workers may well be more powerful when inflation is fast or employment high. The result in the medium run is the business cycle, and in the longer run a fair stability in the functional income distribution. The cyclical picture is as follows: an investment boom in the first instance shifts the income distribution toward capital through forced saving. But as employment rises or inflation speeds up, labor gains strength and forces an increase in the real wage. Profit rates fall, investment stagnates, and output growth declines. Wage claims then erode, the distribution shifts towards profits, and the stage is set for another upswing.

Third—and more specific to the models of chapter 6—conflicting claims
are worked out subject to given institutional rules. One common case is
lagged wage adjustment to inflation, perhaps a wage increase in response
to *past* inflation rates every second quarter or every year. Under this type
of wage indexation, an acceleration in inflation will reduce the real wage
averaged over the indexing period. In inflationary economy practice, rules
are bent according to the macro situation, as in the profit-squeeze mechanism just described. The main point is that the rules have forced saving
through a wage lag built into them.

To explore the implications of these inflation responses, we have to bring
in the financial side of the economy. Two possibilities present themselves,
as described in section 11.2. Short-run monetary expansion, for example,
may reduce prices by moderating interest rate cost-push, or it may not. In
the longer run, these outcomes can be assessed when there is an increased
growth rate of money supply. To do theory tractably, we start from a
postulated initial steady state (described more fully in chapter 6). Across
steady states, can increasing the money supply growth rate *reduce* the rate
of inflation?

Surprisingly, the answer to this question is yes: an initial acceleration in
money supply growth will lead, under rapidly adjusting (or "rational")
expectations, to an initially faster rate of inflation. Given lagged adjustment
of the money wage, the real wage consistent with indexing goes down.
Workers respond by being more aggressive in wage demands, and ultimately the actual real wage (or wage-price ratio) begins to rise. Saving
supply is squeezed and investment slows. The result is reduced demand
pressure on commodity markets and incipient decline in the rate of inflation. The ratio of money supply to value of output rises and, as a consequence, interest rates fall as well. Working-capital cost-push is reduced,
making room for higher real wages and a lower steady-state inflation rate
consistent with the indexing rules.

For this process to occur stably, investors have to be threatened enough
by increased wage demands to cut back aggregate demand and reduce
inflationary pressure; a profit-squeeze theory is involved in this sense. Second, the interest rate decline in response to a higher money/output ratio
must be strong enough to permit a higher steady-state real wage. If not, then
the second phase of the adjustment won't go through and faster money
growth will lead to more rapid inflation, as usually postulated.

This scenario (described fully in chapter 6) shows clear long-run "non-
neutrality" in the economy. Different money supply growth rates are
uniquely linked to different rates of price inflation and output growth—the

signs of the linkages depending on the strength of working-capital cost-push. The mechanisms are structural and plausible in a Third World institutional setting. Orthodox models that leave them out may be a poor basis for formulation of long-term monetary and growth policy.

11.13 Poor Countries in the World System

One final topic is the position of poor countries as a group in the international system. Aggregating all the Third World together is perilous—precisely the point of the previous discussion is that there is great structural diversity in underdevelopment. Nonetheless, for the grand view one has to work with grandly aggregated models. One such is presented in chapter 10. Following structuralist tradition, it tries to spell out the essential asymmetries in the international roles of rich and poor countries (or "North" and "South"), underlining the barriers that hinder the latter group's overall growth. The key assumptions go as follow:

1. The North grows in Keynesian fashion, with excess capacity that can be reduced by brisker export sales to the South. When saving equals investment in macro equilibrium, the North's growth rate, profit rate, and output level are all determined. By contrast, investment and growth follow from available saving in the South, where output is constrained by supply conditions as opposed to demand in the North. Surplus labor fixes the South's real wage.
2. Consumption patterns differ in the two regions, but in the North the Engel elasticity for the South's export is less than one. The South is also dependent on the North for supply of its capital goods. As discussed in section 11.3, the amount of Northern financial capital transferred to the South (that region's trade deficit) is likely to be less than the value of capital goods imports. The actual magnitude is assumed to be determined largely by political forces, and is fixed in the short run.
3. Finally, there is a third region in the system selling an imported intermediate input to the North at a nominal price of its own choosing. Part of the proceeds from sales of the intermediate flow back to the North as export demand. A rise in this price is of course a stylized version of an oil shock.

All these assumptions go together to give conclusions that are very strong:

1. There are not enough degrees of freedom in the international system to allow the South to choose its own growth rate or terms of trade. Macro equilibrium is determined by saving and investment functions in the North, plus its determination of the magnitude of capital flows.

2. A productivity increase or an oil shock by itself will reduce aggregate demand in the North, leading to slower growth in both regions and a fall in the South's terms of trade. In the medium run, the nominal wage rate in the North might be expected to rise following either event, to restore aggregate demand. Any inflationary impact would be beneficial to the South.

3. Faster capital flows from North to South stimulate the latter's growth rate and terms of trade; however, the quantitative response may be small. Capital flows stimulate Northern capacity utilization and output growth. These responses follow from determination of output by aggregate demand in the North, and the role of surplus labor and capital inflows in shaping saving supply in the South.

4. Productivity increases in the South will reduce its terms of trade and growth rate so long as the North's Engel elasticity for consumption of Southern exports is less than one. Such immiserizing effects of technical change have often been invoked in structuralist discussions of the terms of trade.

5. In steady state, the Southern growth rate remains determined by the Northern rate, and the response coefficient is equal to one. A perturbation to steady state such as an oil shock or a Northern productivity increase will reduce the coefficient, so that Southern growth will lag. The South carries a major share of worldwide economic adjustment costs.

The reasons why these conclusions arise are singled out in the formal discussion of chapter 10, but their implications for the South seem clear. Poor countries are caught in a web of economic restrictions from which the exits are difficult and few. Realignment of export patterns to more "modern" products, reduction of the need for imported capital goods, elimination of surplus labor—these changes are as difficult as they are essential to a more equable alignment of international growth. Autonomous development of the South may well require an inward-looking strategy delinked from Northern pressures to the maximum possible extent. South-South trade and relaxation of NIC restrictions on imports from their poorer neighbors would help greatly toward these ends. But in the final analysis, each country has to go it alone and make its own way out of the structural cage it is now within. The failure of the New International Economic Order negotiations of the 1970s showed how tightly Southern countries are bound. The successes will come only when they break their constraints.

Notes

Chapter 1

1. The terminology is due to Hicks (1974). For additional references, see chapter 3.
2. Commodities imported in "non-competitive" or "complementary" fashion cannot be produced domestically within a reasonable time period (for example, a year) or without unreasonable changes in existing techniques. "Competitive" imports are made up of commodities that are (or can easily be) produced at home.

Chapter 2

1. Good references on the microeconomic rationale for markup pricing are Sylos-Labini (1979) and Kalecki (1971a). A useful discussion is given by Lara-Resende (1979), while Ros (1980) provides econometric justification in the case of Mexico.
2. More detail on input-output accounting is given in chapter 4 and Taylor (1979). When intermediate input prices can vary, further complications are added to the adjustment process, as illustrated in chapter 3.
3. Public sector enterprises fit uneasily into standard accounting categories but generate a substantial cash flow. They are handled explicitly in an illuminating study of Brazil by Werneck (1980).
4. Or at least output variation is the main adjustment mechanism in Keynes's *General Theory* (1936). Previously, he had concentrated on forced saving type adjustments in the *Treatise on Money* (1930), as discussed below.
5. See Kaldor (1955). Forced saving is the main adjustment process in Keynes's *Treatise on Money* (1930), where its continual replenishment of profit flows is likened to the biblical parable of the widow's cruse. Lopes (1977) gives a nice synthesis of the arguments involved.
6. Note that in practice the government may serve as another important source of forced saving. If tax receipts rise along with the price level P but government spending is fixed by the budgetary process in nominal terms, then government saving will increase. This tax effect is present in countries like the United States, where income is withheld during the

year, but may work the other way in many developing countries where taxes on incomes earned in one year may not be collected until the middle of the next.

7. This quote is from a political economy analysis in the Indian newspaper, *Economic and Political Weekly* (Special Number, August 1978). The model in the text follows Dutt (1982).

8. Bitar (1979) is a standard economists' reference on the Allende period in Chile. His and other evidence shows that GDP rose by about 8 percent in 1971, Allende's first full year in the presidency. The major stimuli were income redistribution and higher aggregate demand. In 1972, limits on both foreign exchange and capacity were reached, and inflation (fed by full and unlagged wage indexation) accelerated rapidly. Needless to say, substantial internal and external political disruption abetted the inflationary process.

9. The notion that devaluation may lead to simultaneous price increases and economic contraction has appeared for many years in the literature. Early versions in English are Hirschman (1949) and Diaz-Alejandro (1963), and there are papers in Spanish and Portuguese as well. Cooper (1971a, b) provided both theoretical and empirical support for the idea, and discussed the fate of ministers who devalue. The formal model here is similar to that of Krugman and Taylor (1978).

10. Sylos-Labini (1979) argues that there are at most very weak linkages between markup rates and capacity utilization in industrial economies; Ros (1980) finds a *negative* relationship for Mexico.

11. For details on the CES function collected in one place, see Taylor (1979), Appendix D.

12. Another way of putting this result is that the present model is linearly homogeneous in P and w, so the price level will change by the same amount as the wage in percentage terms, and w/P must stay constant. Adding an additional input such as intermediate imports would permit the real wage to change when the money wage was modified (even when the price level is not pegged), but the effect on resource allocation would probably be weak. For algebra on this point see Taylor and Lysy (1979), who paraphrase the elegant argument in Keynes's *General Theory* (1936), chapter 19.

13. The whole argument in this chapter draws heavily on the literature about how different schools of economists close their models in different ways, consistent (usually) with their ideological stance. Sen (1963) is perhaps the first published paper on the topic, while Marglin (1983) gives it an illuminating and thorough treatment. Note also in passing that neoclassical full employment can be assured when there is an independent investment function if both saving and investment are sufficiently responsive to the rate of interest (introduced as an adjusting variable in the system, distinct from the rate of profit). Since interest rates presuppose the existence of money and other assets, their analysis is postponed to later chapters. In practice, private saving is not strongly affected by the interest rate in poor countries, and the classical "loanable funds" adjustment is a weak foundation upon which to construct a full employment general equilibrium. For evidence, see Giovannini (1982), who severely criticizes regression results by Fry (1980) that purport to show interest-responsiveness of saving in several Asian economies.

14. The radical story has its roots in the theory of the political business cycle put forth by Kalecki (1971b), though he argued that capitalists might induce a recession to discipline labor when there is full employment rather than have their own profits squeezed by workers' militancy. Current versions involving a profit squeeze are presented for the United States by Boddy and Crotty (1975) and for Britain in a longer time frame by Glyn and Sutcliffe (1972).

15. A complete, useful review of the American evidence is given by Weisskopf (1979).

16. Note the possibility that $L > \bar{L}$, at least for some period of time—actual employment can exceed the "normal" full employment level.

17. References on the stability of differential equations include Hirsch and Smale (1974) at a fairly rigorous level, Gandolfo (1980), who stresses economic applications, and many other texts. In this book, only local stability analysis based on the Routh-Hurwitz theorem is employed.

Chapter 3

1. Sections 9.1 and 9.2 in chapter 9 extend the model further to deal with questions of inflation and growth.
2. "Short run" in the context of the present model means a period of a year or less, during which farmers are not likely to switch their patterns of input use markedly in response to price or other signals. In the longer run, no one denies that farmers revise input and yield patterns under institutional circumstances that reduce risk and guarantee some security of tenure. Even so, total aggregate output from agriculture will depend on availability of capital, land, and technical change. In a relatively land-scarce economy, a production function specification like (3.2) makes sense.
3. For a version of the model with a class structure in agriculture, see Taylor (1982b).
4. For references on stability of differential equations, see note 17 of chapter 2.
5. For more on the instability of food prices, see the model for India in the following chapter.
6. Reasons why the Law of One Price is frequently violated are reviewed by Kravis and Lipsey (1977) and Isard (1977).
7. Chichilnisky (1981) gives one such model. In the present version, a full linear expenditure system (with another constant term for nonagricultural demand corresponding to Θ for agriculture) would permit existence of the unstable case in which the agricultural market schedule of figure 3.1 would have a negative slope and cut the nonagricultural market schedule from above. A rise in food exports would lead to a lower agricultural price in this case.
8. See Ellman (1975) for discussion of the Soviet first plan experience.
9. Models of the terms of trade between food and nonfood sectors along the lines developed here show up in various contexts throughout development economics. The behavior of the large general equilibrium model for South Korea proposed by Adelman and Robinson (1977) can be understood in terms of the simple model presented here. More interesting political economy appears in Mitra (1977) and in empirical models developed by deJanvry and Sadoulet (1983). Okun (1981) gives a lucid presentation of a developed country version of the model.
10. There is a large structuralist literature about mineral-exporting economies from both Latin American and Carribbean authors. See, for example, Girvan (1973), Brewster (1972) and Sunkel (1969). The present formal treatment closely follows Boutros-Ghali (1981).
11. There is usually a wage differential in favor of the mineral sector (perhaps created by the export companies to maintain a labor queue), which we ignore. For evidence regarding Jamaica on this matter, see Brewster (1968) and, more generally, Nankani (1979). The present model ignores the interesting policy question of what happens when the wage differential is reduced.
12. Or at least 5 percent was the mineral sector wage share in Chile in 1977, according to the input-output table.
13. It is worth noting that in many countries the production of U-sector products is likely to be in the hands of public enterprises, which often engage in transactions that are not rationed by price. If, however, the export sector is given priority when intermediates are in short supply, then most of the results that follow will still go through.
14. These useful terms are from Boutros-Ghali (1981).
15. A good historical review of such developments in non-Persian Gulf oil exporters is given by Gelb (1981).
16. Magee (1973) gives a good empirical description of the j-curve.
17. See Cooper (1971a) for statistics regarding the number of finance ministers who fell not long after effecting a devaluation.

Chapter 4

1. The work reported here draws heavily on joint research with Jørn Rattsø and Hiren Sarkar on contructing a macroeconomic model for India. A directly parallel effort for Mexico is being undertaken by the author with Bill Gibson and Nora Lustig. Models closely related to the present one are described in McCarthy and Taylor (1980) and Taylor (1979), while more distant cousins are scrutinized by Dervis, deMelo, and Robinson (1982).

2. Social accounting matrices derive ultimately from the work of Richard Stone at Cambridge University; see Stone (1966). Expositions of the usefulness of SAMs in developing countries are given by Pyatt and Thorbecke (1976), Pyatt and Roe (1977), and Taylor (1979).

3. Note in passing that the same sector can have both competitive imports and exports—this happenstance is due to aggregation of trade in many commodities over time and space.

4. The SAM in table 4.1 was constructed by a team at the National Council of Applied Economic Research in New Dehli; see Sarkar and Subba Rao (1981).

5. For applied detail in constructing social accounting matrices, see Pyatt and Roe (1977) or Eckaus, McCarthy and Mohie-eldin (1981).

6. For discussion of the RAS procedure (due like social accounting matrices to Richard Stone), see Bacharach (1970).

7. The original presentation of the linear expenditure system is by Stone (1954). A useful monograph is by Lluch, Powell, and Williams (1977).

8. The output iteration just described amounts to a Gauss-Seidel procedure for solving a closed Leontief model in which prices are fixed. Convergence will be rapid so long as "leakages" of income flows to saving (instead of consumer demand) are nonnegligible.

9. The reduced form excess demand equations for sectors one and two with the corresponding prices as endogenous variables are highly nonlinear; hence a fairly sophisticated algorithm must be used to find their solution. The solutions described here were obtained with an algorithm due to Powell (1970). It is no longer state-of-the-art, but has proved effective in several computable equilibrium models besides the one described here.

10. Taylor (1979) discusses the strengths and weaknesses of using SAMs in applied macro analysis in developing countries.

11. Taylor (1979), Appendix B, discusses "guesstimation" of LES parameters in applied models.

12. The Jacobian in table 4.5 is "exact." An algebraic representation of the Jacobian was obtained with the symbol-manipulation computer package MACSYMA at MIT; the numerical version followed from plugging in the base solution parameters and values of the variables from the SAM. The table 4.5 matrix does *not* include effects of wage indexation, rising markup rates, and foodstock speculation as discussed below.

13. In the numerical solutions, initial prices are set to one, while quantities are scaled around unity by figuring magnitude in units of one hundred billion rupees (instead of crores, or ten million, as in table 4.1). In practice, computable general equilibrium models seem to be easier to solve when all variables are normalized around one (or some other convenient order of magnitude).

14. A quick check shows that all 2×2, 3×3, and so forth, principal minors of the Jacobian have alternating signs—these determinants basically show whether or not groups of sectors taken in isolation show stable adjustments. Somewhat more complicated calculations show that all eigenvalues of the matrix are negative, as required for stability. Their values are -0.996, -0.834, -0.701, -0.574, and -0.052. The small magnitude of the last eigenvalue reflects potentially destabilizing feedbacks between sectors one and two, as described in the text.

15. The prices of the infrastructure services aggregated into sector four are fixed by the government; hence, the markup rate is held constant.

16. The Jacobian in table 4.5 underestimates price responsiveness because the inflationary feedbacks discussed here are not incorporated into its underlying equations. The price responses in the expanded model are substantially larger than the values shown in table 4.5.

17. As discussed in chapter 2, the local currency trade deficit can move either way after devaluation. It improves in the India model but deteriorates sharply in the companion model for Mexico described by Gibson, Lustig, and Taylor (1982).

18. For completeness figure 4.2 shows how procurement would have to fall to compensate for production decreases (points to the left of the base run.) Numerical results are not reported, however, since changes in the procurement are not a likely policy under such circumstances.

19. The extent to which the model needs smoothing depends on circumstances. In the Mexico model described by Gibson, Lustig, and Taylor (1982), for example, agricultural price fluctuations are much less brusque than those summarized here. The difference in behavior probably reflects the reduced role of the agricultural sector in the Mexican economy as compared to India's.

Chapter 5

1. The short-run model of stagflationary effects of monetary restriction presented here is a restatement and simplification of Taylor (1981a). The inspiration of that paper owes much to Bruno (1979) and especially van Wijnbergen (1983b). Three-asset models in which changes in the rate paid on bank deposits can reduce overall credit availability have been worked out by several authors, including Buffie (1983), van Wijnbergen (1983a), and Krugman (1981). Friedman (1978) presents similar notions in the context of the American economy.

2. Emphasis on working-capital costs goes back far in structuralist tradition. A good empirical study is by Morley (1971) for Brazil; see also Lara-Resende (1979) on the same country. The current emphasis stems from Cavallo (1977) and the formalization by Bruno (1979) and van Wijnbergen (1983b).

3. In practice, of course, some fraction of working capital will be financed by firms from current income flow—perusal of flow-of-funds data suggests that the self-financed portion may exceed one-half. Both the level and possible interest rate responsiveness of the self-finance ratio are ignored in the following discussion. The main point is that its value is well below one.

4. What may happen when the saving propensity from interest income exceeds zero is discussed in note 6 below.

5. This investment function is a variant on the "q" theory of Tobin (1961).

6. If $f < 1$ is the share of working-capital cost financed by banks and the informal credit market and $s_i > 0$ is the saving propensity from interest income, then the numerator of (5.8) should be rewritten as $[(s - h)(1 + i) - fs_i i]wab$. Its derivative will be positive when $s - fs_i - h > 0$. The results of the text will be unchanged if f and s_i are small enough fractions. In practice, they probably are.

7. See Atkinson (1975) and Thurow (1975) for the relevant data.

8. These particular balance sheets follow van Wijnbergen (1983b). Buffie (1983) uses another financial structure with similar results.

9. In practice, of course, financial markets are segmented with many interest rates and also quantity-clearing from queues, moneylenders' judgments, bankers' committees, and ministers' telephone calls. Using one interest rate is at best a pallid miniature of all this complexity. Regrettably, most of us can't paint like the Younger Brueghel.

10. The monetary contraction could take the form of a lower value of H in (5.11). Strictly speaking, there would have to be fiscal policy changes to permit H to vary over time, but we ignore this complication here. Alternately, the reserve ratio μ could be increased or (in any functioning economy) myriad other instruments could be deployed to induce monetary tightness.
11. See the references in note 2.
12. The quote is from Kapur (1976), which is more or less the approved formalization of the institutional and historical arguments presented by McKinnon (1973) and Shaw (1973). The general equilibrium asset market model used here of course follows in the tradition of Tobin (1975). Recent specific applications to poor countries include Krugman (1981), van Wijnbergen (1983a), and Buffie (1983), all of whom note that changes in the deposit interest rate can move total private sector credit either way.
13. Argentina in the late 1970s was perhaps the nearest thing to complete credit market liberalization. The results were disastrous but complicated by volatile capital flows in and out of the country. See chapter 8 for details.
14. To their credit, McKinnon, Shaw, and their disciples would also push for lower reserve requirements and loosening of credit restrictions to increase bank intermediation and the effectiveness of interest rate reform. But these policies would just look like monetary expansion in figure 5.1. Why bother with the deposit rate incantations?
15. Kindleberger (1978) gives a fascinating history of financial panics from destabilizing speculation.

Chapter 6

1. The growth model presented here has a fairly complicated history. A first version of the medium-run forced saving story of section 6.3 appeared in a 1976 first draft of Taylor (1979), following the institutional analysis of Georgescu-Roegan (1970). Cardoso (1979) added a monetary adjustment mechanism. The institutionally based wage adjustment is based on Bacha and Lopes (1983), with mathematical assistance from Sweder van Wijnbergen. Bacha and Lopes also extend the analysis to include the real balance or inflation tax effects that are part of orthodox monetary growth models. The possibility that faster money growth may slow inflation in steady states is pointed out by Sargent and Wallace (1981). Their mechanism is financial market crowding due to government demands for loans to finance the interest burden of its debt. Working-capital costs give rise to the "perverse" long-run effect of slower money growth in the present model. This channel has apparently not been noted before. Finally, for comparison of the wage dynamics adopted here with more orthodox Marxian model closures, Marglin (1983) is a useful source.
2. The need for such extreme assumptions about investors' perspicacity stems from the way $\hat{P}$ behaves in (6.1) and (6.2). Note that partial derivatives of both expressions with respect to $\hat{P}$ are positive, ruling out simple excess demand based adjustment hypotheses.
3. The loss of real purchasing power of fixed money wages in the face of inflation is an old Latin American notion—diagrams similar to figure 6.3 have been around the continent for decades. The present formalization follows Bacha and Lopes (1983).
4. Chilean labor contracts in the 1960s had their renegotiations spread over a quarter or two following legislation on government wage readjustments that could be passed anytime during the first few months of a new year. For details, see Cortazar (1983).
5. Econometric evidence for South Korea and Argentina comes from van Wijnbergen (1982) and Cavallo (1977), respectively.

Chapter 7

1. Factor income flows are omitted for the moment from (7.4)—repatriated profits from multinationals or interest on sovereign debt going out and emigrants' remittances or intergovernmental transfers coming in. These items are introduced in section 7.4.

2. A wrinkle on (7.5) is that all of the current account deficit (or capital inflows less reserve changes) may not be saved. Griffin (1970) and Weisskopf (1972) in influential papers both pointed out that B in (7.5) should be multiplied by a saving share $s_b < 1$. The foreign exchange inflows not saved would have to be consumed, adding a term $(1 - s_b)eB$ to the right-hand side of (7.3).

3. Evidence that $h > 0$ can be pieced together from such sources as the World Bank's *World Development Report* (1981).

4. When not all "capital inflows" are saved, as suggested by Griffin (1970) and Weisskopf (1972), then the saving parameter $s_b < 1$ will multiply q in the numerator of the expression for the internal balance slope. The distinction between the two balances becomes even stronger.

5. Early two-gap formulations are due to Chenery and Bruno (1962) and McKinnon (1964). The latter paper is the source for figure 7.1. The basic notion of "external strangulation" from lack of foreign exchange is due to the Latin structuralists; an early exposition in English is in chapter 9 of Hirschman (1958).

6. The neoclassical case is argued by Bhagwati (1966) and Findlay (1971). It is further discussed in connection with figure 7.5.

7. This interpretation of the two-gap hypothesis follows Bacha (1983).

8. The condition $\epsilon_0 < 0$ resembles Marshall-Lerner restrictions on elasticities in orthodox balance of payments theory. Dornbusch (1981) gives the canonical explanation.

9. We follow the usual confusing terminology about the exchange rate. *Depreciation* or *devaluation* refers to a rise in q, and *appreciation* to a fall. When q (or e) rises, then our country's real (or nominal) purchasing power abroad goes down; hence, the decline, depreciation, or devaluation of the local money's force.

10. Tricks for formally setting up such cumulative processes as mineral abundance giving rise to slow growth are presented in chapter 9. The obverse story is that a price shock to an oil importer is likely to reduce u but raise q. The resulting stimulus to domestic activity may accelerate growth in the long run.

11. In *nominal* terms, interest payments are a large component of the current account of countries that borrowed heavily in world capital markets during the 1970s, such as Mexico, South Korea, and Brazil. *Real* interest payments are substantially less (the extent depending on the price deflator subtracted from nominal interest rates to make them "real"), but still can amount to more than 10 or 20 percent of exports. In what follows, we implicitly work with a real interest rate i. For more on debt and interest problems, see Bacha and Diaz-Alejandro (1982).

12. For theoretical discussion of how credit rationing naturally arises in international capital markets, see Eaton and Gersovitz (1981) and Sachs (1982).

13. Condition (7.23) follows Bacha (1983). At a full capacity level of the output-capital ratio u, the quantity $iP_1^*(1 - \Theta)/u$ becomes a floor level on the export share ϵ. If its value of ϵ falls below the floor, a country is not likely to get access to foreign commercial loans.

14. For examples, see Michaely (1977) and Balassa (1978).

Chapter 8

1. The name *crawling peg* was proposed by Williamson (1965). Bacha (1979) gives an insightful review of the practical effects of a crawl.

2. Diaz-Alejandro (1981) gives an influential survey of the historical and institutional under-pinnings of responses in Latin economies to a slower crawl. Reviews of the Chilean and Argentinian cases are given by Ffrench-Davis and Arrellano (1982) and Frenkel (1982), respectively. The importance of economists who study real economies is emphasized by the large number of theoretical papers that these studies stimulated, for example, Buffie (1981), Calvo (1981), Krugman (1980), Dornbusch (1981), van Wijnbergen (1983c), and the present treatment, among many others. A related issue is switching by nationals between local currency and readily available dollars. This is an important policy issue in countries such as Egypt or Mexico; see Boutros-Ghali (1980) and Macedo (1983), or Solis and Rizzo (1982).

3. The details are a bit different, but the general approach in the following model comes from Krugman (1981).

4. As pointed out by Dornbusch, et al. (1982), currency outstanding from the United States Federal Reserve Bank is on the order of $500 per American. Even allowing for organized crime, a large proportion of these dollars must be held by private individuals outside the United States.

5. An excess of credit is nearly equivalent to an excess supply of money—if the latter drives up the price level, then so should the former as well. Note from table 8.1 that money supply $D^s = H/\mu$ while (ignoring loans for gold for simplicity) loan supply $L^s = (1 - \mu) H/\mu$. The simplest goods market clearing equation is $PI = sPX$, and loan demand $L^d = \alpha PI$ (ignoring imported capital goods). Then $L^s - L^d = (1 - \mu)H/\mu - PsX$ is excess supply of loans. But this expression is proportional to a typical equation for the excess supply of money of the form $D^s - kPX$ where $k = \alpha s/(1 - \mu)$ can be interpreted as an institutionally determined money demand parameter. The money and credit markets are almost mirror images of each other, especially in an economy with little financial depth, and one can model price pressures in one as well as the other.

6. This assumption precludes discussion of important questions regarding coordination of monetary and exchange rate policy; see Krugman (1981) and Dornbusch (1980) for various rules.

7. Van Wijnbergen (1983c) has an interesting model along these lines.

8. Buffie (1981) reviews this cyclical history in Argentina and Uruguay, and presents a model incorporating traded and nontraded goods and a Phillips curve.

9. The model by Polak (1957) enshrined the IMF approach—this is undoubtedly one of the most practically important macroeconomic papers written since the Second World War. The Fund's nitty-gritty is further displayed by Robichek (1975).

10. Reichman (1978) and Reichman and Stilson (1978) back up the assertions made here in official IMF publications. Buira (1983) presents a thoughtful synthesis of Fund experience.

Chapter 9

1. The label "passive money" and an interesting formalization appear in Olivera (1970).

2. See Deaton and Muellbauer (1980) for a good discussion of true cost-of-living indexes and other demand theory concepts.

3. See Ahluwalia (1979) for evidence on India, for example.

4. This elegant argument follows Cardoso (1981).

5. Land reform as a device to improve agricultural productivity and reduce inflation was at the key of the Latin America structuralist world view. The classic paper is Sunkel (1960). An early (and neat) formalization appears in Garcia d'Acuña (1964).

6. The same general observation applies if a worker/capitalist (or landlord) class structure exists in the agricultural sector. For details, see Taylor (1982b).

7. For the mineral sector long-term story, see Boutros-Ghali (1981). Growth models involving distributional considerations along the lines of sections 9.3 and 9.4 are presented by Taylor and Bacha (1976) and deJanvry and Sadoulet (1983).

8. The sort of model developed here underlies the guarded optimism about equity improvements presented in such books as *Redistribution with Growth* by Chenery, et al. (1974). The input-output studies mentioned in the text are reviewed in part by Morawetz (1974).

9. Lustig (1980) and (1982) reviews this literature and runs it through empirical tests using Mexican data. In a framework similar to the one here, deJanvry and Sadoulet (1983) study inequality using data from several countries.

Chapter 10

1. The model presented here is used in one form or another by Prebisch (1959), Nurkse (1959), and Lewis (1980). Its political economy is discussed by Taylor (1982a). The formalization here follows Taylor (1981b). For a more neoclassical presentation see Findlay (1981).

2. Bhagwati's (1958) model of impoverishing growth (really exogenous technical change) has been very influential, as evidenced by its transformation of the strange word "immiseration" into economic jargon. Bacha (1978) states a similar result in the context of the debate about unequal exchange, further reviewed by Mainwaring (1980) and Gibson (1980).

3. The references are Hobson (1902) and Luxemburg (1921). As pointed out by Hirschman (1976), the philosopher Hegel was an (unlikely?) precursor.

4. More precisely, the terms of trade always shift against the South when its productivity rises. So much is clear from the excess demand function (10.12), where a decrease in b_s cuts Southern workers' total demand for their product, and leads its price P_s to fall. However, the profit rate only falls when Northern demand is inelastic and the fall in price is more than proportional to the productivity gain. Symmetrically to a productivity gain, a decline in the Southern wage rate w_s also reduces the region's terms of trade, profit rate, and growth. Though the mechanisms differ, this is the key result of the Sraffa-type unequal exchange models of Mainwaring (1980) and Gibson (1980).

5. This hypothesis on saving follows Griffin (1970) and Weisskopf (1972). See also chapter 7.

6. If the model is extended to include endogenous capital flows, then it will be stable when the North's export surplus z adjusts according to a rule such as $z = z_0 + \alpha(r_s - r_n)$. In this equation, the parameter α measures the response of the level of capital flows to a profit rate differential, while z_0 represents foreign investors' animal spirits. Adding such a response function to equations (10.11)–(10.13) complicates the model but does not alter its essential results. This more market-oriented variant of the political story in the text still rules out independent Southern investment demand.

Chapter 11

1. For equations describing IMF "financial programming" as just sketched, see section 8.4 here and (in another variant) section 9.2 in Taylor (1979).

2. In most of the following discussion, foreign interest payments and remittances are ignored. For detail on how the former may upset normal macro relationships, see section 7.4.

3. Chapter 2 gives a rationale for markup pricing rules. Note also that we do not permit freely varying competitive imports or exports to close the "gap between the gaps" as in traditional trade theory. For a justification, see section 7.2.

4. In a representative economy, investment might be 20 percent of GDP, made up in turn of 60 percent nationally produced goods (construction and simple machinery) and 40 percent imported goods (sophisticated machinery). The capital goods import share in GDP of 8 percent will exceed the feasible trade deficit for most countries.

5. The policy shift could take the form of devaluation or more sector-specific changes such as export subsidies or acreage controls. Examples might be Bangladesh emphasizing jute production as opposed to rice, or the Central American republics pushing bananas and beef instead of corn and beans.

6. One key reason for these interventions is to avoid inflation. If the real cost of food rises for groups such as urban workers, they can easily bid up money wage demands, which in turn can be passed along to further price increases and an inflationary spiral. Models are given in sections 9.1 and 9.2.

7. In some countries—Egypt is an example—nominal consumer prices of basic food items have been held constant for years. Consequently, the real food price has dropped steadily as the general price level has gone up. Such a secular decline in an important price sooner or later has to be undone, but raising food prices suddenly is political dynamite. One should have sidestepped the problem by slow and gradual price revisions, as in the crawling peg exchange devaluation schemes discussed herein.

8. If the exchange rate is fixed when domestic inflation is substantially higher than that of trading partners, imports steadily become cheaper and exporting less worthwhile. Pressures toward devaluation grow, and asset-holders begin to put wealth abroad through legal channels or by overinvoicing imports, underinvoicing exports, and similar illegal devices if necessary. The capital flight finally forces a maxidevaluation, with the shocks to the economy discussed in section 11.3. Only the wealthy benefit, by bringing home their assets and enjoying their capital gain.

9. A profit squeeze and consequent cutback in investment at the height of a boom is a moderately convincing theory of the business cycle in a capitalist economy. For details, see section 2.4 and chapter 6.

10. One imaginative—and nameless—structuralist economist fancies that the IMF team arrives in a country on mission with briefcases full of whips and leather dungarees. Mel Brooks movies to the contrary, such is not the case. But it is at times difficult to avoid reading self-righteousness or class bias into orthodox policy moves.

11. For references and models, see chapters 2 and 9. Note that distinct consumption propensities between rich and poor for different goods, diverse investment and saving functions and, more generally, demand composition differentials underlie the discrepant theories mentioned in the text. It is hard to sort out the theoretically dominant forces underlying different income redistribution models, let alone their empirical relevance.

12. For details, see sections 3.3 and 3.4.

13. For example, in the numerical model for India in chapter 4, devaluation and an export push are strongly inflationary because they indirectly and directly generate demand for products of the supply-limited agricultural sectors.

14. The implicit assumption is that the world capital market effectively imposes credit limits

on borrowing countries—there is nonprice rationing of Eurocurrency loans. The limits for mineral exporters are relatively generous, but they do exist.

15. See section 11.4 and chapter 3 for reasons why governments usually separate internal and external food prices. For present purposes, we can assume the nonagricultural price to be determined from the world market or (more likely) from a markup rule.

16. The classic Latin American structuralist theory of inflation is based on conflicting claims to product in a situation of lagging agricultural supply. See chapter 9 and section 11.12.

17. One cannot help adding, in the context of Britain and America in the early 1980s, that regressive redistribution has scarcely proved its merits either.

References

Adelman, Irma, and Robinson, Sherman. *Income Distribution Policies in Developing Countries: A Case Study of Korea.* Stanford, CA: Stanford University Press, 1977.

Ahluwalia, Isher J. "An Analysis of Price and Output Behavior in the Indian Economy: 1951–73." *Journal of Development Economics* 6 (1979): 363–90.

Atkinson, A.B. *The Economics of Inequality.* New York and London: Oxford University Press, 1975.

Bacha, Edmar L. "An Interpretation of Unequal Exchange from Prebisch-Singer to Emmanuel." *Journal of Development Economics* 5 (1978): 319–30.

Bacha, Edmar L. "Notes of the Brazilian Experience with Minidevaluations, 1968–76." *Journal of Development Economics* 6 (1979): 463–81.

Bacha, Edmar L. "Growth with Limited Supplies of Foreign Exchange: A Reappraisal of the Two-Gap Model." Mimeo. Rio de Janeiro: Pontifical Catholic University, 1983.

Bacha, Edmar L., and Diaz-Alejandro, Carlos F. "International Financial Intermediation: A Long and Tropical View." Princeton University: Princeton Essays on International Finance No. 147 (1982).

Bacha, Edmar L., and Lopes, Francisco L. "Inflation, Growth and Wage Policy: A Brazilian Perspective," *Journal of Development Economics* 12 (1983).

Bacharach, Michael. *Biproportional Matrices and Input-Output Change.* New York and London: Cambridge University Press, 1970.

Balassa, Bela. "Exports and Economic Growth: Further Evidence." *Journal of Development Economics* 5 (1978): 181–90.

Bhagwati, Jagdish N. "Immiserizing Growth: A Geometrical Note." *Review of Economic Studies* 25 (1958): 201–05.

Bhagwati, Jagdish N. "The Nature of Balance of Payments Difficulties in Developing Countries." *Measures for Trade Expansion in Developing Countries,* Japan Economic Research Center, Center Paper No. 5, (1966).

Bitar, Sergio. *Transicion, Socialismo y Democracia: La Experiencia Chilena,* Mexico City: Siglo XXI, 1979.

Boddy, Raford, and Crotty, James. "Class Conflict and MacroPolicy: The Political Business Cycle." *Review of Radical Political Economics* 7 (1975): 1–19.

Boutros-Ghali, Youssef R. "Foreign Exchange, Black Markets and Currency Substitution: The Case of Egypt." Mimeo. Department of Economics, Massachusetts Institute of Technology, 1980.

Boutros-Ghali, Youssef R. "Single Export Systems and the Dependent Economy Model." "Essays on Structuralism and Development." Unpublished Ph.D. dissertation, Massachusetts Institute of Technology, 1981.

Brewster, Havelock. "Wage, Price, and Productivity Relations in Jamaica." *Social and Economic Studies* 17 (1968): 107–32.

Brewster, Havelock. "The Growth of Employment under Export Biased Underdevelopment." *Social and Economic Studies* 21 (1972): 153–70.

Bruno, Michael. "Stabilization and Stagflation in a Semi-Industrialized Economy." In Rudiger Dornbusch and Jacob A. Frenkel (eds.) *International Economic Policy: Theory and Evidence*, Baltimore and Washington: Johns Hopkins University Press, 1979.

Buffie, Edward. "Price-Output Dynamics, Capital Inflows and Real Appreciation." Mimeo. Department of Economics, Yale University, 1981.

Buffie, Edward. "Financial Repression, the New Structuralists and Stabilization Policy in Semi-Industrialized Economies." *Journal of Development Economics*, in press, 1983.

Buira, Ariel. "IMF Financial Programs and Conditionality." *Journal of Development Economics*, in press, 1983.

Calvo, Guillermo A. "Trying to Stabilize: Reflections on Argentina." Paper presented to a Conference on Financial Policies and the World Capital Market: The Problem of Latin American Countries, Mexico City, 1981.

Cardoso, Eliana A. "Inflation, Growth and the Real Exchange Rate: Essays on Economic History in Brazil." Unpublished Ph.D. dissertation, Massachusetts Institute of Technology, 1979.

Cardoso, Eliana A. "Food Supply and Inflation." *Journal of Development Economics* 8 (1981): 269–84.

Cavallo, Domingo F. "Stagflationary Effects of Monetarist Stabilization Policies." Unpublished Ph.D. dissertation, Harvard University, 1977.

Chenery, Hollis B., et al. (eds.) *Redistribution with Growth.* New York and London: Oxford University Press, 1974.

Chenery, Hollis B. and Bruno, Michael. "Development Alternatives in an Open Economy: The Case of Israel." *Economic Journal* 72 (1962): 79–103.

Chichilnisky, Graciela. "Terms of Trade and Domestic Distribution: Export-Led Growth with Abundant Labor." *Journal of Development Economics* 8 (1981): 163–92.

Cooper, Richard N. "An Assessment of Currency Devaluation in Developing Countries." In Gustav Ranis (ed.) *Government and Economic Development.* New Haven: Yale University Press, 1971a.

Cooper, Richard N. "Devaluation and Aggregate Demand in Aid-Receiving Countries." In Jagdish N. Bhagwati et al., *Trade, Balance of Payments and Growth: Papers in International Economics in Honor of Charles P. Kindleberger.* Amsterdam: North Holland, 1971b.

Cortazar, Rene. "Employment, Wages and Income Distribution in Chile." Unpublished Ph.D. dissertation, Massachusetts Institute of Technology, 1983.

Deaton, Angus, and Muellbauer, John. *Economics and Consumer Behavior.* London and New York: Cambridge University Press, 1980.

deJanvry, Alain, and Sadoulet, Elisabeth. "Social Articulation as a Condition for Equitable Growth." *Journal of Development Economics*, in press, 1983.

Dervis, Kemal, de Melo, Jaime, and Robinson, Sherman. *General Equilibrium Models for Development Policy.* New York and London: Cambridge University Press, 1982.

Diaz-Alejandro, Carlos F. "A Note on the Impact of Devaluation and Distributive Effect." *Journal of Political Economy* 71 (1963): 577–80.

Diaz-Alejandro, Carlos F. "Southern Cone Stabilization Plans." In William R. Cline and Sidney Weintraub (eds.), *Economic Stabilization in Developing Countries.* Washington, D.C.: The Brookings Institution, 1981.

Dornbusch, Rudiger. *Open Economy Macroeconomics.* New York: Basic Books, 1981.

Dornbusch, Rudiger et al. "The Black Market for Dollars in Brazil." *Quarterly Journal of Economics*, in press, 1982.

Dutt, Amitava K. "Stagnation, Income Distribution and Monopoly Power." Unpublished Ph.D. dissertation, Massachusetts Institute of Technology, 1982.

Eaton, Jonathan, and Gersovitz, Mark. "Debt with Potential Repudiation: Theoretical and Empirical Analysis." *Review of Economic Studies* 48 (1981): 298–309.

Eckaus, Richard S., McCarthy, F. Desmond, and Mohie-eldin, Amr. "A Social Accounting Matrix for Egypt, 1976." *Journal of Development Economics* 9 (1981): 183–203.

Ellman, Michael. "Did the Agricultural Surplus Provide the Resources for the Increase in Investment in USSR during the first Five Year Plan?" *Economic Journal* 85 (1975): 844–64.

Ffrench-Davis, Ricardo and Arellano, Jose Pablo. "Financial Liberalization and Foreign Debt: The Chilean Experience, 1973–80." Mimeo. Santiago Chile: CIEPLAN, 1982.

Findlay, Ronald. "The Foreign Exchange Gap and Growth in Developing Economies." In Jagdish N. Bhagwati, et al. *Trade, Balance of Payments and Growth: Papers in International Economics in Honor of Charles P. Kindleberger,* Amsterdam: North-Holland, 1971.

Findlay, Ronald. "The Fundamental Determinants of the Terms of Trade." In Sven Grassman and Erik Lundberg (eds.) *The World Economic Order: Past and Prospects.* New York: Saint Martin's, 1981.

Frenkel, Roberto. "Financial Liberalization and Capital Flows: The Case of Argentina." Mimeo. Santiago, Chile: CIEPLAN, 1982.

Friedman, Benjamin M. "Crowding-Out and Crowding-In: The Economic Consequences of Financing Government Deficits." *Brookings Papers on Economic Activity,* No. 3, 593–641, 1978.

Fry, Maxwell J. "Saving, Investment, Growth and the Cost of Financial Repression." *World Development* 8 (1980): 317–27.

Gandolfo, Giancarlo. *Economic Dynamics: Methods and Models* (2nd revised edition). Amsterdam: North-Holland, 1980.

Garcia d'Acuña, Eduardo. "Inflation in Chile: A Quantitative Analysis." Unpublished Ph.D. dissertation, Massachusetts Institute of Technology, 1964.

Gelb, Alan H. "Capital-Importing Oil Exporters: Adjustment Issues and Policy Choices." World Bank Staff Working Paper No. 475, 1981.

Georgescu-Roegen, Nicholas. "Structural Inflation-Lock and Balanced Growth." *Economies et Societes* 4 (1970): 557–605.

Gibson, Bill. "Unequal Exchange: Theoretical Issues and Empirical Findings." *Review of Radical Political Economics* 12 (1980): 15–35.

Gibson, Bill, Lustig, Nora, and Taylor, Lance. "Impactos Distributivos de las Politicas del Sistema Alimentario Mexicano en un Marco de Equilibrio General." Mimeo. El Colegio de Mexico, Mexico City, 1982.

Giovannini, Alberto. "The Interest Elasticity of Saving in Developing Countries: The Existing Evidence." Mimeo. Department of Economics, Massachusetts Institute of Technology, 1982.

Girvan, Norman. "Multinational Corporations and Dependent Underdevelopment in Mineral Exporting Economies." *Social and Economic Studies* 19 (1970): 490–526.

Glyn, Andrew, and Sutcliffe, Bob. *Capitalism in Crisis.* New York: Panthenon, 1972.

Griffin, Keith B. "Foreign Capital, Domestic Savings and Economic Development." *Bulletin of the Oxford University Institute of Economics and Statistics* 32 (1970): 99–112.

Hicks, John R. *The Crisis in Keynesian Economics.* New York: Basic Books, 1974.

Hirsch, Morris W. and Smale, Stephen. *Differential Equations, Dynamic Systems and Linear Algebra.* New York: Academic Press, 1974.

Hirschman, Albert O. "Devaluation and the Trade Balance: A Note." *Review of Economics and Statistics* 31 (1949): 50–53.

Hirschman, Albert O. *The Strategy of Economic Development.* New Haven: Yale University Press, 1958.

Hirschman, Albert O. "On Hegel, Imperialism, and Structural Stagnation." *Journal of Development Economics* 3 (1976): 1–8.

Hobson, John A. *Imperialism: A Study.* London: J. Nisbet, 1902.

Isard, Peter. "How Far Can We Push the 'Law of One Price'?" *American Economic Review* 67 (1977): 942–48.

Kaldor, Nicholas. "Alternative Theories of Distribution." *Review of Economic Studies* 23 (1955): 83–100.

Kalecki, Michal. "Costs and Prices" and "Distribution of National Income." In *Selected Essays on the Dynamics of the Capitalist Economy*. New York and London: Cambridge University Press, 1971a.

Kalecki, Michal. "Political Aspects of Full Employment." In *Selected Essays on the Dynamics of the Capitalist Economy*. New York and London: Cambridge University Press, 1971b.

Kapur, Basant K. "Alternative Stabilization Policies for Less-developed Economies." *Journal of Political Economy* 84 (1976): 777–95.

Keynes, John Maynard. *A Treatise on Money*. London: Macmillan, 1930.

Keynes, John Maynard. *The General Theory of Employment, Interest and Money*. London: Macmillan, 1936.

Kindleberger, Charles P. *Manias, Panics and Crashes: A History of Financial Crises*. New York: Basic Books, 1978.

Kravis, Irving B., and Lipsey, Robert E. "Export Prices and the Transmission of Inflation." *American Economic Review (Papers and Proceedings)* 67 (1977): 155–63.

Krugman, Paul. (1981) "The Capital Inflows Problem in Less Developed Countries." Mimeo. Department of Economics, Massachusetts Institute of Technology, 1981.

Krugman, Paul, and Taylor, Lance. "Contractionary Effects of Devaluation." *Journal of International Economics* 8 (1978): 445–56.

Lara-Resende, Andre. *Inflation, Growth and Oligopolistic Pricing in a Semi-Industrialized Economy: The Case of Brazil*. Unpublished Ph.D. dissertation, Massachusetts Institute of Technology, 1979.

Lewis, W. Arthur. "The Slowing Down of the Engine of Growth." *American Economic Review* 70 (1980): 555–64.

Lluch, Constantino, Powell, Alan A., and Williams, Ross A. *Patterns in Household Demand and Saving*. New York and London: Oxford University Press, 1977.

Lopes, Francisco L. "Lucro, Juros e Moeda: Um Ensaio em Dinamica Keynesiana." *Revista de Estudos Economicas* 7 (1977): 221–51.

Lustig, Nora. "Underconsumption in Latin American Economic Thought: Some Considerations." *Review of Radical Political Economics* 12 (1980): 35–43.

Lustig, Nora. "Characteristics of Modern Economic Growth: Empirical Testing of Some Latin American Structuralist Hypotheses." *Journal of Development Economics*, in press, 1982.

Luxemburg, Rosa. *Die Akkumulation des Kapitals*, Leipzig: Frankes Verlag, 1921.

Macedo, Jorge Braga. "Currency Diversification and Export Competitiveness: A Model of the 'Dutch Disease' in Egypt." *Journal of Development Economics*, in press, 1983.

Magee, Stephen P. "Currency Contracts, Pass-Through and Devaluation." *Brookings Papers on Economic Activity* 1 (1973): 303–23.

Mainwaring, L. "International Trade and the Transfer of Labor Value." *Journal of Development Studies* 17 (1980): 22–31.

Marglin, Stephen A. *Growth, Distribution and Prices: Neoclassical, Neo-Marxian and Neo-Keynesian Aporoaches to the Study of Capitalism*. Cambridge, Mass.: Harvard University Press, 1983.

McCarthy, F. Desmond, and Taylor, Lance. "Macro Food Policy Planning: A General Equilibrium Model for Pakistan." *Review of Economics and Statistics* 62 (1980): 107–21.

McKinnon, Ronald I. "Foreign Exchange Constraints in Economic Development and Efficient Aid Allocation." *Economic Journal* 74 (1964): 388–409.

McKinnon, Ronald I. *Money and Capital in Economic Development*. Washington, D.C.: The Brookings Institution, 1973.

Michaely, Michael. "Exports and Growth: An Empirical Investigation." *Journal of Development Economics* 4 (1977): 49–54.

Mitra, Ashok. *Terms of Trade and Class Relations.* London: Frank Cass, 1977.

Morawetz, David. "Employment Implications of Industrialization in Developing Countries." *Economic Journal* 84 (1974): 411–52.

Morley, Samuel. "Inflation and Stagnation in Brazil." *Economic Devlopment and Cultural Change* 19 (1971): 184–203.

Nankani, Gobind. "Development Problems of Mineral Exporting Countries." Washington D.C.: World Bank Staff Working Paper No. 354, 1979.

Nayyar, Deepak. "Industrial Development in India: Some Reflections on Growth and Stagnation." *Economic and Political Weekly.* Special Number, August₀ 1978.

Nurske, Ragnar. *Patterns of Trade and Development.* Stockholm: Almquist and Wicksell, 1959.

Okun, Arthur M. *Prices and Quantities: A Macroeconomic Analysis.* Washington D.C.: The Brookings Institution, 1981.

Polak, J.J. "Monetary Analysis of Income Formation and Payments Problems." *International Monetary Fund Staff Papers* 6 (1957): 1–50.

Powell, M.J.D. "A Hybrid Method for Nonlinear Equations" and "A FORTRAN Subroutine for Solving Systems of Nonlinear Equations." In Philip Rabinowotz (ed.) *Numerical Methods for Nonlinear Algebraic Equations.* London: Gordon and Breach, 1970.

Prebisch, Raul. "Commercial Policy in the Underdeveloped Countries." *American Economic Review* 49 (1959): 251–73.

Pyatt, F. Graham and Roe, Alan. *Social Accounting for Development with Special Reference to Sri Lanka.* New York and London: Cambridge University Press, 1977.

Pyatt, F. Graham and Thorbecke, Erik. *Planning Techniques for a Better Future.* Geneva: International Labor Office, 1976.

Reichman, Thomas M. "The Fund's Conditional Assistance and the Problems of Adjustment, 1973–75." *Finance and Development* 15 (no. 4) (1978): 38–41.

Reichman, Thomas M. and Stilson, Richard T. "Experience with Problems of Balance of Payments Adjustment: Stand-by Arrangements in the Higher Credit Tranches, 1963–1972." *International Monetary Fund Staff Papers* 25 (1978): 293–309.

Robichek, E. Walter. "Financial Programming Exercises of the International Monetary Fund in Latin America." Mimeo. IMF Institute, International Monetary Fund, 1975.

Ros, Jaime. "Pricing in the Mexican Manufacturing Sector." *Cambridge Journal of Economics* 4 (1980): 211–31.

Sachs, Jeffrey. "LDC Debt in the 1980's: Risk and Reform." Mimeo. Department of Economics, Harvard University, 1982.

Sargent, Thomas J. and Wallace, Neil. "Some Unpleasant Monetarist Arithmetic." *Federal Reserve Bank of Minneapolis Quarterly Review* (Fall, 1981) 1–17.

Sarkar, Hiren, and Subba Rao, S.V. "Social Accounting Matrix for India for 1980–81." New Delhi: National Council of Applied Economic Research, 1981.

Sen, Amartya K. "Neo-Classical and Neo-Keynesian Theories of Distribution." *Economic Record* 39 (1963): 54–64.

Shaw, Edward S. *Financial Deepening in Economic Development.* New York and London: Oxford University Press, 1973.

Solis, Leopoldo, and Rizzo, Socrates. "Oil Surplus and Financial Openness: The Case of Mexico." Mimeo. Santiago, Chile: CIEPLAN, 1982.

Stone, Richard. "Linear Expenditure Systems and Demand Analysis: An Application to the Pattern of British Demand." *Economic Journal* 64 (1954): 511–27.

Stone, Richard. "Multiple Classifications in Social Accounting" and "British Economic Balances in 1970: A Trial Run on Rocket." In *Mathematics in the Social Sciences and Other Essays.* London: Chapman and Hall, 1966.

Sunkel, Osvaldo. "Inflation in Chile: An Unorthodox Approach." *International Economic Papers,* No. 10 (1960): 107–31.

Sunkel, Osvaldo. "National Development Policy and External Dependence in Latin America." *Journal of Development Studies* 6 (1969): 23–48.

Sylos-Labini, Paolo. "Industrial Pricing in the United Kingdom." *Cambridge Journal of Economics* 3 (1979): 153–63.

Taylor, Lance. *Macro Models for Developing Countries.* New York: McGraw-Hill, 1979.

Taylor, Lance. "IS/LM in the Tropics: Diagrammatics of the New Strucuturalist Macro Critique." In William R. Cline and Sidney Weintraub (eds.) *Economic Stabilization in Developing Countries.* Washington D.C.: The Brookings Institution, 1981a.

Taylor, Lance. "South-North Trade and Southern Growth: Bleak Prospects from a Structuralist Point of View." *Journal of International Economics* 11 (1981b): 589–602.

Taylor, Lance. "Back to Basics: Theory for the Rhetoric in the North-South Round." *World Development* 10 (1982a): 327–35.

Taylor, Lance. "Food Price Inflation, Terms of Trade, and Growth." In Mark Gersovitz, et al. (eds.) *The Theory and Experience of Economic Development: Essays in Honor of Sir W. Arthur Lewis.* London: Allen and Unwin, 1982b.

Taylor, Lance, and Bacha, Edmar L. "The Unequalizing Spiral: A First Growth Model for Belindia." *Quarterly Journal of Economics* 90 (1976): 187–219.

Taylor, Lance, and Lysy, Frank J. "Vanishing Income Redistributions: Keynesian Clues about Model Surprises in the Short Run." *Journal of Development Economics* 6 (1979): 11–29.

Thurow, Lester C. *Generating Inequality: Mechanisms of Distribution in the U.S. Economy.* New York: Basic Books, 1975.

Tobin, James. "Money, Capital and Other Stores of Value." *American Economic Review (Papers and Proceedings)* 51 (1961): 26–37.

Tobin, James. "A General Equilibrium Approach to Monetary Theory." *Journal of Money, Credit and Banking* 1 (1969): 15–29.

van Wijnbergen, Sweder. "Stagflationary Effects of Monetary Stabilization Policies: A Quantitative Analysis of South Korea." *Journal of Development Economics* 10 (1982): 133–70.

van Wijnbergen, Sweder. "Interest Rate Management in LDC's." *Journal of Monetary Economics,* in press, 1983a.

van Wijnbergen, Sweder. "Credit Policy, Inflation and Growth in a Financially Repressed Economy." *Journal of Development Economics,* in press, 1983b.

van Wijnbergen, Sweder. "Capital Flows, the Real Exchange Rate and Preannounced Crawling Peg Policies." *International Economic Review,* in press, 1983c.

Weisskopf, Thomas E. "The Impact of Foreign Capital Inflow on Domestic Saving in Underdeveloped Countries." *Journal of International Economics* 2 (1972): 25–38.

Weisskopf, Thomas E. "Marxian Crisis Theory and the Rate of Profit in the Postwar U.S. Economy." *Cambridge Journal of Economics* 3 (1979): 341–78.

Werneck, Rogerio L. "Rapid Growth, Distributional Equity and the Size of the Public Sector: Trade-Offs Facing Brazilian Economic Policy in the 1980's." Unpublished Ph.D. dissertation, Harvard University, 1980.

Williamson, John. (1965) "The Crawling Peg." Princeton University: Essays in International Finance No. 50, 1965.

World Bank. *World Development Report: 1981.* Washington, D.C., 1981.

Index